THE HAMLYN LECTURES
FORTY-SIXTH SERIES

BLACKSTONE'S TOWER
The English Law School

AUSTRALIA
The Law Book Company
Brisbane · Sydney · Melbourne · Perth

CANADA
Carswell
Ottawa · Toronto · Calgary · Montreal · Vancouver

AGENTS
Steimatzky's Agency Ltd., Tel Aviv;
N.M. Tripathi (Private) Ltd., Bombay;
Eastern Law House (Private) Ltd., Calcutta;
M.P.P. House, Bangalore;
Universal Book Traders, Delhi;
Aditya Books, Delhi;
MacMillan Shuppan KK, Tokyo;
Pakistan Law House, Karachi, Lahore

BLACKSTONE'S TOWER
The English Law School

by

WILLIAM TWINING
Quain Professor of Jurisprudence
University College, London

Published under the auspices of
THE HAMLYN TRUST

LONDON
STEVENS & SONS/SWEET & MAXWELL
1994

Published in 1994
by Stevens & Sons Ltd./Sweet & Maxwell Ltd.
South Quay Plaza, 183 Marsh Wall, London E14 9FT
Computerset by
Wyvern Typesetting,
Bristol
Printed in England by Clays Ltd, St Ives plc

A CIP catalogue record for this book
is available from the British Library

ISBN 0 421 53270 X (H/b)
0 421 53280 7 (P/b)

To Hilary

TABLE OF CONTENTS

The Hamlyn Lectures

The Hamlyn Lectures

The Hamlyn Lectures

The Hamlyn Trust

The Hamlyn Trust owes its existence to the will of the late Miss Emma Warburton Hamlyn of Torquay, who died in 1941 at the age of eighty. She came of an old and well-known Devon family. Her father, William Bussell Hamlyn, practised in Torquay as a solicitor and JP for many years, and it seems likely that Miss Hamlyn founded the trust in his memory. Emma Hamlyn was a woman of strong character, intelligent and cultured, well-versed in literature, music and art, and a lover of her country. She travelled extensively in Europe and Egypt, and apparently took considerable interest in the law and ethnology of the countries and cultures that she visited. An account of Miss Hamlyn by Dr. Chantal Stebbings of the University of Exeter may be found, under the title "The Hamlyn Legacy," in volume 42 of the published lectures.

Miss Hamlyn bequeathed the residue of her estate on trust in terms which it seems were her own. The wording was thought to be vague, and the will was taken to the Chancery Division of the High Court, which in November 1948 approved a Scheme for the administration of the trust. Paragraph 3 of the Scheme, which closely follows Miss Hamlyn's own wording, is as follows:

"The object of the charity is the furtherance by lectures or otherwise among the Common People of the United Kingdom of Great Britain and Northern Ireland of the knowledge of the Comparative Jurisprudence and Ethnology of the Chief European countries including the United Kingdom, and the circumstances of the growth of such jurisprudence to the Intent that the Common People of the United Kingdom may realise the privileges which in law and custom they enjoy in comparison with other European Peoples and realising and appreciating such privileges may rcognise the responsibilities and obligations attaching to them."

The Trustees are to include the Vice-Chancellor of the University of Exeter, representatives of the Universities of London, Leeds,

The Hamlyn Trust

Glasgow, Belfast and Wales and persons co-opted. At present there are eight Trustees:

From the outset it was decided that the Trust's objects could best be achieved by means of an annual course of public lectures of outstanding interest and quality by eminent Lecturers, and by their subsequent publication and distribution to a wider audience. Details of these Lectures are given on page ix. In recent years, however, the Trustees have expanded their activities by organising supplementary regional lecture tours and by setting up a "small grants" scheme to provide financial support for other activities designed to further public understanding of the law.

The forty-sixth series of lectures was delivered by Professor William Twining at the University of Manchester in November 1994.

September 1994   **DESMOND GREER**
Chairman of the Trustees

ABBREVIATIONS

(a) The following abbreviations are used in the text and the notes:

ACLEC	The Lord Chancellor's Advisory Committee on Legal Education and Conduct
ALI	The American Law Institute
ALT	The Association of Law Teachers
BTEC	The Business and Technical Education Council
CNAA	Council for National Academic Awards
CPE	Common Professional Examination
CVCP	Committee of Vice-Chancellors and Principals
ESRC	Economic and Social Research Council
ILC	International Legal Center (New York)
JSPTL (NS)	Journal of the Society of Public Teachers of Law (New Series)
LCAC	Lord Chancellor's Advisory Committee (see ACLEC)
SPTL	Society of Public Teachers of Law
UFC	Universities Funding Council
UGC	University Grants Committtee

(b) Some of the points and themes in the text are treated at greater length in other writings by the author. The following abbreviations are used in the notes:

ALLD	*Academic Law and Legal Development* (Lagos, 1977)
ANALYSIS	*Analysis of Evidence* (with Terence Anderson, Boston and London, 1991)
HDTWR	*How to Do Things With Rules* (with David Miers, 3rd ed., London, 1991)
JJM	"The Job of Juristic Method: A Tribute to Karl Llewellyn" (1993) 48 *University of Miami Law Review* 601

Abbreviations

KLRM	*Karl Llewellyn and the Realist Movement,* (London and Oklahoma, 1973, 1985)
LTCL	*Legal Theory and Common Law* (ed., Oxford, 1986)
RB	"Reading Bentham", Maccabean Lecture, (1989) 75 *Proceedings of the British Academy,* 97–141.
RE	*Rethinking Evidence* (Oxford, 1990; Chicago and London, 1994)
TAR	"Talk about Realism" (1985) 60 *New York University Law Review* 329
TEBW	*Theories of Evidence: Bentham and Wigmore* (London, 1985; and Stanford, 1986)

ACKNOWLEDGMENTS

In the course of this project I have accumulated many debts. I am grateful to the Hamlyn trustees not only for the invitation to give the 1994 Hamlyn Lectures, but also for their support and advice. The staff at Sweet & Maxwell have handled the process of production with speed and efficiency. Thanks are due to the International Legal Center and the Social Sciences and Humanities Research Council of Canada for permission to reproduce copyright material. I am particularly grateful to Tony Becher, Nick Bevan, Kim Economides, Andrew Lewis, Claire Palley, Robert Stevens, David Sugarman and Barbara Tearle for reading one or more draft chapters and making helpful criticisms and suggestions. I have profited from suggestions from Marcel Berlins, Kevin Boyle, John Cairns, Stephen Guest, A.H. Halsey, Bob Hepple, Fiona Hindle, Dawn Oliver, Avrom Sherr, Phil Thomas, Geoffrey Wilson and colleagues at the University of Miami Law School, University College, London, the University of Warwick and many others. Thanks are due to the library staff at the Bodleian Law Library, the Institute of Advanced Legal Studies, the Institute of Education and, in particular the University of Miami Law Library; Beverley Crearer and Evelyn Medina gave considerable help with word-processing. The Netherlands Institute for Advanced Study provided a supportive and congenial environment for completing the project. My greatest debt is to Terry Anderson who devoted most of one holiday to rescuing the penultimate draft from errors, repetitions and inelegancies as well as acting as a sounding-board and help-line throughout most of the process. As ever, the book would not have been completed without the constant help and encouragement of my wife.

W.L.T.
Wassenaar, September 1994

PREFACE

The purpose of this book is to suggest that the study of law is in process of becoming re-absorbed into the mainstream of our general intellectual life, as it was from Blackstone's time until the late nineteenth century,[1] and that this is a welcome development. A central theme is that law as a discipline has become somewhat isolated from that mainstream and that this is in part explained by the peculiar history and culture of the institutionalised study of law as it has developed in England and of its primary base, the law school. The main focus is on the study of law in universities, but the relative isolation of law extends beyond the academic context to the kind of "middlebrow culture" that is roughly illustrated by *The Good Book Guide, The London Review of Books*, the *Times* crossword or the contents of a good general book shop.[2] One way of posing the question is to ask: why does law feature prominently on the front pages of newspapers, yet get hidden away at the back of even the best general book shops?

My interest in this topic was first stimulated in the 1970s by two excellent series of books which claimed to be introductions to "the men who have changed or are changing the life and thought of our age" (*Fontana Modern Masters*) or "to leading intellectual figures of the past" (*Oxford Past Masters*). Although both series included figures who had made important contributions to legal thought, such as Aquinas, Bacon and Weber, law was conspicuously absent from the lists of titles, the authors and, for the most part, the treatment of the subjects. General philosophy, political and social theory, literature, religion, and, less confidently, science, were well represented as contributing to the mainstream of the history of ideas, but law and legal theory were not. The first major exception, John Dinwiddy's excellent *Bentham* (1989), was a late-comer written by a historian.[3]

In preparing this book and its accompanying lectures, I have tried to follow the spirit of Miss Hamlyn's bequest by addressing a non-specialist audience, though perhaps not the Common People.

Preface

There is an irony in arguing that law should be more part of our general culture in a book published by a specialist law publisher and in lectures that are likely to attract a mainly legal audience. I have tried to address the problem by adopting the standpoint of a tour guide introducing the history and culture of the English law school to visitors from outside, especially colleagues from neighbouring disciplines or from other legal systems. So I have tried to make the text both readable and comprehensible to non-specialists, but — as with a *Baedeker*—visitors may wish to skip some of the detail, especially in chapters two, six and seven. Legal colleagues, whether academics, practitioners or students, may treat this as holding up a mirror to a familiar world. Even locals can learn something from a guided tour, especially in a rapidly changing and confusing situation.

For reasons of space I have focused almost exclusively on the small world of the English university law school, and I have on the whole resisted temptations to branch out into such seductive areas as law and literature, law and the media, and the changing world of legal practice. I have also concentrated almost entirely on England and Wales, because it was not possible to do justice to the differences in the history and situation of law schools in Scotland and Northern Ireland, although the affinities and connections are equally significant. Solely for the sake of brevity I have followed legal convention in using "England" and "English" to include Wales and Welsh, but I am well aware of the distinctiveness of some aspects of the Welsh tradition, not least in respect of attitudes to education.

The focus is narrow, but the subject is large. It embraces all law and its relations with other disciplines. It can best be understood in a series of broad overlapping contexts: international trends in legal training, developments in higher education in the United Kingdom and elsewhere, Government policies on legal aid, changes in legal practice and the organisation of the legal profession, broader trends in ideas and technologies, the United Kingdom's relations with post-Maastricht Europe, the instabilities of the British and the world economy and the traumas of world politics in the early 1990s—all of these are relevant to interpreting the situation of English law schools today.

The subject has also become very topical. For over 30 years I have been interested in legal education policy as a participant and commentator. In 1992, I thought that it was time to try to step back and view the subject from a broader perspective with relative detachment. Instead, since starting on this project I have found myself involved in a year-long review of the inter-collegiate LLM of the University of London, a review of the Bar Vocational Course at the Inns of Court School of Law, a Consultative Panel for the Lord Chancellor's Advisory Committee on Legal Education and Conduct (ACLEC), a study of the whole system of legal education and training in Tanzania, and workshops, consultations and conferences in several jurisdictions. In England the most visible sign of public interest and concern is the fact that ACLEC began the first major review of legal education and training in England and Wales since 1971, starting with the initial or academic stage. This exercise has already stimulated a series of surveys, research projects and symposia. It is as much a symptom as a cause of public concern about the future of our system of legal education in a rapidly changing environment and an uncertain economic climate.

This increased interest has made my task easier in some ways and harder in others. On the one hand, I have had access to a mass of new ideas and detailed information; on the other hand, the pace of change and one's own involvement undermine any strong claims to detachment. I shall try to set some immediate issues in a broad context, but the interpretation is that of an involved insider.

Legal tourism as a pastime is a recent development. It is only in the past few years that lawyers' tours to Russia and China or The Hague or Britain have become quite common. It is the lawyer's equivalent of a busman's holiday. If one has done some homework and has a well-informed and forthcoming guide, one can learn quite a lot. But like other kinds of up-market tourism the outcome is at best impressionistic. One visits courts, prisons, ministries and other institutions; one interviews judges, practitioners, scholars and students; one witnesses a trial or two, attends a few lectures or seminars, samples some documents, hears about a recent *cause célèbre* and snatches a few snapshots of the legal system in action.

I propose to adopt the standpoint of a tour guide introducing non-lawyers and foreign colleagues to the world of the English Law School and its academic culture. Like any guide I shall be highly selective, using stories, cameos, case-studies and other particular examples to illustrate some general themes. The approach will be largely ethnographic and historical. I shall try to show a respect for facts, but I shall not conceal my biases. This introduciton should not be interpreted as a series of modest or defensive disclaimers. On the contrary, I hope to make this a rather Grand Tour and like

Preface

Henry James' caretaker I would consider the enterprise a success if it is seen by a few as a Work of Art.[4]

Notes

[1] See, for example, Stefan Collini, *Public Moralists, Political Thought and Intellectual Life in Britain 1850–1930* (1991), especially the treatment of jurists who are almost all late nineteenth century figures, such as H.S. Maine, Fitzjames Stephen, James Bryce and A.V. Dicey.

[2] It is unnecessary, for my purposes, to get drawn into discussing the complexities of the concept of "culture", on which see the discussion in Peter Scott, *Knowledge and Nation* (1990), Chap. 3, which fits this context admirably.

[3] My initial response was to propose a series on *Jurists* to another publisher, but this soon came to be perceived and treated by authors, readers and publishers alike as being more specialised than the *Past Masters* and *Modern Masters* series, and the process became self-confirming.

[4] Henry James. "The Birthplace" (1903), reprinted in *Selected Stories* (ed. G. Hopkins, 1957).

1. Law in Culture and Society

INTRODUCTION

Soon after I had decided to embark on a career as a jurist, I asked one of my mentors, Professor Harry Lawson, for some suggestions for systematic reading over one long vacation. "Start with Blackstone's *Commentaries*", he advised.[1] I failed at the first attempt and I only read through the whole work many years later.

Nevertheless the advice was sound and Blackstone provides an obvious starting-point for exploring the world of the English law school. He was the first great modern English academic lawyer,[2] the first holder of the Vinerian Chair at Oxford (1758), and he tried to establish the study of English Law as a university subject. In this, he was unsuccessful in the short run. His lectures were well-received, but he failed to persuade the University of Oxford to establish a law school devoted to the study of English Law. Blackstone's *Commentaries* became an immediate best-seller, with eight editions published in his lifetime. They purported to systematise the unsystematic by presenting an elegant, readable, comprehensive map of English law as a whole. They soon established themselves as one of the canon of texts for educated English gentlemen—a part of the general culture of the nobility and landed classes. They also became the principal conduit for the spread of common law. Colonists wish to carry their law with them, but they travel light. Blackstone could fit into the luggage of frontiersmen, settlers and colonial lawyers in America and Australia more easily than the bulky, unsystematic reports of cases that were the blood of the common law. And the *Commentaries* could be used to uphold individual rights against the colonial government. As Frederic William Maitland observed: "The Tory lawyer little thought that he was giving law to colonies that were on the eve of a great and successful rebellion".[3]

Blackstone also provided the target for the first major attack on the common law tradition. Jeremy Bentham heard Blackstone's lec-

1

tures and was appalled by the contrast between what he saw as the Vinerian Professor's complacent glorification of the common law and the realities of litigation and legal practice. *The Commentaries*, especially Book I, provided a more specific target for attack than the amorphous common law. Bentham the Censor, or critic, challenged Blackstone the Expositor first in *A Fragment on Government* and later in *Comment on the Commentaries*. Almost exactly two centuries later Professor Duncan Kennedy of Harvard used Blackstone's *Commentaries* as his target, when he introduced deconstruction and "trashing" into the armoury of critical legal studies.[4]

It was Bentham's followers rather than Blackstone's who established the first degree in English law, at the University of London, later University College (UCL). Ironically, the two founding Professors at UCL fitted neither's model of the law teacher. John Austin was Bentham's disciple, but his aim was to establish a descriptive science of positive law. His colleague Andrew Amos, was a practising barrister who brought the "fire and thunder"[5] of the courtroom into the classroom and tried to induct his students into the skills of practice. These four, however, symbolise their successors. Ever since then the expositor, the censor, the scientist and the craftsman have competed to be accepted as the dominant model of the English scholar-teacher of law.

This book examines the nature and potential of the discipline of law as part of our general intellectual heritage and in relation to the legal profession and to society at large. The study of law has a long history throughout the Western world. In England, however, the emergence of university-based law schools is a quite recent phenomenon and, as we shall see, they are still in the process of coming of age. Their development has made apparent the tensions between the study of law and its professional practice. In all Western societies law schools are typically caught in a tug of war between three aspirations: to be accepted as full members of the community of higher learning; to be relatively detached, but nonetheless engaged, critics and censors of law in society; and to be service-institutions for a profession which is itself caught between noble ideals, lucrative service of powerful interests and unromantic cleaning up of society's messes.

These tensions are not necessarily unhealthy. They are reflected in the metaphor of "Blackstone's Tower". I have chosen my title for a number of reasons. First, Blackstone could have been the model for a Hamlyn lecturer. He set out to make the common law

2

accessible to non-specialists and to exhibit its superiority to other systems. My aims are more modest and less chauvinistic, but the concern to make law more accessible is shared.

Secondly, Blackstone as expositor represents the dominant English academic tradition, which has never gone unchallenged.

Thirdly, Blackstone's tower was not and is not a tower of ivory. Here, it symbolises English law schools collectively, rather than any individual institution. Law as a discipline is constantly fed with practical problems and materials from the "real world": actual rather than hypothetical cases; proposals for legislative reform; and social problems from domestic violence and crime to world peace and environmental survival. Blackstone himself was not only an expositor: a scholar by temperament, he had wide experience as a barrister, member of Parliament, judge and academic statesman. He was only moderately successful as a man of affairs, but as a writer all of his work was imbued with practical concerns.

Fourthly, Blackstone's tower is argumentative, dialectical, filled with lively debate; but it is not as chaotic as Babel: some of the debate is formal, structured, even ritualistic; some is conducted in a peculiar tongue, the language of the common law. Legal talk has always been quite varied; recently some spaces have been created in which one can sometimes hear previously unheard voices telling their stories, notably women, minorities and the oppressed. When one contemplates the titles of articles in the rapidly proliferating legal journals, one wonders how to make sense of it all. So much seems specialised or obscure or repetitious or trivial, but it is more like babble than Babel.

A tower is itself an ambiguous symbol, conjuring up images of ancient fortifications, Victorian follies, and modern high rises, such as Centre Point or Canary Wharf. The disorganisation of the common law is often portrayed through architectural analogies. Blackstone himself compared English Law to "an old Gothic castle, erected in the days of chivalry but fitted up for a modern inhabitant".[6] His aim was to exhibit "the model of the old house" and to expose and criticise "the new labyrinth" created by ill-considered piecemeal legislative interventions.[7] Blackstone emphasised the evolutionary nature of the common law and its concern with particular, practical knowledge, both of which are also characteristics of our law schools. Later an American jurist, Karl Llewellyn, contrasted the classical lines of codified civilian systems to the crude architecture of old New England farm-houses . . ." like a kind of Topsy, with neither head nor tail nor plan, that just growed".[8]

3

Law in Culture and Society

The English law school, where the discipline is housed, is in many respects a modern plate glass creation; but it carries with it vestiges of the Middle Ages, heavy encrustations of Victorian thought, powerful capitalist and corporatist influences and even a few embellishments by post-modernism. This institution is not the product of a single age or period-style. Over the past 30 years it has grown rapidly and quite irregularly. John Grisham, one of the new breed of American lawyer-novelists, extends the image in describing another kind of institution:

> "Like most big-city charity hospitals, St Peter's had been built over time whenever funds could be squeezed, with little thought of architectural symmetry. It was a sprawling and bewildering configuration of additions and wings, with a maze of hallways and corridors and mezzanines trying desperately to connect everything. Elevators and escalators had been added wherever they would fit. At some point in history, someone had realized the difficulty of moving from one point to another without getting hopelessly lost, and a dazzling array of color-coded signs had been implemented for the orderly flow of traffic. Then more wings were added. The signs became obsolete, but the hospital failed to remove them. Now they only added to the confusion".[9]

That could well be a metaphor for the common law. These architectural images present a paradox; they signify absence of an architect, a lack of an overall design. But the image-makers are generally scholars of the common law whose mission was to find or construct or impose order in terms of underlying principles, a coherent internal structure, or even a system. English law schools may not be quite as disorderly as their subject-matter, but in many ways they reflect it. Visitors from other disciplines need a guide. My main object is to provide a guided tour of parts of this edifice.

LAW IN SOCIETY: THE NEWSPAPER EXERCISE

Let us begin, then, where I begin with first year law students. As part of preparing for this event, late in January 1994 I sat down and read every word of *The Independent* newspaper for Tuesday, January 18. I read it in a particular way according to a simplified version of instructions I give to law students as their very first exercise.[10] They are asked to read *all* of a non-tabloid newspaper, to mark every passage which, in their view, either deals directly with law or which is "law related", and to answer some specific questions. They are required to stipulate their own definitions of "law" and "law related". For the immediate purpose I adopted a more restricted conception of these terms than is my normal practice, in order not to bore you. The date was chosen at random. This is what I found:

(a) Only a few passages consisted of pure "law talk", that is to say that they were expressed directly in the kind of language used in statutes, the law reports or formal legal documents, such as conveyances, contracts or treaties. There was one report of a Court of Appeal decision on the admissibility of evidence in a child abuse case. It was signed by a barrister and in a form that allows it to be cited in court as a precedent. There were two official legal notices, both relating to the liquidation of insolvent companies. There was a fairly typical collection of statements in small print in several advertisements. All of the public sector job advertisements contained explicit references to equal opportunities, while there was no overt mention of these in more than a dozen advertisements for accountancy and financial posts in the private sector. There was a small notice, "donated by the publisher", inviting complaints about the contents of the newspaper to be sent to the Press Complaints Commission. The standard copyright sign, covering the whole newspaper, was tucked away in very small print below the crossword. I noticed that, in contrast to American practice, the cartoons did not have their own individual copyright claims. There was a list of the day's business in Parliament, which included the second reading of two Government Bills (the Coal Industry Bill and the Police and Magistrates Court Bill) and consideration of the Farm and Conservation Grant (Variation) Scheme.

(b) Proceedings in courts and other tribunals, and litigation generally, both at home and abroad, are one of the main sources of news for journalists. There were over twenty items, of varying length, based on court hearings and a further eight to ten referring to civil claims that were pending or had been settled. As one would expect, there were more than a dozen items dealing with criminal investigations and other law enforcement activities by the police, the Serious Fraud Office, immigration officials and other agencies. John Major's appearance before the Scott Inquiry into the arms-for-Iraq affair merited three items and a picture, but because of the "fast footwork of a cool witness", the confrontation was less sensational than expected and was relegated to page two. Two other ongoing stories attracted substantial space: the aftermath of the arrest and detention before Christmas of 190 Jamaicans at Gatwick

5

by the Immigration Service and a feature commenting on the trial of the Menendez brothers for the murder of their parents in Hollywood, proceedings which had been televised live in the United States over several months. In addition half a page was given to the start of an inquiry by the Monopolies and Mergers Commission into the prices charged by Nintendo and Sega for video games. The long-running conflicts within the Council of the London Zoo highlighted some internal legal and constitutional issues. There were also several short reports of disciplinary proceedings before the Jockey Club and other sporting bodies, but these were less detailed than they sometimes are: the first time I did this exercise, I found a detailed summary by a racing journalist of argument by Queen's Counsel before the Jockey Club.

Homicide and sex had their normal share of cases reported (including a brief reference to the amputative Lorena Bobbitt), but there was a fair spread of topics, including gender discrimination; illegal arms dealing; an I.R.A. explosives trial; an action by Mensa to compel Camden Education Authority to pay school fees for a child with a high I.Q.; the expulsion of three German and Belgian "neo-Nazis"; insider dealing; the banning of a deputy circuit judge for drunk driving; a new chapter in the saga of Lloyds "names"; and a £50 million claim for negligence against a leading City firm of solicitors. There were reports on at least three alleged miscarriages of justice, one dealing with the Carl Bridgewater case and an interesting story about the University of Cambridge giving support to a professor of medicine who had been jailed in France for alleged negligence in respect of the distribution of HIV contaminated blood. This looked like a fairly typical day.

(c) Parliament was in session, but this was a relatively quiet day for legislative activity. Apart from the formal listing of the day's business, mentioned above, the most discussed issues were the age of consent for homosexuals and the debate on the Local Government etc (Scotland) Bill, in which the Government was accused of cynically promoting electoral advantage. A feature article urged the revival of the use of Parliamentary impeachment proceedings for dealing with corruption by ministers and other members of the executive. And there were several items dealing with issues of public policy which were relevant as background to possible legislative action in respect of domestic violence, credit cards, and insolvency.

(d) Legislative activity and proceedings in courts and other tribunals present the most visible and sensational side of the law to the media. They are public and conflict is the stuff of drama. Law has it share of headlines, but its main business is the prevention of disputes and the ordering of behaviour and expectations through rules and routines and ideas that are taken for granted. One can use the business pages to illustrate this point. One of the best compliments that I have heard paid to a law degree by a former student was that by the time he graduated he was equipped to understand every page of the *Financial Times* (including its excellent Arts section). On January 18, 1994 on a single page one finds allusions to white knight rescues, convertible preferred shares, vulture funds, a liquid secondary debt market; there is also the following sentence: "Profits were struck after a £600,000 exceptional charge, forecast on flotation, to meet the costs of unwinding and interest-rate hedge". On the same page there are references to the Take-Over Panel, the Office of Fair Trading, the Independent Television Commission, and the OECD—all institutions whose existence and powers are constituted by law. The law generates terms and concepts that invade specialised areas of activity. In the business pages there are also many words that are part of everyday use (at least for some) which derive their most precise, often technical, meanings from law: company, stocks, dividend, bankruptcy, and privatisation, for example. The same is more generally true of our ordinary language: contract, murder, rape, marriage, tenant, alien, infant, employer, social security.

It would be tedious and unnecessary to take you through the rest of the newspaper in detail: the advertisements, which on this day took up only about one-sixth of the space, could be dissected with a lawyer's eye; one could point to contract, torts, crime and administrative law on the sports pages; the arts section had less than its normal share of contract, employment, copyright and censorship matters; one could point out the range of constitutional, human rights and international law issues and terms that occur in the foreign news; or how in making sense of news from abroad it helps to have some knowledge of Islamic or foreign domestic or private international law. In trying to understand the Rushdie affair, it helps to know the meaning and implications of a *fatwa*. Even with this impressionistic analysis, enough has been said to illustrate the pervasiveness of law.

Let us pass on to a different point. One does not need to get very far into the project to recognise that what is to count as directly "legal" or "law related" depends on how one has defined the terms for the purpose of the exercise. Even if one adopts a very narrow definition, there will be many borderline or otherwise difficult cases. And the consequences of a narrow perspective should make one uneasy. If, on the other hand, one adopts a broad conception of "law", one may start to wonder whether any item in the whole paper is not "legally relevant". That is one object of the exercise. This is not to make the point that any law teacher can conjure up hypothetical legal problems from the most innocent-looking weather forecast or football report or book review. Rather it is to show how law lurks in the background of every event, transaction or relationship in our social life, even in supposedly private spheres, and that legal understanding is very often an important aspect of interpreting such matters.

Later I shall explore to what extent looking at social life with a lawyer's eye may produce any unique or special insights and how this can also be a distorting lens.[11] Here I want to make a more elementary point about law lurking in the background. Let us turn to page one of my newspaper. There were three lead stories on January 18th: by far the most prominent was the San Fernando Valley earthquake, which had claimed at least 22 lives on the previous day; secondly, this was the day on which it was reported that the Prime Minister had overruled his own officials in deciding that £234 million of foreign aid should be given to Malaysia to help fund the Pergau Dam project; a third headline stated that "Venables' £1 million payout opens way for shot at England goal". Although this last report explicitly discusses Terry Venables' legal problems when he was being considered for the post of England's Football Manager (references to which also appeared in the business and sports pages), it is the least legally interesting of the three. The Pergau Dam affair was not only politically embarrassing for the Government, but it brought to public attention a whole series of constitutional issues about accountability for and legality of decisions about foreign aid—issues which were subsequently taken up in Parliament and by constitutional lawyers.

The San Fernando Earthquake is a somewhat different example. This was a dramatic natural disaster in which the human suffering, damage to property and the geological background naturally attracted the most attention on three pages. Two small points caught my eye: on the front page the manager of a newly opened pizza kitchen was reported as saying: "My place is completely destroyed inside". The reporter continued: "which you would think was upsetting. But he shrugged and said: "Insurance". However, on page three it was reported that the initial estimate of the cost of the disaster was $ five billion, but the cost to the insurance industry was likely to be considerably less because earthquake insurance premiums were punitively expensive and many victims were uninsured. It happens that I was on the spot in Coral Gables, Florida during Hurricane Andrew and its aftermath. Its estimated cost was $20 billion. My memories include the visual impact of the devastation, stories of suffering, courage and generosity, and the ordeal of driving in the Greater Miami area with all the traffic lights out of action. But during the ensuing weeks I probably learned as much about insurance law in action as about anything else, although I was merely an observer. This was not so much about litigation as about the interpretation of insurance policies and the processes of negotiation and settlement of claims by adjusters in an emergency. There were, of course, other legal issues arising out of Hurricane Andrew, for example about the relative responsibility of the federal and state governments for disaster relief, and a host of other matters. This illustrates how most news items have obvious and not-so-obvious legal implications and that knowledge of legal rules alone will typically not be sufficient to predict what those might be.

When my students report back on the newspaper exercise, they generally come up with findings similar to those that I have summarised for January 18, 1994. Almost invariably they find contract on every page; they recognise that European Community Law, Public International Law and the domestic law of other countries not only feature in many news items, but also impinge on their lives in many more ways than most of them had previously realised; some acknowledge that they had begun to see that legal knowledge helps one to read a newspaper intelligently; and, to put the matter differently, a good legal education can provide one with a set of lenses for reading and interpreting current events and the contemporary world. They also begin to realise that reading newspapers is an important part of one's legal education.

The newspaper exercise is intended as an eye-opener. It should serve to convey a number of simple messages about their subject to first year law students: about the pervasiveness of law in society, its dynamism, its international character, its diversity and its potential interest. I use it mainly to try to bury two fallacies that are often rooted in the expectations of new law students. First is the Fustian Fallacy, that law as a subject is dry, boring, old-fashioned and esoteric. The exercise demonstrates that the subject-matter of law is dynamic, fascinating and relevant to almost every aspect of public and private life.

The second fallacy is that law is a new subject that they are encountering for the first time. In fact it is so much a part of our environment that our legal education begins at birth. Everyone daily has direct experience of state law. At a more fundamental level, everyone makes, interprets, obeys, manipulates and evades rules; everyone weighs evidence; everyone makes claims, negotiates, mediates, and argues; in daily living, almost everyone has been a claimant, negotiator, advocate and judge.

I can confidently stand in front of a class made up predominantly of 18 to 19 year olds and use a traditional law teacher's incantation: "I have before me a bunch of slanderers, legatees, trespassers, tortfeasors, buyers, sellers, copyright violators, smugglers, debtors and CRIMINALS".

I could say the same and more to my present audience. But my immediate purpose is to focus on law as an academic enterprise, as a subject of formal study and scholarly endeavour. In order to understand the world of the law school one needs to learn something about its history, traditions, dilemmas and quirks. Every adult member of society has some practical experience and a good deal of knowledge of many aspects of law, probably more than most of you realise. So, in an important sense, the subject-matter of the discipline needs no introduction. The treatment of law by the media reflects its pervasiveness in most aspects of our social, political and economic life. This seems to contrast quite sharply with the relatively low visibility of the discipline of law in our intellectual life: law as a subject of study is still widely considered to be technical and esoteric.

In the United States law schools are highly visible institutions. Law schools and law teachers feature in popular novels by Scott Turow and John Grisham; some of you will recall John Houseman as Professor Kingsfield of the Harvard Law School in *The Paperchase*, which was in turn a popular novel, a film and a soap opera, and of which one critic wrote that this was like *Love Story*, with a contracts teacher substituted for leukaemia as the villain.[12] Unlike their American counterparts, our law schools are not particularly prominent social institutions; law schools and law teachers hardly ever feature in British campus novels or soap operas; and the law section, if there is one, is almost always hidden in the remoter regions of even the best book shop. There is a puzzle here. Is there really a sharp contrast between the prominent treatment of law in newspapers and its place in other forms of literature? Let us pause for a moment and consider law in book shops through an anecdote.

LAW IN CULTURE: FANTASY IN A BOOK SHOP

One afternoon some years ago while browsing in a provincial second-hand book shop, I overheard a conversation between the manager and a new assistant. It was the time of year when university students try to sell their books after their examinations are over. The manager was explaining his buying policy for "intellectual" books: "We do not want specialist works", he was saying, "only those with some appeal to the general reader". By this test English literature, sociology, politics (but not economics), Penguin philosophy and works on oriental religions were "in"; technical and scientific books, law, business studies, medicine and Christian theology were "out". History, anthropology, classics and modern languages were tricky—"When in doubt don't buy" he advised.

This struck me as a fair précis of contemporary ideas of general middle-brow culture. I was sorry that law was dismissed so summarily. It was not surprising, for the image of law books is still of large volumes—erudite, expensive and boring—that are almost always to be found in the most remote part of a book shop, if they are stocked at all. One does not find law books on railway station bookstalls.

Reflecting on this later, I began to construct an imaginary conversation with the manager in which I tried to persuade him why and in what respects his attitude to law was wrong. Some of it went as follows:

"You already hold many books about law, only you don't classify them as such. Under literature you have *Bleak House, Billy Budd, Crime and Punishment, Lord of the Flies* and Kafka's *The Trial*; under history you have *Albion's Fatal Tree*, Maitland's *Constitutional History of England* and Herbert Morrison's *Memoirs*, each of which is about different aspects of law-making; the drama section includes *Antigone, A Man for All Seasons, The Merchant of Venice, St Joan, The Trial of Galileo, The Winslow Boy*, and many others—for drama and trials are natural partners. You have whole sections devoted to crime and detection; you

11

have biographies and memoirs of political prisoners, victims of torture, criminals, policemen and even lawyers and judges. You put Kant and Bentham under philosophy, Max Weber under sociology, Walter Bagehot, F. A. Hayek and the *Crossman Diaries* under politics, the *Koran* under religion, *Rumpole of the Bailey, Yes, Minister* and A. P. Herbert under humour; you have the *Encyclopaedia of Rules of Sports and Games* under sport, *Alice in Wonderland* in the children's section and the speeches of Cicero and Demosthenes, *Njal's Saga* and *The Trial of Socrates* under classics. Karl Marx is almost everywhere."

"What have all these to do with law?"

"Each of them deals with important law-related themes: *Lord of the Flies* is about anarchy—absence of law; *Antigone* is a classic treatment of civil disobedience and a citizen's obligation to obey the law; *Crime and Punishment* is about responsibility, retribution and expiation; *Bleak House* is about the abuses of legal procedure; and the *Crossman Diaries*—like many political memoirs—tell us a lot about the workings of the Constitution and the making of laws. Max Weber is perhaps the leading pioneer of legal sociology, and Frederic William Maitland is indisputably our greatest legal historian".

"These may all be relevant to law or about law in some rather general way, but surely they are not law books".

"The distinction between law books and books about law is a useful one, although it is beginning to break down",[13] I replied, "but a legal background is helpful to understanding and appreciating each of the works I have mentioned; and one cannot begin to understand law if one only studies 'law books' in the very narrow sense in which you envisage them".

"You cannot understand law merely by reading books", he commented. "Is there not a cliché about the gap between law in books and law in action?"[14]

"That is also true. And this brings me to another point. You have an outdated image of specialist law books. Some years ago nearly all law books were heavy technical treatises. They were mainly works of reference or traditional student texts; they were strictly confined to expounding legal rules; they told us little about the actual operation of the law in practice and, of course, they hardly qualified as bedside reading. That has changed. There has been something approaching a revolution in law publishing. History, politics, sociology, statistics, philosophy, literary theory, critical commentary on current affairs and much else besides have found their way into books that still can only be classified as legal works; at the very least this new material provides some necessary background to legal rules, so that law is now said to be studied in its political, social, economic or other contexts.

The distinction between law in books and law in action is dissolving as more of the action gets into the books. There is thus much greater variety in legal literature than there was twenty years ago. Law books have come out of the age of the wing collar and the quill pen: their jackets are often in bright, even garish, colours and a few years ago one leading law publisher allowed pictures on the cover for the first time in nearly 200 years! So we are not very far from having law books, as well as books about law—if the distinction still holds—on railway station bookstalls.

All of this is part of a trend towards a closer integration of law and other subjects. We have not quite reached the point where the law is once again seen as one of the great humane subjects, along with history and literature, as it was in Classical and Medieval times, and as Blackstone tried to make it in the eighteenth century. But the study of law has become much broader and more diverse than it used to be. One result has been to make much legal literature more accessible to ordinary readers. Law is far too important, too far-reaching and too interesting not to be part of general culture".

The original episode took place about 12 years ago. Book shops have not changed very much, but it is probably true to say that there has been a significant increase in exposure of law on television, as is illustrated by such popular series as *Crimewatch*, *L.A. Law*, and *Streetlaw*. Since then there has also developed a "Law and Literature Movement" which has been hailed by some as a significant breakthrough in academic law and which has been attacked by an American academic and Judge, Richard Posner, as fundamentally misconceived.[15]

Even more striking is the extraordinary recent success of American lawyer-novelists, particularly John Grisham, Scott Turow, Philip Friedman, and Richard North Patterson, who singly and collectively have broken a number of publishing records in the United States. Novels, and films based on them, such as *The Firm, The Pelican Brief* and *Presumed Innocent,* have penetrated the British market.[16] It has been suggested that one reason for the popularity of the genre is that the ambiguities and dilemmas of legal practice suit the modern mood better than the heroes and villains of classic westerns or the intellectual puzzles of the ordinary detective story. With the ending of the Cold War the lawyer can replace the spy or double agent as a morally ambiguous protagonist, operating in a dramatic setting with endless narrative opportunities. The American lawyer novel has the advantage of being able to deal with a very wide range of subjects, many of which are topical, complex and controversial, because in America, at least, almost any public issue can be transformed into a legal issue, as de Tocqueville noted long ago. Unlike some other kinds of best-seller, it appeals to both men and women.[17] This interpretation may exaggerate the long-term staying power of the genre. Be that as it may, the book shop fantasy echoes the newspaper exercise in reminding us of the ubiquity of law in intellectual and popular culture as well as in everyday life.

It might be objected that newspapers, books, plays and TV programmes do not accurately reflect the realities of law in society any more than they mirror other aspects of everyday life. Newspapers emphasise the unusual, the dramatic, the sensational. On the whole, what works well, the routine, and the commonplace are not "news". "Driver observes speed-limit" or "John Brown not burgled last night" or even "Businessman honours contract" are not the stuff of headlines. Yet one of the main functions of law is to produce such orderly behaviour. Similarly courtroom dramas feature prominently in fiction, film and plays just because they are seen as dramatic. But few real life trials are sensational or even interesting for spectators, and we sometimes forget that the contested trial is wholly exceptional in legal life.

It might be argued, not only is law treated highly selectively in the news and other media, but what is depicted may be misleading or inaccurate. One should not confuse journalism or fiction with sociology. This point applies with special force to television and other forms of popular culture from which many people get some of the most vivid impressions and images of law. As an American commentator, Lawrence Friedman, put it:

"Suppose our legal sources were all destroyed in a nuclear nightmare which wiped out [all the standard legal reference works and sources];

later generations digging in the ruins, discover intact only the archives of NBC Television. The diggers would certainly get a distorted picture of the legal system. They would learn little or nothing about property law, tax law, regulation of business, and very little about tort law or even family law; but they would find an enormous amount of material on police, murder, deviance, rape and organized crime ... Crime shows, for example, overrepresent violent crimes; shoplifting is no great audience-holder, but murder is. A study of prime-time TV in 1972 counted 26 murders and 20 cases of aggravated assault out of 119 total crimes in a single week; there were only two burglaries and three cases of drug possession".[18]

Similar considerations apply to the portrayal of law in programmes such as *Rumpole* or *L.A. Law*, in classic and popular novels and in courtroom scenes in films and soap operas. In that context Friedman's warnings are important: we should not assume that newspapers, the media or fiction deal with all aspects of law in society or legal practice; nor should we expect them to present a sociologically accurate or balanced picture of the realities of the law in action; nor, merely by looking at books and films, can we tell to what extent they either reflect or influence how ordinary people perceive or understand law.

Nevertheless the newspaper exercise and the book shop fantasy illustrate some valid points: first, the law is ubiquitous—it pervades nearly all aspects of our lives, whether or not we realise it. Indeed, it may be because we are so dependent on law that it is so prominent in the media, even if its reflection is distorted. Secondly everyone in society has had a great deal of direct and indirect exposure to matters legal, but what they have learned, the impressions they have gained may not be representative or accurate. "Life in America, and in the West in general", says Friedman, "is a vast diffuse school of Law".[19] But, one might add, you do not want to believe all you learn in school. Thirdly, law as a subject of formal study is important and can be interesting; yet there is a puzzle about the relationship between law as a discipline and law in culture and society. For example, if one does penetrate to the law section in a remote part of a good second-hand book shop one is still likely to find plenty of evidence for the old image of heavy, daunting, impenetrable, technical, fustian, tomes with incomprehensible titles that suggest a subject that is mysterious and remote from common sense and everyday experience. More like an old testament litany, perhaps: Byles on Bills, Cheshire on Conflicts, Bodkin on Champerty, Gale on Easements, Scrutton on Charterparties,

Snell on Equity, Mather on Sheriff and Execution Law, Kerr on Receivers and Withers on Reversions. This raises some questions that we shall need to consider: what is the relationship between law as a discipline and general intellectual culture? Is there a major gap? If so, is this necessary and is it changing?

THE SCOPE OF LAW: THE LAW IN ACTION, LAWYERS' ACTION, AND LAW AS A SUBJECT OF STUDY

So far I have touched on the relationship between law as depicted in newspapers and other cultural media and law in society—what is sometimes referred to as law in action. We should not assume that because law is ubiquitous in social life that practising and academic lawyers are necessarily regularly concerned with all aspects of law in society. Indeed, it is a commonplace that "lawyers' action" tends to be much narrower in scope than the law in action. Even in the United States most citizens rarely, if ever, consult a lawyer. There are large areas of legal regulation which are either handled by other kinds of specialist (for example, in health and safety legislation or atomic energy law) or do not, for one reason or another, become a focus for any kind of legal practitioner; there are many kinds of needs or potential demands for legal services which for economic or other reasons have not been met by the legal profession. Significant parts of welfare, employment, debt, and consumer law are examples: some lawyers deal with such problems, but their contribution is tiny in relation to potential demand or need. There are possible markets for legal services which from time to time have been dominated by other professionals: for example, accountants have traditionally captured a major share of the market for tax advice and insolvency; and rent reviews are more often dealt with by surveyors than by solicitors. So we need to distinguish between the law in action in society and that part of it which is "lawyers' action". And we need to recognise that the relationship between the two changes from time to time and from place to place.

What is studied in law schools overlaps with both of these, but tends to be narrower than either. On the whole this is because institutionalised academic law has been strongly influenced by what is covered by the professional examinations and the perceived needs of fledgling practitioners. Law degrees have concentrated on the alleged "core" of general practice—providing building blocks and leaving out great areas of specialisation. Thus succession, tax, civil procedure, commercial arbitration, and construction law, are examples of recognised areas of specialised legal practice which traditionally have received relatively little sustained scholarly attention. Academic fashion sometimes lags behind areas in legal practice; sometimes it anticipates them. But at any given period in the history of legal education and legal scholarship in England, the focus of legal scholarship has tended to be narrower than the scope of legal practice—both in respect of fields of law and of sustained treatment of the law in action from practitioners' points of view. There are, of course, some areas of legal scholarship—criminology, sociology of law, labour law, Chinese law— where the academics' focus of attention has been much broader than that of practitioners. But these have tended to be minority options, which usually attract few students.

The newspaper exercise illustrated among other things some of the difficulties of differentiating law from other phenomena. It raises in this context the specific question: what is the scope of the discipline of law? or to put it differently: what precisely are we studying when we study law? A natural response to such questions is to seek a general definition of the word "law". But experience has taught us that this is not likely to be very helpful.

There are some obvious reasons why this is so. First, the word "law" is regularly used in many different senses in many different contexts. There is no clear criterion for deciding which of these meanings we should choose here.

Secondly, and more important, puzzlements and disagreements about the scope of the discipline of law relate to issues of substance (what should we be studying when we study law?) rather than about the meanings of words. What should be the scope of the study of law is regularly contested among legal scholars, as we shall see. Some, for example, think that the study of law should be confined to legal rules made by the State; some would include "non-state law" such as custom, international law and religious law; most would include the policies, principles or reasons behind the rules as well as or as an integral part of the rules themselves; others would include institutions such as courts, the legal profession, and the judiciary; and many would include the social, economic and political context and consequences of legal rules, pro-

17

cesses and institutions. And who would exclude the history, philosophy or anthropology of law as being of no concern to legal scholars?

Thirdly, in respect of any of these different conceptions there will be many borderline cases, yet the problem of whether or not some particular example is to be treated as falling inside or outside a precisely drawn boundary is often quite trivial. Precise boundary-drawing by courts sometimes has important practical consequences, but in many other contexts whether a borderline case is classified as "legal" or "non-legal" is not important. It does not matter for the purposes of the newspaper exercise whether one treats a report of a routine police investigation of a murder or a hostile take-over bid as being "legally relevant" or not.

I propose to adopt a broad conception of the subject-matter of the discipline of law without entering into complex issues of legal theory to justify this position. In due course we shall come across alternative, generally narrower, conceptions of the subject and we can consider some of the pros and cons of such alternative perspectives. Nor will I concern myself very much with outer boundaries of my discipline and with borderline cases. Rather, following the American jurist Karl Llewellyn, I shall adopt the broad and deliberately vague conception of law as a social institution specialised to the performing of certain tasks or meeting certain needs in human groups, especially those groups which we call societies.[20] These tasks include dispute-prevention, dispute-settlement, allocation of power and authority, and the technology involved in performing these tasks, including the skills, devices and artefacts that have been produced by the systematic study of law.[21] In this view the subject-matter of the study of law includes ideas, principles, rules, personnel, processes, institutions, skills, and much else besides. Later we can consider whether and when we can sensibly place any limits on the field and whether it can be said to have a core.[22] This broad conception, to which I am generally sympathetic, fits my present purpose because I am here concerned with what is in fact studied in law schools—and all of these matters are in fact studied in at least some law schools.

I shall not try here to justify my choice of perspective theoretically. But it may be useful to illustrate its application by reference to a research project in which I was recently engaged. As part of a wider project on archives policy in the Commonwealth, a team of us undertook a case-study of legal records in Accra, Ghana.[23] One of the main objectives of the project was to persuade archivists that they should conceive of "legal records" as extending far beyond the records of courts and land registries, which have traditionally been treated by archivists as being the main or only kind of "legal records". The concern was practical, viz. to draw attention to a wide range of documents that have tended to be ignored or neglected in selecting those to be saved for posterity.

In order to set some limits to our enquiry and to obtain the necessary clearances we had to clarify what we meant by "legal records". We avoided attempting a general definition of types of document, as that would have entailed endless debates about whether bus-tickets, lawyers' personal papers, official notices, financial records of a law school or anthropologists' field notes on customary law were "legal records". Rather we said that we were interested in the records of all institutions "specialised to law" and the criteria for selecting them for preservation or destruction. This greatly simplified our enquiry and fitted in well with archivists' ways of doing things, because the first principle of archives management is to classify records by provenance (or source) rather than by subject. We resolved other borderline cases pragmatically, usually in terms of their potential scholarly interest.

Although we had limited time and resources and had to be highly selective, we were able to achieve our main aim of illustrating the range of potentially interesting law-related documents that need to be considered in formulating selection criteria for archival purposes in Ghana or any other similar jurisdiction. In the past, attention had been focused almost exclusively on the courts. The Accra study suggested that there were institutions of comparable interest in the governmental, parastatal and private spheres. To give a few examples: governmental institutions specialised to law include the Ministry of Justice, legal departments of several ministries, the Land Registry, the Ombudsman, the Committee for the Defence of the Revolution and the Peoples' Tribunals, as well as institutions concerned with law reporting, law-making, law-enforcement, licensing and tax. The parastatal sector included major projects with an international dimension such as joint ventures with agreements involving enormous sums of money, sometimes with provision for arbitration abroad and under foreign law. For example, we found important collections in the legal departments of the Volta River Authority and the State Insurance Corporation. Of particular interest was the Ga House of Chiefs, which held extensive records of traditional dispute-settlement processes some, but by no means all, of which were either recognised or incorporated into the national court system, a fascinating example of the interaction between the State and "customary law". The Faculty of Law of the University of Ghana also contained a rich and, in some respects, surprising confusion of documents.

In the private sector, in addition to the records of law firms, were to be found non-governmental organisations offering legal advice or acting as pressure groups for reform, a women's group involved in a legal awareness programme, letter-writers sitting outside the court and even professional witnesses (although they generally do not keep written records). Lawyers have played a particularly important role in the history of Ghana and whether or not one counts the personal papers of a lawyer-politician as a "legal record", few can doubt that such collections are potentially of great archival interest.

The findings of the Ghana study were mirrored in a subsequent study of selected legal institutions in England and Wales.[24] Records which provide crucial evidence of the law in action in all its many aspects are created, but are not always managed or preserved, by a vast range of organisations including, for example, a number of well-known voluntary bodies concerned with civil liberties, law reform, miscarriages of justice or filling in gaps in legal services to the less well-off. Many of these had only rudimentary or no records management policies. Nearly of all them had failed to attract the sustained attention of archivists, perhaps because the latter have had a narrow, court-centred picture of law.

The legal records project illustrates a number of further points First, it reinforces one lesson of the newspaper exercise: that litigation is only one small and exceptionally visible part of legal activity in any society. Secondly, I would suggest that all of the examples listed above are relatively clear cases of institutions specialised to law or at least clearly law-related and as such of potential interest to students of law. However, thirdly, most of the records identified in this survey were potentially of at least as much interest to historians and social scientists as to legal scholars. Indeed one can predict with some confidence that academic lawyers in most countries will make less use of legal records preserved in national archives than will other kinds of scholars. This is significant not merely as a reminder of the obvious point that law is of interest to students and scholars from other disciplines, but also that there are factors in academic legal culture that may militate against the rich variety of legal records being much exploited by the law school community. Primary legal documents such as contracts, wills, trade agreements, commercial paper and even trial records, have to an extra-ordinary extent been neglected in legal studies and, in due course, we shall need to consider why this might be.

CONCLUSION

In this chapter I have tried to illustrate the potential of law as a subject of study—its pervasiveness, its variety, its vitality, its relevance to social life at all levels. I have also suggested that the study of law can provide one kind of way of looking at both practical problems and social events. Legal thought and language can provide one set of lenses for interpreting the world. I have introduced a set of distinctions—between the law in action in society, lawyers' action and academic law—which overlap in quite complicated ways. The significance of these distinctions should become clearer as we continue on our tour. In the next chapters, we shall look at English law schools as institutions. I shall start with some history. For I believe that one can only make sense of the institutionalised study of law and its relationship to law in society and legal practice, by outlining the story of the development of law schools in the context of higher education as well as of the legal profession and legal system. We shall also need to look at the culture of law schools: their roles and values as institutions, the economic and political factors that affect them, the aspirations and dilemmas of teachers and students, and the ideas that underpin the discipline.

Notes

[1] W. Blackstone, *Commentaries on the Laws of England* (1st ed., 1765–69) (references are to the Facsimile of the First Edition (ed. S. Katz, 1979)).
[2] Canon and Civil Law had been taught in English universities long before Blackstone. English Law had been taught at the Inns of Court from the Middle Ages. There had been institutional works before Blackstone, for example by Coke, Wood and Hale. Blackstone, however, was the first university Professor of English Law and his *Commentaries* were more comprehensive and, in some respects, more systematic than previous English expository works.
[3] F. W. Maitland, "English Law", *Encyclopaedia Britannica* (11th ed., 1910), Vol. 9, at pp. 601–607. A. L. Smith said of this article, which first appeared in the 1902 edition, that it was "the irreducible minimum which every educated man should read." (*F. W. Maitland*, 1908).
[4] Duncan Kennedy "The Structure of Blackstone's Commentaries" (1979) 28 *Buffalo L. Rev* 205.
[5] John Baker, "University College and Legal Education, 1826–1976" (1977) *Current Legal Problems* 1.

21

6 3 *Comm.* 268. Blackstone's home at Wallingford from 1761 was called Priory Park; the original house survives with some alterations and is variously known as Priory Place or Priory Castle. See David Lockmiller, *Sir William Blackstone* (1938) Chap. VI.
7 See G. Jones (ed.) *The Sovereignty of the Law*, (1973) at pp. xxxiii–iv; cf. 3 *Comm.* 267–268. Blackstone's use of architectural metaphors is discussed by David Lieberman, "Blackstone's Science of Legislation" Part II (1989) *Law and Justice*, 31, at pp. 36–37. Dr. John Cairns has pointed out to me the extensive use of similar architectural metaphors in Sir Walter Scott's pamphlet, *The Visionary* (1819).
8 Karl Llewellyn, Unpublished lecture, (undated, circa 1955) quoted in KLRM at p. 309.
9 John Grisham, *The Client* (1993) at p. 76.
10 One version of the instructions is printed in HDTWR at pp. 386–387.
11 Below, especially Chaps. 5 and 7.
12 Burton F. Brody, review of *The Paperchase* (1974) 26 *Jo. Legal Educ.* 605. The original novel by John Osborn was published in 1971.
13 R. Abel, "Law Books and Books about Law" (1974) 26 *Stanford L. Rev.* 175.
14 The phrase was first used to indicate a gap between what legal rules prescribed should happen and their actual impact. The extension of the term to refer to other "gaps" is usefully discussed in David Nelken, "The 'Gap Problem' in the Sociology of Law: A Theoretical Review" (1981) 1 *Windsor Yearbook of Access to Justice* 35.
15 R. Posner, *Law and literature: A Misunderstood Relation.* (1988)
16 The original novels that have been made into films were by John Grisham, (*The Firm* and *The Pelican Brief*) and Scott Turow (*Presumed Innocent*). Others are on the way and there are many imitators. Perhaps the best-known precursor was Harper Lee's *To Kill a Mockingbird*, starring Gregory Peck, which became a film classic about racism and rape (1962).
17 This paragraph draws on an interesting television programme, "The Best-seller Brief", which included interviews of several leading lawyer-novelists by Mark Lawson (BBC, Late Show, 1994).
18 Lawrence M. Friedman, "Law, Lawyers and Popular Culture" (1989) *Yale L. J.* 1579 at p. 1588.
19 *ibid.* at p. 1598.
20 The most important statement of the law-jobs theory is Karl Llewellyn, "The Normative, the Legal and the Law-Jobs", (1940) 49 *Yale Law J.* 1355; for a recent discussion and elaboration see JJM at pp. 126–136.
21 *Ibid.*
22 Below, Chap. 7.
23 The final report was by P. Akotia, H. Akussah and V. Dankwa, *Legal Records in Accra* (1992), (ACARM and CLEA, London). A shorter version is included in W. Twining and E. Quick (eds.), *Legal Records in the Commonwealth* (1994), Chap. 4; the theoretical framework is developed in *ibid.*, Chap. 1.
24 Clare Cowling, *ibid.* Chap. 5.

2. Law in the Universities: The Historical Context

"Americans who have walked through the quads and gardens of Oxford and Cambridge, and who know that Harvard was modelled on a Cambridge college, often think of British universities as immeasurably older than our own. But in fact higher education as a system is much younger in the United Kingdom than in the United States. The U.S. organisational revolution took place 100 years ago, roughly between 1870 and 1910; the emergence of the British system is still underway." (Martin Trow)[1]

Martin Trow is one of those who have argued that the modern English university system is largely a post Second World War creation—especially in respect of its "public life", that is to say its governance, finance, organisation and scale. From this perspective the modern English law school is even younger.

Two great theses of Max Weber help to explain Trow's conclusions. First, in 1918, Weber predicted the Americanisation of the European university as part of the adaptation of traditional corporate bodies to the economy of modern capitalist societies: the result would be increasing demand for high-level manpower, the bureaucratisation of institutions of higher education and the "proletarianisation" of the academic profession in respect of both teaching and research.[2] America was somewhat ahead in a process that was one part of modernisation. It is widely accepted that Weber's interpretation was essentially correct, but that Britain has resisted this kind of change longer than most industrialised countries. We are still moving uneasily and jerkily from a small, elite, accretion of autonomous institutions towards a more centralised, mass system of higher education. The process has been evolutionary and not necessarily unilinear.

Secondly, in writing about law before 1920, Max Weber contrasted the civil and common law systems largely in terms of differences between their "legal honoratiores"—his mildly sardonic term for dominant legal elites.[3] The civil law system was operated by university-trained personnel and dominated by jurists who systematised, codified, and refined the law in a "formal rational" manner. In England, on the other hand apprenticeship was the almost exclusive mode of legal training; legal practice and legal development were also dominated by pragmatic, case-oriented lawyers. Legal culture was tradition-bound, technical and, in Weber's view, "irrational".[4]

Some aspects of Weber's thesis are controversial, but given the limited scale and prestige of English law schools when he wrote, and indeed for a further 50 years, there is no denying the past dominance of the practising profession, especially the bar and the judiciary, over legal training and our legal culture generally. We shall see later that during the key period of expansion of university legal education, several other factors combined to assign law schools a severely limited role. However, both of Weber's generalisations have proved to be broadly correct over the long haul.

ACADEMIC LAW BEFORE 1945

If one were to write the history of academic law in England from the mid-nineteenth century until 1945 in terms of outstanding individuals and their ideas, a passable array of talent could be assembled: Blackstone, Bentham, Austin, Maine, Stephen, Pollock, Dicey, Bryce, Anson, Vinogradoff, Holdsworth, Maitland and Jennings would make a reasonable team. Their names are remembered, some of their works are still read, but they left a legacy of ideas rather than institutions.

Instead, the story of the institutionalisation of the discipline of law in England is generally presented as a dreary procession of disappointments and missed opportunities. The standard version might be restated as follows: the study of English Law can be traced back over several centuries; its failure to become established or accepted in universities is the central theme. One can begin with the rise and decline of the Inns of Court as centres of learning. Canon Law was studied at Oxford and Cambridge from the twelfth century until the Reformation. The study of Civil Law continued much longer.[5] But the story of English Law in the universities is an unhappy one. Blackstone's lectures and the creation of the Vinerian Chair at Oxford in the 1750s failed to establish the study of English Law on a secure footing at Oxford. The Downing Chair at Cambridge, founded in 1800, fared no better. For much of the nineteenth century it was a sinecure. University College, London is sometimes credited with setting up the first modern English law school in 1826. After a brisk start, it rapidly declined. The first graduating class with the LLB in 1839 totalled three; by 1900 it had produced a mere 135 graduates in law—about the same as the present faculty graduates in a single year. John Austin, who resigned his chair at UCL in despair,[6] wrote: "Turning from the study of the English to the study of the Roman law, you escape from the empire of chaos and darkness, to a world which seems by comparison, the region of order and light."[7] In 1846 the House of Commons Select Committee on Legal Education described a situation that approximated the Bellman's map. . . . a perfect and absolute blank: "No legal education worthy of the name, is at this moment to be had in either England or Ireland."[8]

In the second half of the nineteenth century, and especially from 1866, serious efforts by some extraordinarily talented men at Oxford, and to a lesser extent at Cambridge, showed by example that the study of law could be a worthwhile and serious enterprise.[9] They published some influential works, but by and large they failed to attract able students or to gain full acceptance by fellow academics or by the practising profession. The strong note of disappointment in Bryce's valedictory lecture at Oxford in 1893 contrasts sharply with the optimism of his inaugural lecture in 1871.[10] In the early years of the twentieth century several attempts to establish a national centre of legal education in London foundered on the mutual distrust of practitioners and academics.

One of the recurrent themes that runs through debates and histories of legal education in most comon law countries is the low prestige of law schools and the low status of academic lawyers, both within the university and in the eyes of the profession. The theme has sometimes been overplayed,[11] but the images are powerful, and no doubt self-confirming: John Austin, the neurotic introvert paralysed into silence; C. P. Snow's Lewis Eliot, the leisured foreground observer, is a failed practitioner put out to grass in Cambridge by kind friends; even Christopher Columbus Langdell, the pioneer of the great American law school, is depicted by Jerome Frank as a withdrawn neurotic, who, having failed in practice, cherished "inaccessible retirement."[12] Such images were damaging and, in England, persistent.[13]

This broad picture is supported by the available statistics. In 1909 there were reported to be 109 teachers of law, although how many were genuinely full-time is uncertain; by 1933–34 this had only increased to 130 and the number seems to have been about the same in 1945. As we shall see, the contrast with developments after the Second World War could hardly be greater. In business terms, legal education as an industry has diversified and in 1994 was at least 25–30 times as productive as it was in 1945.

Naturally these generalisations and bare statistics need to be taken with a pinch of salt. Histories of legal education prior to 1945 are patchy, and the complex story of developments in the last fifty years has yet to be told in any detail. Nevertheless, the standard accounts provide strong support for the proposition that the modern English law school is in most important respects a post Second World War creation. I propose to accept this interpretation, subject to two caveats: First, this kind of analysis is by no means unique to law. As late as 1900 most of the academic subjects we know today had either barely been accepted in the university or had not been invented. A similar story could be told about the struggle for acceptance and the institutionalisation of English literature or psychology or sociology or geography, to say nothing of more recent or more esoteric subjects.[14] Secondly, there are some important continuities. Some surviving ideas, attitudes and practices can be traced back much further than 1945: the pre-eminence of Oxford and Cambridge; ideas about institutional autonomy and academic freedom; single honours degrees; English legal positivism; and professional scepticism about the relevance of university law as a preparation for practice are relevant examples.

THE POST-WAR PERIOD

In preparing this study, I read extensively in the literature on higher education in Britain, especially works dealing with its "public life" since 1944. On the whole, Carswell, Halsey, Trow, Stewart, Scott, and the Leverhulme studies of the early 1980s tell a fairly consistent story.[15] Eric Ashby and others provide a broader sweep in both time and space.[16] Legal education has also been much written about. One's first impression is of two extensive bodies of literature that hardly interconnect. Public policy discussions and reports about legal education and training and about the discipline of law have tended to be inward-looking and parochial, often downplaying or ignoring key factors in the wider institutional context and over-estimating the room for manoeuvre and the scope for special policies for law within the general system of higher education. The three most important reports on legal education since 1945—Ormrod (1971), Benson (1979), and Marre (1988)—were all primarily concerned with problems of the legal profession and paid hardly any attention to trends and policies affecting higher education as a whole.[17]

The massive, obsessively repetitious secondary literature on legal education is similarly inward-looking and cocooned, presenting a not particularly appetising picture of lawyers and law teachers talking past each other or to themselves, airing their prejudices and promoting sectional interests. There have been power struggles, conflicts about objectives and priorities, and genuine puzzles and dilemmas. As we shall see, there has also been a propensity to misread the situation, not least in respect of power and finance.[18]

Most reports and debates on legal education ignore the broader educational context, preferring to focus on the relationship between academic law and private legal practice. There have been two main exceptions to this: law teachers, struggling to fight the "trade school" image, regularly invoke classic values of liberal education and occasionally cite Thorsten Veblen, John Henry Newman and others as authority. More recently, those concerned with pedagogical techniques and with skills training have begun to draw on standard educational literature and the writings of a few gurus, such as B. S. Bloom, Robert Mager and Donald Schon.[19]

Conversely, and somewhat surprisingly, law hardly gets any mention in the literature on higher education. The library of the Institute of Education in London subscribes to none of the legal education journals and stocks almost none of the standard works on the subject. Law barely features in the indexes of most general works on higher education in Britain.[20] Even the literature on professional education typically pays much more attention to medicine, engineering and business education; and, as we have seen, in contrast to the United States, our law teachers and law schools hardly feature at all in campus novels. Most significant of all, for most practical and statistical purposes in higher education policy, law has been lumped in with arts or social science. Educationalists and other non-lawyers have made a minimal impact on discussions of legal education and vice versa. Law is almost invisible in the literature and in discussions of policy in higher education.

There are several plausible explanations for the invisibility of law: in contrast to Continental Europe and the United States, the subject was a late-comer to English universities and for a long time it had low prestige within the academy and in the eyes of the legal profession. Law schools have not so far been perceived as, or performed the role of, professional schools and for a long time law's credentials as a proper university subject were questioned by colleagues in science, social science and the humanities. Even since the period of high demand and rapid expansion after 1945, law has only been a small part of the total picture: until recently law students and law teachers have hardly ever exceeded 3.5 per cent of the total, and have generally been nearer to 2 per cent; their share of the budget has been even less.[21] Where a law school has achieved separate status as a faculty, it is typically the smallest and is considered to be an anomaly. Perhaps commentators on higher education, like historians, have considered law to be a mysterious closed world that it is difficult for outsiders to penetrate.

The low visibility of law in discussions of higher education policy is of considerable significance in interpreting the present situation of law schools. For most practical purposes, law in universities and polytechnics has been treated as just one, relatively small and insignificant part of the humanities and social sciences. This suggests a crucial hypothesis: changes in undergraduate legal education closely reflect changes in higher education because most important decisions affecting the discipline of law in universities— on admissions, numbers, student-staff ratios, gender ratios, resourcing, teaching methods, quality assurance, terms of service and career development of academics—have much more closely reflected changes in higher education than changes in legal practice and the legal system. Insofar as this is true, most policy debates on legal education have had little impact on the development of law schools. There are some exceptions, notably the rigid division of legal education and training into separate stages after 1971, but as we shall see this served to reinforce the closer integration of law into the academy. Against this background let us briefly consider some of the main developments in higher and legal education since the Second World War.

1945–60: Quiet Expansion.[22]

From 1943 it was foreseen that there would be a major demand for the expansion of higher education and plans were drawn up to cope with the post-war bulge and to increase numbers. The 1944 Education Act was designed to reshape the whole educational system and in particular to prepare many more for entry into further education. For the first time the universities were included in political and economic planning as part of a national system.

Immediately after the war, there was rapid expansion followed by a period of consolidation. Stewart highlights five key areas of change between 1945–60:

> "First, the massive public concern about increased and improved provision of education, particularly higher education; second, the amount of new ground broken both within the institutions and in their relationships with one another; third, the evidence of an increase in central planning; fourth, the growth of applied sciences and social sciences in universities; fifth, the commitment to longer-term educational policies with the pledges by future governments which that implies."[23]

This was the period of the Welfare State, the Cold War and public demand for increased educational opportunity. Perhaps the most important development was the increasing commitment of governments to carry the major burden of funding higher education. Successive plans projected that two-thirds of the increases in student numbers should be in the sciences and applied sciences, but largely because the school system (especially girls' schools) was unable to deliver, the bulk of expansion was taken up by arts and the fast-developing social sciences, including law.

The 1950s saw the beginning of what Noel Annan called "the Age of the don",[24] which continued until the early to mid-seventies. The decade was also later referred to as "the silent fifties", a label which refers more to political style and lack of interest in university governance than to general political apathy. It was, in fact, a period of very significant change in higher education, but with very much less public debate and controversy than in the years that followed. There was a largely silent revolution in which the ground was laid and the momentum was built up for the more spectacular changes of the heady sixties. For some, the most visible revolution in universities was "the revolution in philosophy".

Legal education between 1945–60 mirrors the general pattern. The number of undergraduates reading law rose from 1515 in 1938–39 (62 per cent at Oxbridge) to about 3,000 in 1959–60 (42 percent at Oxbridge), almost an exact reflection of undergraduate expansion.[25] Figures on "full-time" university law teachers are similar, but less reliable: they had remained fairly constant in the 1930s, and they too had approximately doubled between 1945 and 1960 (272 in 1963). There was uncertainty, but relatively little public debate about the contents and methods of legal education. In the 1950s academic law was still not highly regarded by either the universities or the profession: academically able intending barristers typically read other subjects before proceeding to a cram course at Gibson and Weldon, the efficently anti-intellectual commercial tutors; most of those who qualified as solicitors were nongraduates; and several law faculties saw their main function as preparing local articled clerks for the Law Society's examinations.[26]

Addresses by Presidents of the Society of Public Teachers of Law sometimes lamented the low prestige and underfunding of legal education, but by and large there was an atmosphere of quietism among leaders of the profession, ranging from complacency to mild depression about lack of prestige and influence. It is in this period that some of the best known derogatory statements about academic law and lawyers were made.[27]

There was one notable exception to this quietism. In his inaugural lecture, published in extended form in 1950, Professor L. C. B. Gower of LSE launched a powerful attack on "English Legal Training", in which he castigated practitioners and academics alike.[28] He proposed a clear separation between "preliminary theoretical training, which should be left to the universities, and subsequent practical training and qualifications for entry, both of which should be controlled by practitioners."[29] He also argued for the study of law in its social context, four year degrees and differential pay for law teachers. This lecture seems to have made no immediate impact, but it came to be treated by the next generation of law teachers as one of the few important statements about their enterprise. In retrospect, Gower's lecture reads like a self-fulfilling prophecy, for all but the last two of his suggestions became the foundation of a new orthodoxy. Gower himself went on to make major contributions to changes in legal education and training, first at LSE, then in West Africa in the early sixties, and eventually in England through his membership of the Ormrod Committee—but that was 20 years later.[30]

Not only was there little sustained discussion about legal education among law teachers, let alone law students, during the fifties, but there were very few significant intellectual developments in the discipline. The most notable event was the appointment of H. L. A. Hart, who was at the time virtually unknown outside a small circle in Oxford, to the Corpus Chair of Jurisprudence at Oxford. He brought the revolution in philosophy to legal theory and within a remarkably short time made a profound impact on the subject, introducing a new note of vigorous intellectualism into academic law.[31]

Thus on the surface the period 1945–60 was marked by steady expansion, but little intellectual ferment. Visiting Americans made unfavourable comparisons to their own law schools with varying degrees of diplomacy.[32] However, as with the university system, the seeds of change were sown. In particular, the legal profession was expanding and more and more of those who had chosen to read law went on to qualify professionally. The pattern of the law degree as the normal route of entry began to develop slowly. For many years solicitors' clerks had been able to study for Part I of the solicitors' finals by attending lectures at an "approved law school", but as the university law schools focused more on undergraduate teaching, mutual dissatisfaction built up, and the system broke down, ending a long period of close association between the Law Society and provincial university law schools.[33]

Expansion also involved recruitment of more teachers. Most of the next generation of academic lawyers graduated in the fifties and started teaching then or in the early sixties. A significant number had experience of American law schools or of teaching in Africa or elsewhere in the Commonwealth or both—experiences which opened their eyes to new possibilities.[34]

The Turbulent Sixties

Euphoria, turbulence, and change mark the decade of the sixties. It is impossible in a short summary to do justice to the richness and complexity of the story of higher education in this period. The most persistent theme was expansion. This is also the era of the Robbins Report,[35] the creation of the binary system (despite Robbins), the establishment of the Open University (which by arrangement with the London External Division did not include law) and, of course, student unrest. This period also saw a slow, often imperceptible, weakening of university autonomy, and the start of what Halsey has called the "decline of donnish dominion"[36]:

Few academics saw the writing on the wall.[37] Stewart suggests that the keynotes in higher education from 1960–65 were "optimism, new ideas, expansion and opportunity."[38] To start with law expanded at a slightly lower rate than average, but in most other respects the story is similar to higher education as a whole, usually after a slight lag.

31

During the 1960s overall undergraduate numbers in law almost doubled from just over 3000 to just under 6000. There were similar increases in respect of law teachers and postgraduates. The London External Degree also grew rapidly prior to the introduction of polytechnic based law degrees. New law schools were set up in several existing universities; in all but one of the plateglass universities in England, in two of the former CATS, and in most polytechnics, so that by 1970 there were nearly 40 law schools teaching at degree level.[39]

Expansion brought with it new institutions and new ideas. But law got off to a slow start. The Society of Public Teachers of Law submitted memoranda to both the Robbins Committee and the Heyworth Committee on Social Studies, which reported in 1965. Neither seems to have been impressed. The Robbins Committee barely mentioned law explicitly. The Heyworth Committee observed that in the United Kingdom "the study of law has mainly been concerned with the professonal training of barristers and solicitors" and that it lagged behind other countries in considering the wider social implications of the subject.[40] Initially the "new" universities were reluctant to include law in their first programmes and in 1963 the Society of Public Teachers of Law felt it necessary to set up a committee to press for an expansion of the number of law faculties. The Society had felt handicapped in submitting evidence to the Robbins Committee and the National Incomes Commission "by an almost total lack of information concerning the present organization of law schools and the opinions of those engaged in teaching".[41] A grant from the Nuffield Foundation was obtained, a high-powered Advisory Committee was set up and Professor John Wilson of Southampton undertook the first major modern survey of legal education. Wilson's "Survey of Legal Education in the United Kingdom" was, as its title implies, almost entirely factual and made few recommendations.[42] It provided a fairly comprehensive snapshot of the situation in 1963–65, but made no attempt to set this in its historical context or to describe long-term trends. Nevertheless, it made a considerable impact and was used by the Ormrod Committee as one of the main sources for its own work in 1967–71.

The period after 1965 was, however, one of ferment in legal education. A great deal of dissatisfaction was expressed about both law degrees and the system of professional training and qualification, especially apprenticeship. Jurisprudence had come alive, particularly after the publication of Herbert Hart's *The Concept of Law* in 1961. There was much debate about research and teaching of law in its social context, about curricular innovation, methods of teaching and assessment and about law reform. Public assertions about the value of the law degree as a form of general education became more frequent; much was said and something was done about building links with the social sciences. During this period the university law schools sought greater acceptance within the academy and in the process, not without controversy, some deliberately distanced themselves from the profession.

In the late 1960s the new polytechnic law schools sought both to establish their academic credentials through the Council for National Academic Awards (CNAA) and to build up an image of vocationalism. It is probably fair to say that the search for academic respectability initially led to a cautious, rather traditional approach in CNAA law degrees, but some (such as Middlesex and Birmingham Polytechnics) were quite adventurous and there was generally a greater willingness to provide services to the practising profession in respect of vocational training and continuing legal education.

The pressure for change received a powerful impetus in 1963. In a polemical book entitled *Law Reform Now*, Gerald Gardiner Q.C. and Andrew Martin argued forcefully for a thorough overhaul of the legal system, including institutions of law reform and legal education.[43] When Gardiner became Lord Chancellor in 1964, he was responsible for the establishment of the Law Commission in 1965, in which academics came to play an increasingly prominent role. Lord Gardiner also appointed a committee chaired by Mr Justice Ormrod to conduct the first major review of legal education since the Atkin Committee of 1934—or, as that had been rather feeble, one might say the first since 1846. The Ormrod Committee was set up in 1967, but did not report until 1971. Except in respect of speed, it performed for legal education a role analogous to Robbins for higher education. The report and its aftermath belong to the seventies, but the existence of the Committee and rumours about its internal politics focused the attention of both academics and practitioners on issues of legal education. It is not insignificant that the Ormrod Committee sat throughout the period of student unrest.

THE ORMROD COMMITTEE AND AFTER

The Ormrod Committee and Preparation for Practice

The Ormrod Committee has a special place in the history of legal education in this country. Most official reports on legal education and training focus on the *process* of professional formation, only part of which takes place in law schools in any system—a quite small part in ours. Conversely, law schools as *institutions* are not solely concerned with professional formation, for their role and clientele may be much more varied. Few official reports on legal education and training say much about research, post-graduate studies or law for non-lawyers, for example. However, the vexed questions of professional formation and institutional function are so intimately related that it is often difficult to keep them distinct. The Ormrod story is no exception. The Committee was mainly concerned with preparation for private practice, but it had a powerful impact on the role and situation of university law schools.

Reports of official committees can be interpreted as political events as well as authoritative texts. The Ormrod exercise would make a good subject for a book-length case-study of the politics and economics of professional education. Ideology, competing political interests, economics and tradition were mixed in with and often overshadowed educational concerns. Much of the detail need not concern us here. For our purposes two underlying issues can be treated as central: first, how to reconcile the universities' interest in institutional autonomy and academic freedom with the concern of two independent professions to control training, entry and professional competence? Secondly, how far is it in the public interest to fund or subsidise training for the legal profession? Both issues are alive today.

The Committee on Legal Education was appointed by Lord Gardiner, the Lord Chancellor, in December, 1967. The Chairman, Sir Roger Ormrod was at the time a High Court Judge, who had originally qualified as a doctor of medicine. Of the 13 other members, one was the Emeritus Regius Professor of Medicine at Oxford. The rest were lawyers, six of whom were senior academics including L. C. B. Gower, who was then a Law Commissioner, Professor John Wilson, and Professor (later Sir Arthur) Armitage, the Vice-Chancellor of the University of Manchester. No committee on legal education in this country, before or since, has had such a strong academic representation.[44]

On a literal reading of the terms of reference of the Ormrod Committee, the exercise was an almost total failure. The stated objectives were "to advance legal education in England and Wales by furthering co-operation between the different bodies now actively engaged upon legal education" (para 1); to make recommendations for "*a professional qualification* in the two branches of the

legal profession"—which could have been interpreted as an invitation to devise a largely common system of professional education and training for barristers and solicitors (para. 2)[45]; and to serve as a standing advisory committee to the Lord Chancellor on matters relating to legal education (para. 3).

None of these objectives were achieved. The three main interest groups failed to agree to co-operate[46]; instead they recommended a rigid three-stage structure—academic, professional, continuing—which defined and further entrenched three separate spheres of influence. The academic stage was to be the primary responsibility of the universities and of the polytechnics, who were supervised by the CNAA. This was subject to the *caveat* that the professional bodies would have the power to grant or withhold recognition of law degrees as satisfying the first stage. The representatives of the Bar and the Law Society failed to reach agreement on a joint professional qualification: instead they insisted on separate courses and examinations for the second or vocational stage in their own independent, privately financed law schools outside the university system, despite the fact that this would kill any hope of substantial public funding of the vocational stage.[47]

No doubt fatigued by more than two years of wrangling, the Committee recommended its own liquidation: in its place they recommended that there should be a less formal Advisory Committee to serve as a link between the educational institutions and the profession; they also proposed an ad hoc committee to draw up a scheme for an Institute of Professional Legal Studies. The latter never materialised, the former was a disaster.[48]

Not only did the Ormrod Committee fail to carry out Lord Gardiner's agenda of creating an integrated and unified system of legal education and training, but by no means all of its 43 conclusions and recommendations were accepted: some were implemented immediately; some were watered down or introduced after a long delay; others were rejected or merely forgotten.[49] For example, the Law Society reversed its own decision to treat the vocational stage as a substitute for articles and instead made it a preparation for apprenticeship, thus adding an extra stage to the process. There was a delay of almost 20 years before the Bar and later the Law Society took skills training seriously and implemented the Ormrod proposals on skills at the professional stage. Instead of accepting the principle of recognition of law degrees, both branches of the profession insisted on more detailed control through a system of subject-by-subject exemptions. This has continued to be a persist-

35

ent, largely unnecessary, source of bickering between academics and practitioners that has reinforced rather than lessened mutual distrust.[50] No committee to design a national Institute of Professional Legal Studies was ever set up.[51]

Despite this catalogue of failures, I consider that the Ormrod exercise marked a turning-point in the history of legal education and that its influence was largely beneficial. There are four main reasons for this judgement.

First, the very existence of the committee made legal education a focus of public attention. Argument replaced apathy. The process concentrated the minds of the main interested parties and over time it significantly raised the level of debate. For the first time for over a century there was a sustained and comprehensive consideration of the central issues, based on a serious attempt to collect information about the situation in England and Wales and about other professions and jurisdictions. The data were uneven and not always reliable. Today the final report seems educationally unsophisticated, but in other respects it was on the whole thorough and thoughtful. Since 1971 most subsequent enquiries on legal education and training, in UK and several other jurisdictions, have taken the Ormrod report as their starting-point.

Secondly, if the outcome was a political compromise reminiscent of the Treaty of Versailles, a carving up of territory between largely sovereign powers, at least a pattern was established and some stability introduced into the system. It has been accepted as a reasonable, if uneasy, compromise and since 1971 most conflicts about legal education have seemed like border skirmishes, occasionally interrupted by a civil war.

Thirdly, much of the Ormrod philosophy became accepted as orthodoxy: that the legal profession should become a graduate profession (at the time only 40 per cent. of solicitors were graduates)[52]; that law degrees should be the normal route of entry and should involve "academic" study rather than practical training; that the professional bodies should recognise all existing law degrees and any new courses of at least three years duration which covered the core subjects (at first five, but later this crept up to more than six)[53]; that non-law graduates should be allowed to join the vocational stage after a conversion course; that the vocational stage should emphasise skills training rather than cramming (this has taken almost twenty years to implement); and that the number of law students should continue to expand. These are all important ingredients in the situation today.

Finally, university law schools were given a good deal of space in which to exercise autonomy and academic freedom. Subject to the core subjects requirement, the Ormrod philosophy positively encouraged innovation and experiment in respect of curriculum, teaching methods and research. It also encouraged the study of law in its social context. This at least created space for internal disagreements between academics. Almost as important was the fact that university law schools were given far less responsibility in the process of professional formation than in most countries in the world. This undoubtedly reinforced the trend towards assimilation of law schools into the academy as liberal arts departments rather than professional schools. Ironically the provision for non-law graduate entry strengthened academic freedom: law schools did not have a monopoly over the academic stage, but the existence of conversion courses for non-law graduates served as a buffer against direct professional influence on law degrees—for it would have been unreasonable to prescribe more for a law degree than what could be covered in a one-year conversion course.[54] There has been much debate about the costs and benefits of the Ormrod settlement,[55] whether it could be interpreted as a charter for irresponsibility and whether it makes sense to conceive of a core of law as a subject of study.[56] Suffice to say here that law schools in England and Wales were given much greater freedom than in most countries to define their role, interpret their subject and choose their clientele. That role was explicitly "academic". How they have used their relative freedom will be considered later.

The Legacy of Ormrod: 1971–94[57]

The post-Ormrod settlement clearly eased the way for the closer assimilation of university and polytechnic law schools into the academy. High demand for law and low costs in a period of expansion made law popular with administrators and ensured a supply of able students. It is hardly surprising, then, that law school development between 1970 and 1992 is more intimately linked to developments in higher education than to changes in legal practice or in the legal system. The outlines of that broader story are depressingly familiar: continuing, if uneven, expansion in a period marked by economic crises, austerity and stop-go policies; the creation and formal termination of the binary system; increased centralisation of power and the further erosion of institutional autonomy, exemplified by the end of the quinquennial system, the decline and death of the University Grants Committee, the Education Act of 1988, and the Further and Higher Education Act of 1992. In *Decline of Donnish Dominion* A. H. Halsey documents trends in the British academic profession from 1970 to 1988: in this period funding, salaries, research facilities, staff-student ratios, public respect, and almost every dimension of professional status of academics all deteriorated.[58] The euphoria of the fifties and sixties gradually degenerated into a major crisis of morale.[59] Students fared no better.

Adaptation and change are often painful. No doubt some of this account describes the almost inevitable costs of a move away from an elite system in a time of economic difficulties. Much of it is reflected in broad international trends. During the Thatcher years the nature of the process was often obscured by an atmosphere of mutual hostility and distrust between the academic community and government. At the time of writing the process is continuing and the atmosphere has not improved.

Nevertheless, the story of higher education after 1970 is not one of unremitting gloom: the policy of expanding the system had general support; most academics maintain that in the event more did not inevitably mean worse[60]; the gender ratio improved dramatically, as did the proportion of mature students entering higher education; serious efforts were made to improve access, with mixed success; the post-Robbins euphoria extended well into the seventies and beyond as new and old institutions experimented with different patterns and fresh ideas; the polytechnics proved to be more flexible and adventurous than some of the older universities and introduced further diversity into the system; the extensive network of contacts between universities in the English-speaking world continued in the post-colonial period; and membership of the European Community further expanded horizons. Universities are extraordinarily robust and adaptable institutions. On a broad view we are still in the process of change to a new system which has retained at least some of the strengths of the past.

For most practical purposes university and polytechnic law schools between 1970 and 1993 were treated as an integral part of the higher education system by successive governments and by educational administrators. Law departments generally were treated much like other non-science departments in respect of most matters to do with their terms and conditions of employment and general university policy, finance and infrastructure.[61] So far as public policy and general culture are concerned they continued to be largely invisible. They shared in the post-Robbins euphoria, they shared the pains of cuts and squeezes and down-grading, and, above all, they expanded.

Thus, developments in law schools from 1970 to 1992 in many respects parallel those in higher education, but there are a few significant differences. The detailed story is quite complex, but a future historian of the period would need at least to take account of the following:

(i) *Expansion.* During the early period of post-war expansion law schools developed in ways that were roughly commensurate with the higher education system as a whole, judged by such measures as numbers of students and staff, and the output of graduates. Law got off to a relatively slow start in the boom period, but accelerated rapidly from about 1968.[62] In 1970–71, the year of the Ormrod Report, there were 6,000 full-time undergraduates reading law, 5000 in universities. Ten years later, this had more than doubled (12,603), and by 1991–92 this had almost doubled again, with over 20,000 undergraduates reading for law degrees or mixed degrees with a substantial law content and considerably more part-time students, postgraduates and other categories. During this period law schools increased in both size and number.

To start with, the law teaching profession expanded roughly in step with student numbers, but in recent years there has been a steady deterioration in staff-student ratios.[63] In 1993 there were estimated to be slightly under 2000 full-time academic lawyers in the university sector, approximately a fifteen-fold increase since 1945. The figures are not very reliable and are open to varying interpretations on points of detail. Nevertheless, we can say that on a very crude estimate, academic law in England and Wales has increased more than twenty fold since the Second World War and, as significantly, the scale is at least three or four times what it was at the time of Ormrod. Nearly all of this expansion had little to do with manpower planning or the absorptive capacity of the legal profession. From time to time leaders of the profession complained of an over-supply or a shortage of law graduates, but for a long time this seemed to make little impact on demand for undergraduate places.[64] Law became one of the most competitive subjects, and towards the end of the period the proportion of law students in the system rose from about 2.6 per cent. in 1950–51 to almost 5 per cent. in the 1980s.[65]

Thus the Ormrod Committee reported at the time that law schools were just beginning to achieve "critical mass" and before the most dramatic period of expansion. In this sense, the contemporary university law school is in many key respects a post-Ormrod creation. Ormrod established the structure of professional training and assigned law schools a relatively clear but limited role within it, but left them with a good deal of space to develop as they saw fit. (ii) *Diversification.* It is not surprising, then, that a second post-Ormrod theme is academic pluralism. This takes three main forms: variations in the shape and content of undergraduate law degrees; diversification of intellectual approaches to the study of law; and extension of law teaching beyond undergraduates.[66]

Over time undergraduate degrees in law diversified in respect of both form and content: today there are full-time single honours degrees, English and Foreign law degrees, inter-disciplinary or mixed degrees with a substantial law content. There are part-time and sandwich courses, as well as a variety of conversion courses for law graduates. Modularisation may further increase the variety.

In many respects the most interesting developments since Ormrod have been in the field of ideas. Later we shall see how different approaches to law challenged the traditional emphasis on "blackletter" doctrine in both scholarship and education: for example, at undergraduate level, Kent pioneered a multi-disciplinary, critical approach and for a time experimented with clinical work; Warwick tried to "broaden the study of law from within"; Birmingham Polytechnic (now the University of Central England) went further than anyone in requiring a "clinical" element in all three years; the School of Oriental and African Studies managed to design a B.A. in Law which both satisfied professional exemptions and reflected the title of the institution.

At least until recently, university and, to a lesser extent, polytechnic, law schools saw themselves as mainly undergraduate institutions with the LLB as the main, sometimes the only, offering. Gradually they have diversified their clientele. There has long been a modest legal contribution to subjects such as business studies, accountancy and engineering. Traditionally this was referred to by the derogatory term "service teaching", and the offerings have often been rather unimaginative. Some other professions still maintain an outdated picture of law as a knowledge-based subject. That is changing. Perhaps even more significant is the trend away from almost exclusive emphasis on undergraduate teaching: since 1971 there has been a considerable expansion of postgraduate legal education[67]; by 1993, about 20 universities were offering "Legal Practice courses" that satisfy the Law Society's requirements for the second, or vocational, stage; individuals and to a lesser extent institutions have been involved in continuing legal education, judicial training and other specialised offerings, although these are not yet highly developed.

Similarly, there has been a great increase in non-degree level legal education, including A level law, access courses, paraprofessional training and other programmes.[68] I shall suggest later that law schools, especially in the "old" universities, have been rather slow to move away from the perception of themselves as being primarily undergraduate institutions, although they have greatly diversified their clientele in the past 20 years. One implication of this is that the market for legal education is much more varied than it was traditionally perceived to be and law schools may have a more secure economic base than they imagine.

(iii) *Finance.* Debates and reports on legal education have regularly underestimated the importance of economics. In most countries law has traditionally been perceived as one of the cheapest disciplines. It is thought to have modest requirements in respect of staff-student ratios, accommodation and equipment, except books. This image is so deeply entrenched that it is almost impossible to change. In England, legal education and training have made modest demands on public funding for two further reasons: in some countries, such as the United States, law teachers are paid higher salaries than colleagues in most other disciplines in order to at least mitigate the fact that legal practice can be highly lucrative and that law teaching involves financial sacrifice for most of those who make it a career.[69] In England until now law teachers have generally been on the same salary scales as colleagues in the humanities and social sciences, but this may change in the context of an emergent free or freer market for academic salaries. Furthermore, during the Ormrod exercise the representatives of the Bar and Law Society were responsible for what many consider to be a self-inflicted wound. By insisting that the vocational stage should take place within independent professional schools that they controlled, they gave successive governments the opportunity to refuse to provide direct public funding for post first-degree professional training.[70] Since 1971 law has been the poor relation of medicine and engineering. This has greatly inhibited the development of the vocational stage and has led to one great injustice: as money has become tighter local authorities have increasingly refused to give discretionary grants for the vocational stage, thereby denying many less well-off students access to the legal profession.[71] This remains a blot on our system.

41

In 1984 the Heads of Law Schools argued that law is one of the most cost-effective disciplines, but its development was being impeded by the fact that almost all innovations in legal education—for example, EC Law, the use of new technology, new kinds of skills training—involved a marginal increase in unit costs.[72] Even if it was special pleading, the case was cogent. For a time vice-chancellors and even the UGC were reluctantly responsive. However, from 1993 the Government reinstated the traditional view, by placing law and politics at the bottom of the scale of public funding.[73] Thus for the last 20 years or so at both the academic and vocational stages we have had a modified version of Ormrod-on-the-cheap.

Economic factors have not all been adverse. Over the years demand for legal studies has been both buoyant and steady not only at home, but also from overseas students, many of whom from Hong Kong, Singapore and Malaysia have been able and willing to pay "full-cost" fees. This combination of strong demand and low costs has probably been the single most important factor in the continuing expansion of university law schools within a publicly funded system. It has also protected law more than most other disciplines from the worst effects of financial cuts and squeezes, as we have moved away from an elite system in the direction of a mass system of higher education, without a proportionate increase in public funding. But not all law faculties got a correlative benefit from funds accruing to the university and, as in other countries, law's revenues have often been used to subsidise other departments. The continuing demand for undergraduate places may also have been a conservative force in that it has meant that university law schools have not been under any sustained pressure to explore other outlets for their services.

CONCLUSION

In 1994 there is a sense that, despite a period of adversity, law as a discipline in this country (as in other relatively wealthy anglophone countries) is generally more diverse, more interesting and more ebullient than it was 23 years ago. The most significant developments have been in the realm of ideas, and I shall deal with these in later chapters. So far I have been concerned with institutions and infrastructure. In this respect one can make some quite confident generalisations about a rapidly changing scene. If one compares the situation in 1994 with that at the time of Ormrod one finds: that the scale of the academic enterprise has almost quadrupled; it has diversified in respect of clientele, types of undergraduate degrees and above all ideas; it has become more sophisticated educationally, somewhat more prestigious and much more self-confident. Law is still one of the cheapest disciplines and much in demand at a number of levels. Legal scholarship, legal literature, and law publishing have all diversified and expanded. Law schools have tended to increase in size, but are still quite small by international standards. There are clear indications that Law has been fairly comfortably integrated into the university. If that is so, we have indeed said goodbye to Lewis Eliot. However, academic law is so intimately related to the worlds of legal practice and public affairs as well as to the academy that we must dig deeper into academic legal culture. In the next chapter, "What are law schools for?", we shall look at different models of university law schools in the context of prevailing conceptions of the role and values of universities.

Notes

[1] Martin Trow, "Comparative Perspectives on Higher Education Policy in the U.K. and U.S." (1988) 14 *Oxford Review of Education* 81, at p. 82.

[2] Max Weber, "Wissenschaft als Beruf", a speech at Munich University in 1918, reproduced in H. Gerth and C. Wright Mills, *From Max Weber* (1947) as "Science as Vocation". A. H. Halsey uses this together with Veblen's attack on "the conduct of universities by business men" in *The Higher Learning in America* (also published in 1918), as the keynote theme for considering the current discontents of British Universities (Halsey, *Decline of Donnish Dominion* (1992)). Professor Halsey very kindly made available some data on law teachers extrapolated from his 1989 survey and I have used these at various points below, see especially Appendix.

[3] The locus classicus is Max Weber, *Law in Economy and Society* (ed. M. Rheinstein; trs. M. Rheinstein and E. Shils, 1954). Chap. VII.

[4] "Wherever legal education has been in the hands of practitioners, especially attorneys, who have made admission to practice a guild monopoly, an economic factor, namely their pecuniary interest, brings to bear a strong influence upon the process not only of stabilizing the official law and of adapting it to changing needs in an exclusively empirical way but also of preventing its rationalization through legislation or legal science", (*ibid.* pp. 202–203). David Sugarman supports Weber's linking of "rationality" to modernity and his characterisation of the common law as "irrational", but criticises him for overlooking the convergence of common law and civil law: "In the Spirit of Weber: Law, Modernity and 'The Peculiarities of the English' " (Wisconsin Working Papers in Legal History, 1987).

[5] The study of "civil law" (*i.e.* law belonging to the Romanist tradition or family) could be said to be undergoing a revival with a great increase of interest in

43

contemporary civilian systems as well as in the law of the European Union. The tradition at Oxford continued much later: for example, as an undergraduate at Oxford in the 1950s only about half of my time was spent on the study of contemporary English Law, mainly Private Law; in addition I took three papers in Roman Law, one in Legal History and one in Jurisprudence.

6   Austin was appointed in 1826, first lectured in 1828, probably ceased lecturing in 1832 or 1833, but formally terminated his position later. A. D. E. Lewis, "John Austin (1790–1859): Pupil of Bentham." (1979) 2 *The Bentham Newsletter* 19.

7   John Austin, *Lectures on Jurisprudence* (5th ed., R. Campbell, 1885) at p. 58n.

8   *Report from the Select Committee on Legal Education*, no. 686. (1846) B. P. P. Vol. X. On subsequent committees, see B. Abel-Smith and R. Stevens, *Lawyers and the Courts* (1965) *passim*.

9   F. H. Lawson, *The Oxford Law School, 1850–1965* (1968); H. G. Hanbury, *The Vinerian Chair and legal education* (1958).

10 James Bryce, "Valedictory Lecture" *Studies in History and Jurisprudence* Vol. II (1893); *cf.* Maitland, who had modest expectations of legal education, *e.g.* "Law at the Universities" (1901) 3 *Collected Papers* 419.

11 Some of the pioneers, especially Bryce, Pollock, Dicey and Maitland, had considerable professional standing, and most derogatory comments probably refer to the status of law teaching after the departure of Bryce.

12 Jerome Frank, *Courts on Trial* (1949) at pp. 225–227.

13 See, *e.g.* Abel-Smith and Stevens, *op. cit.* at p. 375, writing of the situation up to 1965.

14 On the relatively late development of most subjects now included in "Arts", see Peter Scott, *Knowledge and Nation* (1990) Chap. 2.

15 The post-war public history of higher education in Great Britain is well-documented. In addition to Halsey's work, I have drawn on W. A. C. Stewart, *Higher Education in Post-war Britain* (1989), J. Carswell, *Government and the Universities in Britain* (1985), Tony Becher, *Academic Tribes and Territories* (1989), Peter Scott, *The Crisis of the University* (1984) and the series of Research into Higher Education Monographs (*The Leverhulme Reports*) published by the Society for Research into Higher Education, 1981–1983.

16 Eric Ashby, *Technology and the Academics* (1963); (with Mary Anderson), *Universities: British, Indian, African* (1966).

17 *Report of the Committee on Legal Education* (hereafter, Ormrod Report) (1971) Cmnd. 4594.; *Report of the Royal Commission on Legal Services* (Benson Report) (1979) Cmnd. 7648; *Report on the Future of the Legal Profession* (Marre Report) (1988). The last was an unofficial report commissioned jointly by the Bar Council and the Law Society.

18 The typical lawyer's account of such turf battles suggests a conflict between three main interest groups: the Bar, the solicitors and the academics, with occasional references to the public interest. A broader perspective suggests that power has been more widely diffused through different departments of central and local government, various parastatal and semi-official bodies, such as the funding councils and the CVCP, and private sector organisations such as charitable foundations, trade unions and, most important of all, students and parents.

19 *e.g.* B. S. Bloom, *A Taxonomy of Educational Objectives* (1956); Robert Mager, *Preparing Instructional Objectives* (1962, misc. eds); Donald Schon, *The Reflective Practitioner* (1983), *Educating the Reflective Practitioner* (1987).

20 *e.g.* the works by Stewart, Halsey, Carswell, Halsey and Trow, and Scott, cited above nn. 2 and 15. Law was hardly mentioned in the Robbins Report and was

Law in the Universities: The Historical Context

dismissed in a paragraph by the Heyworth Committee on Social Studies in 1965, below at n. 40. Tony Becher's *Academic Tribes and Territories, op. cit.* and discussed below, is one exception, but he does not draw on the extensive internal literature on legal education.

[21] The best available estimates are for the U.K. as a whole and are not precise. Guy Neave in R. Abel and P. Lewis (eds.) *Lawyers in Society: Comparative Theories* (1989), Chap. 4.

[22] This section follows fairly closely the very useful overview by Stewart, *op. cit.*

[23] Stewart at p. 86

[24] Noel Annan, *Our Age* (1990).

[25] The first Wilson Report see below, n. 41.

[26] Abel-Smith and Stevens, *op. cit.*, Chap. 13.

[27] *ibid.*

[28] (1950) 13 *M.L.R.* 137–205.

[29] *ibid.* at p. 162.

[30] L. C. B. Gower, *Independent Africa—The Challenge to the Legal Profession.* (1967); "Looking Back", Presidential Address to the S.P.T.L., discussed below n. 48.

[31] D. N. MacCormick, *H. L. A. Hart* (1981).

[32] *e.g.* K. C. Davis, "The Future of Judge-made Law in England: A Problem of Practical Jurisprudence," (1961) 61 *Columbia L. Rev.* 201.; A. Goldstein, "Research into the Administration of Criminal Law: A Report from the United States," (1966) 6 *Brit. Jo. Criminology* 27, at p. 37.

[33] J. C. Hall, "The Training of a Solicitor", (1962) J.S.P.T.L. (N. S.) 24. The function was taken over for a time by local colleges.

[34] Issa Shivji (ed). *Limits of Legal Radicalism* (1986) contains an interesting collection of reminiscences; cf. J. Bainbridge, *The Study and Teaching of Law in Africa* (1972) and Gower, *op. cit.* n. 30.

[35] *Higher Education* (Robbins Report) (1963) Cmnd. 2154. Contrary to popular belief this did not lead to expansion, but rather placed a brake on the move away from an elite system.

[36] *op. cit.*

[37] One example illustrates what was a general form of academic myopia. In 1969, Shirley Williams, then Secretary of State for Education, published Thirteen Points which Stewart summarises as follows:

"[t]hey suggested reductions or removal of student grants and the introduction of loans both for undergraduates and postgraduates; restrictions on admission of overseas students and progress towards full-cost fees for them; limitations of the range of employment for grant-aided students similar to the pledge for student teachers which had been abandoned ten years before; part-time and correspondence courses; shortening of degree programmes to two years for able students; the option of two-year non-degree diploma courses for less able students; a pre-university year which would discriminate more accurately and would exclude unsuitable candidates; more intensive use of buildings and sharing of staff and facilities between institutions; increases in staff/student ratios; economies in residential facilities, including more home-based students and more loanfinanced accomodation . . . the CVCP responded in 1970 giving a cold reply to nearly all of the proposals." (Stewart, op. cit. at pp. 160–161). Today these proposals seem prophetic. At the time they seemed like an assault on "standards", the hallmark of elitist attitudes. Shirley Williams was a Labour Minister, but most of the ideas included in this statement were part of D.E.S. policy over a longer period.

[38] *op. cit.* at p. 154.

[39] There is no accepted definition of a law school: in 1975 Wilson and Marsh reported that 21 universities in England were running full degree courses, and 3 in Wales; by then there were also 19 polytechnics and local authority maintained institutions offering degree courses in law, with others in the process of securing recognition (*op. cit.,* below n. 41 at pp. 242–243). These figures exclude commercial colleges and tutors and the University of Buckingham, which was founded in 1973 as a private university.

[40] *Report of the Committee on Social Studies* (Heyworth Committee) (1965) Cmnd. 2660, para. 38.

[41] J. Wilson "Survey of Legal Education in the United Kingdom", (1966) 9 J.S.P.T.L. (N. S.) p. 5 (hereafter First Wilson Report); this was followed by "A Second Survey of Legal Education in the United Kingdom" (J. F. Wilson and S. B. Marsh reprinted in (1975) 13 J.S.P.T.L. (N. S.) pp. 241–331 and two supplements (1978 and 1981). John Wilson published a third survey in (1993) *Legal Studies* 143, which deals with the old universities only and needs to be read with P. Harris and S. Bellerby, *A Survey of Law Teaching, 1993,* which covers the former polytechnics and most, but not all, other public sector institutions in the United Kingdom (hereafter *ALT Survey,* 1993).

[42] *ibid.*

[43] G. Gardiner and A. Martin, *Law Reform NOW* (1963), Chaps. 1 and 11.

[44] This contrasts strikingly with the present Lord Chancellor's Advisory Committee (ACLEC) which, under the Courts and Legal Services Act, 1990, only has places for two law teachers and has a majority of "lay" members.

[45] Gardiner and Martin, *op. cit.,* Chap. 11, argued that a law degree should (with a few exceptions) be a prequisite of entry to both branches of the profession, but they stopped short of advocating a common system of training.

[46] The main factors were probably fear of fusion, especially on the part of the Bar; distrust of academics; internal divisions within the Law Society; and resistance to the trade school model by law teachers.

[47] It is now widely believed that if the Ormrod Committee had taken more account of Treasury Rules governing funding of higher education we might have had a very different system and rather more generous public financing of professional training. Law, unlike medicine, engineering, education and architecture, has been left largely to professional organisation and private finance outside the state higher education system. It is difficult on the available evidence to judge whether, if the Committee had unanimously and strongly recommended an integrated system of professional legal education and training under the UGC, perhaps on an analogy with medical schools, they could have persuaded a reluctant government to fund all or most of the process. Five years earlier it might have been a realistic option; but by 1971 the costs of higher education had become a major concern. Scotland and Northern Ireland learned from this mistake and have publicly funded vocational courses within universities (without much sacrifice of professional control). I was a member of the Northern Ireland Committee, chaired by Sir Arthur Armitage, who had served on the Ormrod Committee. With the help of an experienced civil servant who understood public finance, all proposals for vocational training outside the university system were shot down on the ground that they would not secure public funding.

[48] Several years later Professor Gower acknowledged in public that the decision to liquidate the standing committee was "a fatal error": "Instead of the Advisory Committee proving to be a forum in which the professional bodies and the uni-

versities and polytechnics can iron out any difficulties in implementing the Ormrod recommendations, it has become one in which the professional bodies can seek legitimation for watering down those recommendations—notwithstanding that they were based largely on their own submissions. The first step was to add a further core subject to the five unanimously suggested after lengthy discussion by Ormrod. This was just silly rather than calamitous. The latest step, which was more serious, was an apparent attempt to dictate to the universities and the polytechnics how they should assess their students—something which the members of Ormrod never contemplated for one moment and to which they would have taken the gravest exception." L. C. B. Gower, "Looking Back", Presidential Address to S.P.T.L. (1978) 14 J.S.P.T.L.(N.S.) 155, at p. 158.

[49] For a summary in 1982, see P. A. Thomas (ed) *Law in the Balance* (1982), Chap. 8.

[50] On the core subjects, see Chap. 7, below.

[51] The Institute of Advanced Legal Studies has taken several steps in the direction of creating a national centre for the study of legal education, first by setting up a Legal Skills Research Group, and recently by raising funds for a Chair of Legal Education and an archives project.

[52] Abel (1988) *op. cit.*, n. 62, below, produces some complex and incomplete figures on the educational background of barristers and solicitors up to 1984. There has been a steady trend toward a graduate profession, but in recent years the number of non-law graduates seeking to qualify has increased to the extent that it is not quite true to say that the law degree is the "normal route of entry".

[53] The phenomenon of the "creeping core" refers to an accumulation of pressures which both overload and constrain the undergraduate curriculum: English Legal System (or equivalents) are core subjects sub silentio; Trusts was added formally; EC/EU Law has been proposed and, although not formally required, is almost *de facto* a core subject; some subjects, especially Public Law, Restitution and Human Rights, have expanded in scope and importance. In the process Roman Law, legal history, and most theoretical and socio-legal courses have come under pressure, although Jurisprudence survives as a compulsory subject in about half the undergraduate law degrees. The process has been one of attrition, and the influence of the core subject requirement can easily be exaggerated. Law schools have more freedom to manoeuvre than they acknowledge, but they do not always use it. See further, below Chaps. 4 and 7.

[54] See below, Chap. 3, n. 23.

[55] See W. Twining, "The Initial Stage: Notes on the Context and a search for Consensus", ACLEC Consultative Conference, July 1993, *Report*, pp. 1–13.

[56] Discussed below, Chap. 7.

[57] For a more detailed overview of developments in academic law between 1972 and 1993, see "Remembering 1972", in D. Galligan (ed.) *Socio-legal Studies in Context: The Wolfson Centre Past and Future* (forthcoming, 1995) and references there.

[58] Halsey at pp. 1–2.

[59] A recent international survey reports that the morale of U.K. academics is very low, even compared to other countries during a period in which higher education is in crisis internationally (T.H.E.S. June 24, 1994).

[60] Halsey's surveys suggest that academic opinion was split about the effect of expansion on the quality of students, but that by 1989 "academics of all political shades were beginning to adopt more cheerful views." (*op. cit.* at p. 242–243.)

[61] Halsey, *op. cit.*, above n. 2.

[62] Available statistics are spotty and do not always clearly differentiate between the United Kingdom, Great Britain and England and Wales. The best collation to date is to be found in Richard Abel, *The Legal Profession in England and Wales* (1988). The third Wilson report *op. cit.* gives detailed figures for 1980–81 and 1990–91 for "old" universities; the ALT study, which is continuing, deals with the former polytechnics and colleges of further education, but omits some categories. In most public policy and statistical documents law is lumped together anonymously under the social sciences and is to a remarkable extent invisible.

[63] Harris and Bellerby, *op. cit.,* and Wilson, *op. cit.,* emphasise the difficulty of constructing meaningful figures on SSRs, but there is no doubt that there has been a significant deterioration.

[64] See below Chap. 3.

[65] Above n. 21.

[66] Writing of the former polytechnics and non-university sectors, Harris and Bellerby reported in 1993: "Since 1981 there has been a 50 per cent. growth in law degree students and a five-fold increase in numbers on mixed/joint degrees. Part-time expansion has significantly outstripped growth in full-time provision. Growth in student numbers has not been matched by similar rates of growth in teaching staff." *op. cit.* at p. viii.

[67] See W. Twining, "Postgraduate Legal Studies" in P. Birks (ed), *Reviewing Legal Education* (forthcoming). The term "postgraduate studies", which used to refer exclusively to advanced academic programmes, is gradually being extended to include primary practical training courses (such as the Legal Practice Course), some of which may lead eventually to a Master's degree.

[68] Harris and Bellerby, *op. cit.,* Chap. 4. Much of this takes place in Colleges of Further Education and other non-university institutions.

[69] Derek Bok, *The Cost of Talent* (1993) Chap. 8.

[70] Above n. 47.

[71] For a vivid account of the problems, see Philip Thomas, "The Poverty of Students" (1993) 27 *The Law Teacher* 152.

[72] Heads of University Law Schools, *Law as an academic discipline* (1983) The bulk of the report was published in the S.P.T.L. *Newsletter,* Summer, (1984); see also the submissions by the Law Society to the U.F.C. and P.F.C. in 1991 (0228R and 0234R), quoted by Philip Thomas, *op. cit.,* at p. 154.

[73] From 1993 the unit of resource of fees-only social science students was reduced by approximately 30 per cent. (£1300 compared to £2,770 for laboratory and workshop-based courses) in order to deter expansion of social science departments, including law (Thomas, *ibid.*)

3. What are Law Schools for?

THE ACADEMIC ETHIC

"When we anatomise British universities to discover what their purpose is we receive a mixed answer. There has been an accretion of functions over the centuries. From Bologna and Salerno comes the function of the university to train students for certain professions, like the church, medicine and law. From Oxford and Cambridge comes the university's function as a nursery for gentlemen, statesmen and administrators. From Göttingen and Berlin comes the function of the university as a centre for scholarship and research. From Charlottenburg and Zurich and Massachusetts comes the function of the university to be a staff college for technological experts and specialists. Some of these functions were created by the scientific revolution; others were deeply influenced by it. The universities have responded to all of them and repudiated none; but adaptation is by no means complete. Form is not everywhere fitted to function. Indeed the cardinal problem facing universities today is how to reconcile these four different functions in one and the same institution."[1]

Sir Eric Ashby wrote this in 1963. Twenty years later an international group of senior Western academics produced a report on *The Academic Ethic*, drafted by Professor Edward Shils. It begins with a clear restatement of one traditional conception of the role of universities in society. "Universities have a distinctive task. It is the methodical discovery and the teaching of truths about serious and important things."[2]

This conception of the role of universities was seen to be coming under strain from a number of trends that affect modern societies in differing degrees. The mass university of 20,000 or more students tends to create a gulf between academic staff and students. Increased pressures to provide non-academic services within the university (*e.g.* placement) and to the wider community (from community hospitals to narrowly focused inservice training) distracts the institution from its central responsibilities for teaching and discovery. The politicisation of the university may serve as a further

49

distraction and, if this involves the belief that all claims to detachment and objectivity are vain and illusory, it "hits at the very heart of the academic ethic."[3] Government influence through manpower planning, "science policy", ad hoc research sponsorship, national curricula, or direct political interference can undermine institutional autonomy and academic freedom, the twin pillars of free enquiry.

The bureaucratisation of universities, which Max Weber had predicted, typically involves the proliferation of non-academic administrators and of paperwork. Reductions and uncertainties in the provision of public funds, after the boom of the sixties, created a crisis of morale in many western universities and tended to distort the age profile of the academic profession, leading in some instances to the danger of the loss of a whole generation of scholars. As universities have become more newsworthy, increased publicity has bred concerns about public relations. The growth of "the Research University" in some countries has often led to the neglect of students by ambitious scholars; it threatens Wilhelm von Humbolt's doctrine of "the unity of teaching and research"; it encourages a culture of grant-seeking and "increased indifference to the affairs of one's own university".[4] Finally, the internal unity of institutions and, ultimately, "the unity of knowledge"[5] are threatened by a series of forces that promote "the disagregated university". These include "large numbers, specialization, external financial support for particular research projects, and the intensification of attention to government and politics which is characteristic of all modern societies."[6]

The common element in this catalogue, according to Shils, is not that all these features of university life are in themselves undesirable or avoidable, but rather that cumulatively, in varying combinations, they place an increasing strain on university teachers in performing their fundamental tasks of teaching and research. Despite these strains, Shils concludes, universities persist as the major centres of learning in most societies.[7]

The Academic Ethic is a clear and forceful reaffirmation of von Humbolt's vision of the university as society's House of Intellect. Shils' analysis identifies some familiar points of tension in British academic life: the relationship between teaching and research; public accountability and the limits of institutional autonomy and academic freedom; forms of university governance; externally sponsored research; the relationship of the university to government and the community; politicisation and bureaucratisation; the vocational and service roles of university courses; challenges to the possibility of neutrality, objectivity or even relative detachment; and the fragmentation of knowledge.

Shils' interpretation restates what is still the prevailing orthodoxy in this country, despite the pressures.[8] It can accommodate a wide range of differences about means and structures and intellectual agendas, but it is unequivocal in its rejection of analogies with factories or businesses or political parties or evangelical churches or guerrilla bases. The overriding purpose of the enterprise is the advancement of learning.[9] In talking of British universities Ashby came to a similar conclusion,[10] while emphasising the pluralism of our institutions of higher education and the fact that, in contrast with Continental Europe, technology was adopted if not totally assimilated into our university system rather than being assigned to *Technische Hochschulen*.[11] This interpretation of the academic ethic accommodates "useful knowledge", professional training and applied as well as pure research. Insofar as it is correct to say that law schools and law teachers are now largely integrated into the university, this analysis of the situation and the ethic applies *pari passu* to them.

LAW SCHOOLS AS INSTITUTIONS: TWO MODELS AND SOME VARIANTS

A panorama of the world's law schools would reveal an extraordinary diversity in respect of size, relative wealth, the average age of students, functions and even architecture.[12] When I face our first year undergraduates at UCL I tell them that their average age is only 19–20 (despite the welcome leavening of a number of mature students); whereas I sometimes teach the entering class of the University of Miami Law school, whose average age is often 26–28. In 1993 the Faculty of Law in the University of Milan admitted approximately 4000 first year students; the average intake in British law schools, outside Oxford and Cambridge, is around 100[13]; In Cairo, Paris, Leiden and Oslo law students are reported to number thousands—despite attempts to end open entry and to limit numbers. One Minister of Justice, himself a former Dean, told me that in his country law, as a cheap subject, was the main dumping ground for excess demand for higher education and the main function of legal education was to reduce juvenile delinquency by keeping youngsters off the streets—one version of the custodial view of education. To visit an ivy league law school in the United States, a mass law school in Italy or the Netherlands, a proprietary school in India,[14] or a Shi'i College in Iran is to enter four unrecognisably different kinds of small worlds.[15]

As we have seen, for most of our history apprenticeship was the prevailing mode of training. Disdain for formal legal education has not been a uniquely English phenomenon: during the period of Jacksonian Democracy in the United States when the legal profession was under attack even requirements for apprenticeship were abolished in a majority of states and by 1840 a mere 345 students, in the country as a whole, were studying law in university affiliated institutions.[16] When, during the Mao period, the International Legal Center commissioned a report on legal education in the Chinese People's Republic it received a succinct reply: "There is no legal education in China".

Law schools are both varied and dispensable. Here I am concerned with function: what are law schools for? In modern industrial societies, despite the complexities, two main conceptions of the role of the law school have competed for dominance: the first is the law school as a service institution for the profession (the professional school model); the second is the law school as an academic institution devoted to the advancement of learning about law (the academic model). Each type has significant variants; most actual law schools are hybrids combining elements of both models. Many of the recurrent tensions and controversies in legal education are rooted in disagreements about objectives and priorities that centre on these two competing views of the nature of the enterprise. It is advisable to treat these as "ideal types".

At the time of the Ormrod Report there were three main variants of the professional school model:

(i) First, and most prestigious, is an institution which purports to be the practising legal profession's House of Intellect, providing not only basic education and training, but also specialist training, continuing education, basic and applied research and high level consultancy and information services. The nearest analogy is the medical school attached to a teaching hospital which, *inter alia*, gives a high priority to clinical experience with live patients as part of an integrated process of professional formation and development. In no modern Western country has this model been realised in law.

(ii) An intermediate form is the graduate professional school. Typically it is within a university, but stands somewhat apart. Its main function is to provide basic vocational education for intending practitioners, who have obtained at least a first degree in some other subject. The graduate business school is the prototype. The classical American law school approximates to this model. Because the first law degree is postgraduate and is explicitly vocational, it carries a higher proportion of the responsibility for primary professional training than is the case in countries where law is an under-graduate subject. Although the profession has a significant influence in practice through the accreditation process, American law schools have been formally integrated into the university in respect of finance, tenure and the twin principles of institutional autonomy and academic freedom.[17] Postgraduate work, law for non-lawyers, specialist training and even continuing legal education have tended to be marginalised. Most attempts to introduce a substantial clinical element into the first degree have failed, and law schools have generally been inhospitable to clinical teachers.[18] With only a very few exceptions, Jerome Frank's vision of clinical lawyer schools has not been realised.[19] British academics tend to cast envious eyes at the better American law schools—with good reason in respect of resources, pay, willingness to experiment and a generally more "grown-up" atmosphere. But, even more than in our generally modest institutions, the structure in the United States has created an acute and persistent tension between the vocational and academic functions, not least in respect of scholarship. In my experience, the most persistent pressure point in American law schools is the clash between the interests and expectations of vocationally oriented, fee-paying students and a full-time faculty who wish to be accepted as true academics.

(iii) A third, and minor, variant is the independent professional school run for—and typically by—the practising profession. Examples of this include the Law Society's College of Law and the Inns of Court School of Law in England and some professional schools in the Commonwealth. These institutions have often performed a useful role under difficult conditions. But only very occasionally in history have they flourished in the long-term—one exception being the Inns of Court in their heyday. The reasons for this are obvious: the price paid for being outside the university system is almost invariably inadequate funding and diminished prestige.

The professional school model can be contrasted with the academic model. Again there are variants, mainly in terms of ambition and prestige. The most ambitious version of this is set out in a report by the International Legal Center (I.L.C.) on *Legal Education in a Changing World*, which states:

> "Law schools, perceived as multipurpose centers, can develop human resources and idealism needed to strengthen legal systems; they can develop research and intellectual direction; they can address problems in fields ranging from land reform to criminal justice; they can foster the development of indigenous languages as vehicles for the administration of law; they can assist institutions involved in training paraprofessionals; they can help to provide materials and encouragement for civic education about law in schools and more intelligent treatment of law in the media; they can organize, or help organize, advanced specialized legal education for professionals who must acquire particular kinds of skills and expertise."[20]

This vision of law schools as multi-purpose centres of learning might be grandly labelled the law school as the legal system's, as opposed to the legal profession's, House of Intellect. I shall refer to this as the I.L.C. model. It overlaps with the professional model in that it includes practical training and other services to the legal profession as part of its remit. But it differs in three key respects: it is independent of the legal profession, it has a much wider clientele and its mission is more in tune with the academic ethic. As with the medical school model, I know of few law schools that have committed themselves wholeheartedly to so ambitious a mission, with the possible exception of the National Law School of India University in Bangalore.[21] As law schools in this country diversify their services and their clientele they have the opportunity to move in this direction, without necessarily seeking, at least individually, to take on such a wide variety of tasks.

A second version of the academic model is the Law Faculty as a full part of the university pursuing original research and offering a general education in law at undergraduate level and a range of postgraduate courses, including research training, advanced academic studies, multi-disciplinary work and some kinds of specialist education and training. This has been the aspiration of most Continental European Law Faculties, with many variations in time and place.

A third variant is the law school which is essentially an undergraduate teaching institution. This may or may not have a commitment to research and, typically, it sees other teaching activities as secondary or even, as still often happens in our tradition, as "outside work". The danger of this kind of self-image is that an institution may get the worst of both worlds, if it treats undergraduate teaching as its main function and the undergraduate degree is perceived and used mainly as the first stage of professional formation. For what is such an institution except a primary or even nursery school for the profession?[22]

It is not clear how many of these types were really feasible options at the time of the Ormrod exercise. What is clear is that the post-Ormrod settlement gave university law schools a specifically "academic" role. In particular, various possible structures were ruled out: a university-based integrated system of education and clinical training on an analogy with Medicine; making the law degree a post-graduate qualification, as in the United States; the Continental model of a much longer academic stage followed by varying (often specialised) provisions for further training; nongraduate entry through apprenticeship and examinations. Even the standard option of making a law degree a necessary qualification for entry to the profession was not accepted: instead the Ormrod Committee recommended that nongraduate entry should be wholly exceptional, that the law degree should be the normal route of entry, but that provision should be made for graduates in other subjects to be able to take a two-year conversion course to qualify for exemptions.[23] The outcome was that we are almost the only country in the Western world that does not require a law degree for intending practitioners of law. Nor does our system give university law schools a monopoly over the academic stage of professional formation. Until recently the structure virtually excluded them from the three later stages of professional training—vocational, apprenticeship, and continuing. That structure has become established and would now be rather difficult to change.

During the period of expansion and diversification of the past thirty years many of the ambiguities about the objectives and priorities of law schools could be glossed over or left unresolved. Demand for legal studies was high at a number of levels and on the whole the higher education system and the legal profession responded to much of the demand.

There was a sharp change in the situation in the early 1990s brought about by a series of factors, mainly economic, of which the recession and government policies affecting legal services, legal aid, the professions, student funding and higher education were the most prominent. As the Lord Chancellor's Advisory Committee on Legal Education and Conduct (ACLEC) began the first major review of legal education and training in England and Wales since Ormrod,[24] it was becoming increasingly apparent that the legal profession would only be able to absorb a relatively small proportion of those aspiring to practice, or at least to qualify, perhaps as few as a third. At the same time law was being given an increasingly high profile in the media, in popular culture and on the international scene. While there was increasing talk of "overproduction" of law graduates, talk which assumed that the main function of undergraduate law degrees was to prepare people for the profession, there was also talk of the need for more continuing education, specialist training, judicial studies, paraprofessional training, human rights education and legal literacy. The market for legal educational services was expanding in some directions while contracting in others. University law schools had only been one kind of institution among several that provided legal education and it was only in the late nineteen-eighties that they had begun to move away from their self-image as being essentially providers of undergraduate and other forms of primary legal education. Questions therefore arose about the future shape and scale of the national system of legal education provision and the role of university law schools within it.

In 1994 it seemed that the range of strategic possibilities was quite limited.[25] It was going to be difficult to break out of the Ormrod structure. On the one hand, the clinical medical school model, the postgraduate professional school, the five-year undergraduate programme and other expensive options could be ruled out as not being feasible within a system which was still largely dependent on public finance, at least at the primary stage. On the other hand, it seemed equally unlikely that English universities would move directly to a mass system involving open entry and very large first year classes. Although there was a strong trend towards eroding the legal profession's monopolies on some legal services, the tendency was to make entry to the legal profession more competitive and professional training more rigorous. It was extremely unlikely that there were would be a return to non-graduate entry on a large scale, but it was also improbable that a law degree as such would be required for entry to the profession.[26] It also seemed unlikely that law schools would be content with being little more than nursery schools for the profession, contracting in size and accepting such a limited role.

This left three main possibilities for English university law schools:

(i) to move in the direction of being mainly service institutions for the profession, curtailing undergraduate numbers, but becoming more involved in vocational training at all stages, including advanced and specialised training;

(ii) to continue to be mainly primary schools, largely confined to introductory legal education, but to diversify their clientele by more wholeheartedly offering "law for non-lawyers", especially by making undergraduate legal education more attractive as a form of general or liberal education and competing for students with the social sciences and humanities; or

(iii) to move more boldly in the direction of the ILC model by diversifying upwards as well as outwards, placing greater emphasis on advanced studies both for lawyers and non-lawyers and taking all law, not just lawyers' law, for their province.

It should be fairly obvious that my sympathies lie with the more ambitious I.L.C. model and that I personally favour diversification of function and much greater emphasis on advanced and inter-disciplinary studies. But my purpose here is to interpret the situation rather than to make a plea for a particular strategy. It is difficult to predict how the situation will develop during the next few years, except that it seems unlikely that the outcome will conform neatly to any single one of these models.

Some things are reasonably clear, however: First, although the models are not mutually exclusive, there are profound differences between a professional school, an undergraduate liberal arts department, and a multi-functional institution concerned with the study of all aspects of law at a variety of levels. These differences relate to objectives, scale, and finance and, above all, to what I shall refer to as academic culture.[27] Secondly, although government policy, the economy, and choices by individual institutions will play their part, the future shape of legal education is likely to continue to be largely demand-led, that is to say that to a very large extent developments will depend on the perceptions of parents, students and employers about the relevance of different kinds of legal studies to their needs and aspirations. Thirdly, even if the institutionalised discipline of law expands outwards and upwards to encompass a more diverse clientele and a greater emphasis on advanced studies, primary legal education is likely for the foreseeable future to be at the core of the funding of university law schools as institutions. If a law degree is perceived as being mainly the first stage towards qualifying as a barrister or solicitor and if the opportunities to qualify and to earn a good living in legal practice continue to shrink, then there could well be a very sharp drop in demand for this kind of education.[28] In short, strong versions of the professional school model imply a quite radical contraction in the scale of the legal education system as it is today.

Against this background, I propose to consider first the claims that law is potentially a good vehicle for general education and then, in the next chapter, how far contemporary academic legal culture promotes or obstructs the realisation of this potential.

THE CASE FOR LAW

In the 1970s it was a widely held view among governments of newly independent states and donors of foreign aid that law was largely irrelevant to development: at best a low priority, at worst a brake.[29] It was in this context that the International Legal Center Committee on Legal Education in Developing Countries, of which I was a member, felt that it should devote a whole chapter to articulating the case for allocating resources to legal education even in very poor countries.[30] The argument was built around five main themes: first, in many countries law-trained people gravitate to positions of pre-eminence in public life, so legal education is an important avenue to the world of affairs; secondly, because of the pervasiveness of law in society, legal education is a good vehicle for the study of affairs in society: in this respect, "the study of law can be a particularly useful discipline to enable its students to relate general theory to particular, sometimes intractable, concrete problems"[31]; thirdly law has a number of characteristics that combine to make it an excellent vehicle for general education[32]; fourth, "development" implies material and cultural change, involving issues of social justice; law and the legal system are important features of these processes, especially when guided by basic values of fairness, justice and equity[33]; and finally, legal education can be a particularly good vehicle for developing important human skills:

"People in law roles are often active participants in transactions which may be very significant to development. They may define and analyze problems; counsel and plan a course of action; negotiate and settle disputes; define and advocate a position; frame and implement rules. Good professionals exercise these skills—indeed, such skills are part of the essence of 'lawyering'; good legal education can encourage (in the view of some, it should demand) the use and development of these skills through various methods of legal education."[34]

At the time this kind of argument was unfashionable. "Development" was generally conceived almost entirely in economic terms and law schools were seen as institutions for producing lawyers, a low priority in the public service, and potential parasites and trouble-makers in the private sector. This somewhat idealised claim for the potential of legal education—the report was highly critical of much existing practice—could be brushed off as special pleading by a group of law teachers.

Since then the mood has swung to the other extreme in some circles. Under the slogan of "democracy, human rights and good governance" some Western governments and organisations such as the World Bank have placed law and the administration of justice quite high on the agendas of foreign aid and "restructuring".[35]

In my view, chapter II of *Legal Education in a Changing World* still contains the best general statement about the potential importance of law in society, the role of law schools and the values of legal education.[36]

In the present context two passages are immediately relevant. The first, which has already been quoted in part, puts forward the model of law schools as multi-functional centres concerned with the study of all aspects of law both domestically and globally. Most English law schools are agreeably small and intimate by international standards, and few can hope to take on all of these functions on their own. The model, like the metaphor of Blackstone's Tower, applies to our national system rather than to individual institutions which are and should be quite diverse. In order to realise their potential, our law schools need to maintain a reasonably stable economic base. This will depend on their ability to provide legal education services for which there is a demand.

Secondly, *Legal Education in a Changing World* summarises the general educational values of studying law as follows:

"90. Typically, the discipline of law is regarded as part of the humanities. This is so because: (a) law covers so many human activities and relationships; but (b) it also deals with much the same phenomena as the social sciences and is increasingly informed by them; and (c) it is intellectually demanding—requiring abilities to draw from a variety of sources in analyzing problems, evidence, and arguments to make careful distinctions and to handle abstract concepts; and (d) it is directly related to the world of concrete practical problems; and (e) it is concerned, as perhaps no other subject is concerned, with the practical operation of processes and procedures; and (f) it has a rich heritage of literature, philosophy and historical experience.

91. While none of these elements is, on its own, peculiar to law, perhaps no other discipline combines them in quite the same way or to the same degree. The study of law can be (a) as intellectually exacting as philosophy, but more down to earth; (b) as concerned with contemporary, real-life problems as medicine or engineering, but with a greater diversity of concerns and with closer links to the humanities; (c) as concerned with power and decision-making as political science, but more concerned with the processes and practicalities of wielding power and, indeed, often more concerned with the limits and abuses of power and the importance of accountability to processes which are seen to be fair.

92. The strength of law as a discipline lies in the fact that it is so multi-dimensional. The teacher is called upon (a) to strike a balance between the elements which make up law; (b) to be informed about and deal adequately in today's world, with the closely related subjects from which law must draw much of its wisdom; (c) to provide both "academic" and "practical" insights; and (d) to use methods which motivate, stimulate and engage students in issues of theory, doctrinal learning, skill-development and engagement with concrete problems."[37]

The case is cogent and there is no need to overstate it. A similarly strong argument might be made for several other disciplines in the humanities and social sciences or for some combinations of them. Some disciplines may be better vehicles for enlarging the imagination or developing numeracy or for rigorous application of disciplined method. Many of the so-called "transferable" skills of reading, writing, talking, thinking clearly, enquiring, analysing and arguing and, in the modern jargon, "learning how to learn" can be developed through the study of any number of subjects. The idea of a liberal education relates to how and in what spirit one studies rather to any particular subject-matter. The "case for law" quoted above is not that it is superior to other disciplines, but rather that it can claim to be potentially as good a vehicle for a general education as English or History or Politics or Sociology. It is rather more flexible and wide-ranging than some other subjects that are also seen to be vocationally oriented.

At a debate in April, 1994, organised by the Association of Law Teachers in a Committee Room of the House of Lords, a motion that "This House believes that we are producing too many law graduates" was defeated unanimously by an audience of about 50 people, by no means all of whom were law teachers (who might be thought to have a vested interest in voting as they did). In opposing the motion, Professor Dawn Oliver, as a good advocate, concentrated on a single theme. "Why pick on law?", she asked, and went on to argue that it is strange to suggest cutting the number of law graduates at a time when the United Kingdom is generally thought to need more well-educated people with transferable skills. It was for the professions, not the universities, to deal with their problems of selection and of alleged overcrowding. Students should be free to choose what they read at university and a law degree was a popular choice for many who did not intend to practice or who had not yet settled on a career. She then summarised the reasons for claiming that a law degree is potentially at least as good a vehicle for general education as History or English or Languages or Business Studies. The argument carried the day.

The key word here is potentially. For it is by no means clear that this potential is realised in practice nor that the image of legal education both inside and outside law schools fits these fine aspirations. In short, law schools proclaim that they provide a general or liberal education, but there is often a credibility gap between such claims on the one hand and the actual practices and attitudes of law students, potential applicants and even some law teachers. In order to probe the relationship between potential, practice and public image it is necessary to look in some detail at the culture of English law schools as it is today.

Notes

[1] Eric Ashby, *Technology and the Academics* (1963) at p. 68.

[2] Edward Shils, *The Academic Ethic* (1983) at p. 3.

[3] *ibid.* at p. 22.

[4] *ibid.* at p. 35

[5] This is a central theme in Allan Bloom's polemic, *The Closing of the American Mind* (1987).

[6] Shils, *op. cit.* at p. 37.

[7] *ibid.* at p. 39; *cf.* Peter Scott, *The Crisis in the University* (1984).

[8] Support for this interpretation can be found in university mission statements, surveys of academic opinion, and at least some party political manifestos; even the bureaucratisation of "accountability" through academic audit, teaching quality assurance and research assessment exercises is by and large premised on the assumption that universities are centres of learning whose primary role is teaching *and* research. This carries with it some clear implications about principles of institutional autonomy and academic freedom and about academic obligations and priorities. See further, Conrad Russell, *Academic Freedom* (1993).

[9] For present purposes Shils's formulation will do, if "truths", "learning", or "knowledge" are interpreted broadly to include know-what, know-why, and know-how. The term "advancement of learning" will be used here to include invention, interpretation and stimulation as well as discovery of pre-existing "facts" and dissemination of what is accepted as settled "knowledge".

[10] Ashby, *op. cit.* at p. 41.

61

What are Law Schools for?

11 *ibid.* Chap. 3.

12 see below, Chap. 4.

13 Undergraduate intakes range quite widely. In 1991–92 the average intake for former polytechnics was 73, for "traditional" universities the average for middle range law schools was about 130–150, but the populations varied from over 700 in Oxford and Cambridge to under 200 in City, SOAS, Lancaster, and Surrey. P. Harris and S. Bellerby, *A Survey of Law Teaching 1993* at p. 36, Wilson, *op. cit.*, at pp. 156–158.

14 Jill Cottrell, "10 + 2 + 5; a Change in the Structure of Indian Legal Education", (1986) 36 *J. Legal Educ.* 331.

15 C. Mallat, *The revival of Islamic Law* (1993) Chap. 1.

16 R. Stevens, *Law School* (1983) at p. 8.

17 On the history of accreditation of law schools by the American Bar Association see Susan K. Boyd, *The ABA's First Section: Assuring a Qualified Bar* (1993); for a more critical view, see Robert Stevens, *Law School* (1983), *op. cit.*

18 *e.g.* Stephen Maher, "Clinical Legal Education in the Age of Unreason" (1992) 40 *Buffalo L. Rev.* 809.

19 Jerome Frank, *Courts on Trial* (1949) Chap. xvi. The most important attempt to apply Jerome Frank's ideas was Antioch Law School, which closed down in 1988; it was in due course was replaced by the District of Columbia School of Law, which was prepared to conform more to established orthodoxy. On Antioch see T. Anderson and R. Catz, "Towards a Comprehensive Approach to Clinical Education: A Response to the New Reality," (1981) 59 *Washington U. L. Q.* 727

20 International Legal Center, *Legal Education in a Changing World* (1975) at p. 39.

21 On NLSIU, Bangalore see (1989) Commonwealth Legal Education Association *Newsletter*, pp. 11–12.

22 See further, William Twining, "Developments in Legal Education: Beyond the Primary School Model", (1990) 2 *Legal Education Review* 35.

23 The Ormrod Committee originally recommended that "conversion" should take two years (paras. 112–115) but this was reduced to one year; for a critique of the present situation see Peter Birks, "Short Cuts" in P. Birks (ed) *Reviewing Legal Education* (1994).

24 Legal education was within the terms of reference of the Royal Commission on Legal Services (Benson Committee, reported 1979) and the Committee on the Future of the Legal Profession (Marre Committee, reported 1988), but neither made much impact.

25 The recent ACLEC Consultation Paper on *The Initial stage* (June, 1994) states that it has not ruled out any models, but sees lack of available resources hampering any substantial move away from the present structure (para. 1.19).

26 By 1994 strong pressure had built up, mainly from the Society of Public Teachers of Law, to extend the period of "conversion" of non-law graduates to two years. Since many universities already provided for an accelerated law degree for graduates this could have the effect of the universities acquiring a virtual monopoly over the initial or academic stage of professional formation. However, even if conversion were made more rigorous, it would not necessarily be the case that the non-law graduate route would be effectively closed off, for conversion courses could be offered by non-university institutions or conversion might not involve any formal instruction. See generally the papers by Peter Birks and Robert Stevens in *Reviewing Legal Education* (1994), *op. cit.* at n. 23. The Advisory Committee in its consultation paper on *The Initial stage* was unequivocal about the survival of the non-law graduate route: "Nevertheless, the law degree route cannot be the only one." *op. cit.* n. 25 at para. 4.27.

[27] Below, Chap. 4.

[28] In the U.S., tightening of the job market in law has in recent years had a delayed effect on the size of the applicant pool. Experience suggests that decreased opportunity may lead to increased competition for entry to the more prestigious schools and pressure on less prestigious schools to lower entry standards or cut both faculty and student numbers. The process is complex, not least because application to law school has to be made in anticipation of the state of the job market several years ahead.

[29] As recently as 1987, it was felt necessary to criticise this attitude, see Keith Patchett, "The role of law in the development process" (1987) 48 Commonwealth Legal Education Association *Newsletter* 33.

[30] *op. cit.* Chap. III.

[31] *ibid.* at p. 35.

[32] *ibid.* at p. 36, see further below pp. 59–60.

[33] The text was so worded as to try to accommodate a broad range of theories of law and of perspectives on development.

[34] *ibid.* at p. 38.

[35] This shift of emphasis is quite closely associated with the propagation of free market ideologies in the wake of the collapse of socialism. An example is the FILMUP Project in Tanzania, which treats the upgrading of financial and legal management, including judicial administration, as a high developmental priority in a free market economy. I personally have some reservations about the policies recently pursued by the "North" in the name of democracy and good governance: "Constitutions, Constitutionalism and Constitution-mongering" in Irwin P. Stotzky (ed.) *Transition to Democracy in Latin America; The Role of the Judiciary* (1993) pp. 383ff.

[36] I was a member of the team that drafted the report, but this chapter states the position better than I could have done on my own. Twenty years on, it still represents my views subject only to minor changes of wording and emphasis.

[37] *op. cit.* at p. 36 (paras. 90–92).

4. Law School Culture: A Visit to Rutland

ACADEMIC TRIBES AND TERRITORIES

When I was at the University of Warwick in the 1970s, I was reminded each time I arrived at the campus of a dictum commonly attributed to Robert Maynard Hutchins when he was President of the University of Chicago, to the effect that a university is "an aggregation of sovereignties connected by a common heating plant."[1] At the time Warwick was a "new university" and our administrators had so arranged the one-way system that almost the first building that greeted the visitor was the boiler-house—an assurance that, despite appearances, this was a real university.

Most modern universities are too large to have only one central-heating system. Hutchins, as a university administrator, was complaining about the rugged independence of academic departments that strongly resisted both central bureaucratic rule and the breaking down of disciplinary boundaries. The departmental system in English universities may be as strong as it ever was, but in other respects this complaint may seem out-dated here as academic autonomy is being steadily eroded by government encroachment on higher education, line management, performance indicators, external auditors, quality assessors and other signs of the movement towards bureaucratic standardisation.

Yet the dictum retains an important core of truth about the distinctiveness of academic cultures. Wander through a modern university from History to Engineering to Spanish to Physics to Social Studies to Philosophy to Medicine to the Business School to Women's Studies, and one seems to enter a series of small worlds, with academic tribes, as Becher calls them, occupying and defending separate territories.[2] Each seems to have its own quite distinctive culture. Even the external signs tell you something: the notice boards, the marks of hierarchy, the conventions of dress, the relative lavishness or penury of the furnishings, the noise levels, staff office hours, the image presented in the departmental prospectus. Wander into a senior common room and play the game of guess-the-discipline, judging academics by their physical appearance. Dig a bit deeper and one is likely to find variations between departments in respect of individual background, career patterns and expectations, work habits, forms of gossip, terms of praise and abuse, political and moral values among both academics and students. But one has to dig deeper still into questions of history, social functions, finance, the distribution of power and, above all, ideas and ideologies, in order to penetrate a particular academic culture.

One example of culture shock will suffice: in the mid-seventies I had to supervise the arrangements for temporarily billeting our small law school in part of the Engineering Faculty, a move of barely a hundred yards to a building designed by the same architect and clad on the outside with identical white tiles. When I arrived to make a reconnaissance, I was greeted by a person of military bearing who spoke like an adjutant. He treated me as if I were the Commanding Officer from another regiment. Although I had put on a sports jacket and tie, I felt improperly dressed. As he showed me round a series of offices that seemed much larger and better appointed than our then accommodation, my guide kept apologising for the modesty of the quarters and the inadequacy of the plant. At the end, he asked what equipment would be needed to be in place before our transfer. He looked mildly surprised when I said that we would only need some bookshelves for the offices and somewhere to make coffee. He kindly undertook to ask his quartermaster to requisition some suitable shelving (books, for the use of) from the departmental store. After all, he implied, we both knew that we have to keep our academics happy by pandering to some of their eccentricities. During our stay, we were well-looked after, but had hardly any social or intellectual contact with our hosts.

This unreliable recollection may tell you something about the prejudices of one academic lawyer. Becher is persuasive in talking of university departments as strongly tribal, with distinctive cultures, stereotyped, often hostile views of their neighbours and a tendency to stake out and defend both physical and intellectual territory. In Becher' scheme engineering is a "hard-applied" discipline, while law is "soft-applied", in contrast, for example, with history, which is "soft-pure" and Mathematics and Physics which are "hard-pure". Another distinction he draws is between "urban" and "rural" disciplines: "urban" subjects have a high people-to-problem ratio, and their "researchers characteristically select a narrow area of study, containing discrete and separable problems, where their rural counterparts typically cover a broader stretch of intellectual territory in which their problems are not sharply demarcated or delineated."[3] According to Becher, Law is predominantly rural, Engineering and most aspects of "big science" are urban, while History is semi-rural.[4]

This chapter is concerned with the culture of English University law schools. I am no Pierre Bourdieu or Michel Foucault. Our law schools, despite sharing a common culture, are probably too diverse to lend themselves to reliable generalisation. So, continuing to adopt the standpoint of a tour guide, I shall fall back on the common lawyer's standby: the case study. I shall begin by giving an impressionistic tour of an imaginary law school, Rutland, focusing on plant, people and events.[5]

RUTLAND

The University of Rutland is a civic university of the middling sort, founded in 1930. In 1993 it had about 8000 students, and was still expanding slowly. During the 1960s it rapidly outgrew its original suburban campus, captured further territory, some neighbouring and some far-flung, where it demolished, converted and erected a motley collection of unmemorable buildings. The main university site houses the library, the administration and most of Arts, Science, Engineering and Social Sciences. The area to the north of the campus is dominated by Medicine. The Law School is a quite small outpost on the southern border, just off the original campus, not as central as Arts, nor as peripheral or far-flung as Agriculture and Astronomy. It is less expansive and expensive than Medicine, but imposing enough to present the appearance of a dignified, but modest, professional school.

The law faculty was founded in 1934. It began by providing part-time instruction for local articled clerks. Then it started courses for the London External LLB. From about 1950 it abandoned both of these and concentrated on teaching its own undergraduate LLB, as well as offering introductory courses to several other departments. Since 1980, it has added a four year degree in English and French Law, three joint-honours degrees, and taught postgraduate courses in Family Law and European Law. In 1994, it neglected to celebrate its sixtieth birthday.

The expansion of the law school is reflected in the numbers of full-time staff: from 1934 there was a lone professor who was joined in 1938 by a junior lecturer. This remained the situation until 1948, when a period of steady expansion began: there were four full-time staff in 1950, seven in 1960, twelve in 1970, twenty-six in 1980. In 1992-93 there were thirty-three, including five professors, responsible for a total "student load" of about six hundred; of these about half were registered for the three year LLB, sixty were postgraduates and the remainder were reading for joint honours degrees in Law or else taking one or two modular law options.[6] The law school also offers a few short courses for solicitors as part of their continuing legal education. Let us start our tour with the physical facilities.

PLANT

Until recently the Rutland Law School fitted quite comfortably into three converted terrace houses just off the edge of the campus. With expansion the accommodation became increasingly cramped. In 1985 a rather ugly purpose-built building was tacked on to provide extra office and teaching accommodation. Almost every American law school is built around the Law Library. This is every law dean's dream and university librarian's nightmare. In Rutland, as in most United Kingdom law schools, the central library won on grounds of economy. There is no room for a proper law library in Denning House, as the law school complex is called, so the faculty is precluded from arguing with fervour that the library is the lawyers' laboratory and can legitimately be separated from the main collections since only lawyers consult law books.[7]

Concern about parking is one of the unifying links of the world academic community. The Law School is one of the few departments at Rutland to have the privilege of its own parking spaces; a small lot by the building can squeeze in up to five compact vehicles. Since 1969, these have not been reserved for any particular officers, but are used by faculty on a first-come-first-served-last-in-first-out basis, providing an on-the-spot case-study of dispute-prevention and resolution for disinterested colleagues who choose to use public transport. Parking studies have a special place in law school legend.[8]

One enters the Faculty by the extension. Denning House has inscribed above its main entrance Coke's admonition to King James—NON SUB HOMINE. . . . SED SUB DEO ET LEGE—an idea cribbed from Harvard's Langdell Hall.[9] At the entrance, below the

inscription—and, in the view of some, contradicting it—is a slate
plaque which in gold letters announces:
DENNING HOUSE
FACULTY OF LAWS
It is worth pausing to consider this text. The not inexpensive
plaque was introduced in the belief that in times of financial crisis
one needs to invest in one's image. The extension was named after
Lord Denning, patron judge of law students, just a year or two
before it became fashionable to exchange such honours for endow-
ments: a chair for a name, as well as a name for a chair. House
was considered less pretentious than Hall. Although since 1990
the institution has been officially called the School of Law, the title
of Faculty has been kept as a reminder of Laws' entitlement to
representation on various university bodies as an independent unit,
despite being no bigger than some departments.

Except for a few imitators, University College London is almost
unique in the world in having a Faculty of Laws rather than a Faculty, School or Department of Law. Rutland is one such imitator.
Leges displaced *Ius*. Francophones classify their discipline as *droit*
rather than *lois*; Italians *diritto* rather than *legge*; Germans *Recht*
rather than *gesetzen*. Here we have a clear reminder of a strong
positivist heritage. Austin, following Bentham, insisted on a sharp
distinction between the study of law as it is and law as it ought to
be, but his conception of the subject allowed for both a Science
of Law and a Science of Legislation within General Jurisprudence.
Austin's followers narrowed his vision by confining the discipline
to the particular "scientific" study of the Laws of England as they
are. For a long time Rutland, like UCL, did indeed have a strong
positivist tradition. Legend has it that the founding dean, Professor
Stern, used to bang the table as he drummed into first year students
the message: "This is *not* a Faculty of Justice; this is *not* a Faculty
of Law; this is the Faculty of *Laws*." The message is clear enough,
but it is no less strange than if a Medical School were to designate
itself the Faculty of Medicines.[10] Today positivism lingers on in
some of the practices, but not in the proclaimed beliefs, of a poly-
glot faculty. Indeed, no-one commented on the jurisprudential significance when the Faculty of Laws was renamed the School of
Law.

On entering the building, one finds a quite spacious, oval circulation area. To the right, behind a grille, is the post of the guardian
of the building, who is still called the Porter, although he does not
carry anything heavier than the mail. He is now backed up by

video cameras and other modern security equipment. To the left are several large, cluttered notice boards. The time-tables show that every undergraduate takes four courses every year, each involving two lectures and one tutorial spread over twenty two teaching weeks. Nine of the twelve courses are compulsory, comprising six "core subjects" required by the profession, together with Legal Method, European Union Law, and Jurisprudence.[11] The student notices relate mainly to the sale of books, places on vocational courses, recruiting visits by law firms, the schedule of the campus law clinic, and Law Society events. Given time we could learn quite a lot about the life of the school by decoding these messages in some detail. The initial impression is of orderly, efficient, unobtrusive regulation.

Front right are two recent exercises in public relations: a framed collage of photographs of all members of academic, administrative and secretarial staff, some 40 in all, indicating titles, but arranged strictly in alphabetical order. This gives a rather favourable impression of the gender and ethnic balance of the academic staff. Immediately opposite is a case exhibiting a sample of recent publications by the Faculty, four slim monographs, about a dozen fat books addressed to the student market (three of which are past their third edition), and a number of offprints with obscure titles, which some might think are self-addressed. No room could be found here for rather more lucrative publications such as nutshells (or other student aids), contributions to loose-leaf practitioners' services, and occasional journalism. First impressions suggest that this is primarily a teaching institution, which is quite vocationally oriented, but which is trying to build up its research profile. These impressions are generally correct. In 1993 Rutland was judged to be "excellent" in teaching, but was disappointed to have been awarded a rating of three in the Universities Funding Council Research assessment exercise in 1992, rather than a coveted four or five.[12]

Facing the front entrance is an already decrepit, but sturdy, 1980s lift which grunts and rattles and pauses as if to complain at having to cope with the demands of several hundred inmates and numerous other invitees, licensees, trespassers and sneak thieves. If we take the lift to the third floor and cross to the attic of one of the old residences, we shall find a small staff reference library—a convenient facility that provides the basic tools of the orthodox academic lawyer: law reports, statutes, a few mainstream journals, the London *Times, Current Law,* a recently installed Lexis terminal (giving access to the standard legal database) and hardly any books.

The top two floors are taken up mainly by a fairly standard mixture of offices and small classrooms. Every full-time teacher has an office; part-timers share. A fair number of offices in the older part are on a quite generous scale by academic standards. By and large their allocation reflects the internal hierarchy—professors and senior office-holders (Dean, Associate Dean, Adviser to Undergraduates, Admissions Tutor) occupy the more attractive older rooms. Other colleagues occupy small, purpose-built offices in the extension. There are notices on most office doors indicating, with varying degrees of cordiality, times at which the occupant would be available to see students without an appointment. Despite standard issue furniture, what becomes of these rooms is a matter of individual expression and use, defying general description. It would be rare to find an office that did not have at least one wall of filled bookshelves, several coffee cups, and a word-processor; few have the uncluttered desk of the modern executive. But the amount of space taken up by piles of paper, food, drink, pictures or bedding is quite varied. Most offices now have computers, but sea mail is still preferred to e-mail.

Most of the Faculty Officers are non-professors: this might be thought to be an inversion of hierarchy or a sign of "democracy", but most professors have opted out of departmental administration with a variety of justifications and excuses. One Dean in the 1970s caught the spirit when she headed the annual list of offices "CHORES": administration is now equated more with obligation than power, and offices rotate with increasing rapidity. Three of the four current office-holders are women.

The first floor contains the office of the Dean and Head of Department (one person). One enters this through the office of the Faculty Secretary, the linchpin of the administration. There is a modest working library for undergraduates, and two common rooms, one for staff and one for postgraduates, a genuine, but not entirely successful effort to foster *communitas*. During term-time, the corridors and stairs of these upper floors are crowded with students, moving between classes, looking for staff, or standing or sitting on the stairs, for the building is bursting at the seams. There is a distinctly cosmopolitan atmosphere about the place. In 1992–93 the Faculty had undergraduates and postgraduates from over 30 countries, with large numbers from Hong Kong, Singapore, Malaysia, Nigeria and Israel, as well as a fair spread from Continental Europe; it also played host to an American summer school. While Rutland may be exceptionally cosmopolitan, mainly for economic reasons, nearly all English law schools have significant numbers of students from overseas. This continuing reminder of our colonial past and present penury tends to obscure the smaller number and special problems of ethnic minority "home" students.[13]

The teaching rooms are unremarkable. The two main lecture-rooms in the old building are squeezed into the basement, along with a xerox room, lockers and lavatories, all windowless and cramped. The lecture-rooms are ugly, uncomfortable and too small. Seminar rooms are spread around the building, although not much small-group teaching satisfies the normal definition of a "seminar". The teaching rooms, the circulation areas and even the graffiti could be in almost any academic department.

Returning to the ground floor, one finds three major public rooms. The Faculty Office, which houses one administrator and five secretaries; the staff common room, somewhat more elegantly furnished, which is used for receptions, parties and a few seminars; an open area, known as "Reality Checkpoint" (again a sign of American influence),[14] which provides the main, rather limited social space for undergraduates; and perhaps the one feature of the new extension that clearly identifies this as a House of Laws. This is the Moot Court, which was designed to look something like a court-room, but doubles as the main lecture theatre and meeting-room. This peculiar hybrid has an elevated bench, a fair imitation of a jury-box, and cramped uncomfortable pews for counsel; but the "public" sits in the standard banked seats of a modern lecture theatre. Here students argue simulated appeals before real or simu-lated judges with some eagerness; much less frequently, they stage an occasional mock trial. Mooting here, as in other English law faculties is, perhaps surprisingly, not officially part of the curric-ulum, but most undergraduates take the opportunity to participate in at least one mooting competition, and some devote a great deal of time to it.[15]

In recent years a sustained effort has been made to create a dis-tinctive ambience. This is most clearly revealed in the pictures, nearly all of which depict heads of male lawyers. The passages of the upper floors are decorated with framed photographs, which with the exception of a row of Daumier prints are almost all of former teachers or reasonably successful alumni, occasionally upgraded by reproductions of famous judges or jurists. The Moot Court is hung with class photographs, through which one can trace the gender revolution: less than 2 per cent. women undergraduates in 1960, about 50 per cent. today. A perceptive observer will notice that these photographs are only of those reading for the LLB; all other students taking law courses, including postgraduates, are not sufficiently visible to be photographed, although there is no evidence that they are less photogenic. On the ground floor the suggestion that the building can be viewed as a minor portrait gallery is reinforced. A bust of Lord Denning smiles benignly on Reality Checkpoint; facing him is a portrait of Professor Stern, the Founding Dean, looking grimly paternalistic.

Law is not photogenic. Nearly all law schools that take trouble with their decor have a problem of restrictive choice: cartoons, Daumier prints, pictures of courts, scenes of famous trials have all been tried, but have almost always failed to undermine the conclusion that the icons and emblems of the law school world are almost inevitably inward-looking, homogeneous, male and dull.[16]

During my career I have taught law in several purpose-built American law schools, at least one of which could claim architectural distinction. I have also taught in a converted army barracks, a political party headquarters, the vault of a disused bank building, a series of converted terrace houses, a prison, purpose-built 1960s academic buildings and, more luxurious than most, a former trade union headquarters. I am not sure that the surroundings made much difference to what went on in the classroom, although it clearly did affect the library facilities, personal relations and general ambience. One suspects that even Michel Foucault would not have found much of positive significance from a study of law school architecture in the United Kingdom, except a seeming indifference to plant and to equipment other than books.

At Rutland there is a further paradox: the Faculty building is somewhat apart from the rest of campus, but almost nothing in its architecture distinguishes it from any other functional academic building—remove the emblemata, and a large department or a small faculty in the arts or social sciences could move in without requiring any structural alterations. The law collection is housed in the main university library, yet this is the most distinctive and exclusive feature of the law school's intellectual life. Before visiting the library, which deserves a chapter to itself, let us consider briefly the occupants of the building and some of its events.

PEOPLE

About 1,500 people regularly frequent Denning House and, in any one year, one could expect at least as many visitors, by far the largest group being the several hundred applicants who come to see the school on open days.[17] Almost all of the visitors have a direct connection with the study of law; those who have been admitted to membership as full-time or part-time teachers, researchers, undergraduates, postgraduates and even secretaries refer to the rest of humankind as "non-lawyers". Yet, one wonders, does this conceit express a distinctive identity? I shall argue that on the whole it does not.

Secretaries

The secretaries provide the first evidence of this theme. As in other academic departments they provide both order and continuity. They keep regular office hours during both term-time and vacation; they welcome visitors and field telephone calls; they know the students and recognise the alumni/ae; they pin up postcards from wandering scholars; several of them have been there longer than most of the faculty and the two senior secretaries, who are in fact administrators, have kept things going steadily over the years as deans and other officers have come and gone. They run the place, keep out of departmental politics, and more than anyone else contribute to a friendly atmosphere.

Students

There is a good deal of information about LLB students at Rutland, much less about the other 50 per cent. In 1991–92 the figures for the entering LLB class of 120 were as follows: 52 per cent. women; 20 per cent from independent schools (UK); 15 per cent. "mature" (*i.e.* over 21); 12 per cent. from home ethnic minorities; 20 per cent. from overseas.[18] This was broadly in line with local and national trends.[19]

Such bare statistics hide a much more complex reality. For example, an American visitor would immediately be struck by the extreme youth of the student body; the age of "maturity" in England is well below the average age of most entering classes in American law schools. The presence of a large number of overseas students from diverse ethnic backgrounds (most of the full-time postgraduates fall into that category) makes the atmosphere quite cosmopolitan. As was noted above, it also tends to mask the special problems of home ethnic minority students, many of whom can justifiably claim various kinds of relative deprivation in their background, situation and prospects.[20] The bare figures can also be misleading about class. There is a good deal of evidence to suggest that the great majority of law students and an even higher proportion of practising lawyers in most Commonwealth jurisdictions come from the upper middle class and above.[21] Rutland does not have many so-called "Oxbridge rejects", but in most respects, despite some attempts to disguise the fact, it is predominantly middle class, both demographically and culturally—an elite institution, somewhere in the middle of the Premier League.

In a useful preliminary cohort study of law students, published in 1994, David Halpern found that undergraduates' expressed views suggested that they "were a vocationally orientated group and, to some extent, more vocationally orientated than those who were teaching them."[22] This is a judicious way of pointing to a divide which varies considerably between institutions and which is naturally glossed over by publicity literature, except the occasional "alternative prospectus".[23]

Student culture is a powerful force in law schools. Here I shall focus on just one aspect: the seeming disjunction between its strong vocational bias and the actual careers of law graduates. Rutland provides a clear example. Most national figures about graduate employment are "first-job" statistics, which merely reveal that between 1980 and 1990 a majority of law graduates proceeded to "further training" and that very few were unemployed.[24] These figures are almost useless, since they provide no information beyond the first year after graduation. Of the 60–70 percent of law graduates who sought a professional qualification, some failed to obtain a place on a vocational course, some dropped out or failed at that stage, many were unable to obtain pupilages at the bar or training contracts with solicitors' firms; there was further "wastage" before qualification and a great many young barristers and solicitors left private practice within a few years. The market has fluctuated over time, and has recently declined sharply, so that by 1993/4 it seemed quite possible that in future only about 30–40 per cent. of law graduates would even have an opportunity to qualify.

Concerned about this perceived decline in opportunities, the Rutland Careers Office undertook a survey of the career patterns of its UK graduates over the period 1980–1993.[25] Despite the practical difficulties of contacting alumni, there was a reasonable response rate. The results surprised both the Careers Office and the Law School. For no single cohort between 1980 and 1987 had more than 35 per cent. of Rutland graduates been in private practice for five years or more. For most years, less than 60 per cent. had obtained a professional qualification and in several years the figure was between 40–50 per cent. Whether this reflects national patterns is not known, because law schools have almost universally failed to keep track of the subsequent careers of their alumni. Nevertheless, it seems quite likely that in the 1980s, less than 50 per cent. of law graduates would follow a legal career for more than five years and that in the 1990s the proportion might decline significantly.

In view of these figures, it may seem strange that law student culture in the early 1990s was very strongly oriented towards the legal profession, especially private practice, and to an unintellectual, sometimes anti-intellectual, conception of what legal practice involves. This appears inconsistent with claims that the undergraduate law degree was intended to provide a liberal education in law, including for intending practitioners. The degree course appeared to be being used for a quite different purpose.

At Rutland the evidence for this disjuncture is persuasive: we have already seen that the undergraduate notice boards are dominated by items to do with vocational courses, training places, interviews, mini-pupilages, and other matters almost exclusively related to the private practice of law. There is one solitary notice, significantly headed "alternative careers", which, equally significantly, includes jobs for employed lawyers.[26] The undergraduate "alternative prospectus", while paying lip-service to the liberal pretensions of the law degree, defines vocational relevance almost exclusively in terms of private practice and even speaks of the possibilities of "opting out" at various stages. The same document emphasises that studying law is hard work and again links this to professionalism. Most undergraduates choose options that they think will "look good on the c.v.", and these are typically related to private practice, despite the protestations of law firms that they want graduates with a broad general education.

Every four or five years the issue whether Jurisprudence should remain compulsory is debated. To date it has survived at Rutland, but not at a majority of law schools in the country.[27] In the early 1980s the Faculty decided to make one of the core subjects optional in order to increase student choice. The subject, Equity and Trusts, lacks universal appeal, especially when, as at Rutland, it is taught in a dry and technical way.[28] This experiment was abandoned after two years, because 95 per cent. of students chose to take it, the most common explanation given being that this was a form of insurance in case non-intending practitioners decided to qualify later.[29] However, in response to the current "crisis", which some see as an opportunity, a group of lecturers has proposed that three of the "core" subjects should be made optional, thereby signalling that the Law School is serious about the LLB providing a general education as well as greatly increasing student choice. The issue is unresolved, but the indications are that about half of the academic staff are opposed to any such change.[30]

The Rutland Faculty

There is a large literature on the academic profession and on students in higher education in Britain, much of it based on empirical research. There is a remarkably extensive, neurotically introspective, and mainly speculative literature on law teachers and law students in the United States.[31] With a few exceptions, mainly relating to gender, race and access, there have been hardly any empirical studies about English law students and law teachers as such, except some irregular statistical surveys.[32] At least two studies of academic lawyers in England are in progress.[33] There is, of course, a mass of information—historical, anecdotal, biographical, statistical and interpretative—scattered in the literature. However, as with law schools as institutions, the scholarly literature about higher education generally assumes that law teachers and law students are not an especially distinctive part of the academic scene. Becher is an exception. Law teachers are almost as inconspicuous in the sociological literature on the legal profession.[34]

In his surveys of British senior common rooms in 1964, 1976 and 1989 Professor Halsey treated law as one part of the social sciences and humanities, and law teachers remain largely invisible in his *Decline of Donnish Dominion* and its predecessors.[35] He has very kindly extrapolated the sample of academic lawyers from his 1989 survey and made it possible to contrast them with a total sample of 2,674 respondents. A preliminary analysis of this rich set of data produces some interesting results, including a few surprises, but by and large it confirms the hypothesis that in most of Halsey's categories academic lawyers are near the middle of the academic spectrum.[36]

The faculty at Rutland is reasonably representative of the national profile of academic lawyers and, in particular, of those in "old" provincial universities. In 1992–93, 12 of the 33 full-time faculty were women, and three were from ethnic minorities (one from overseas). Only nine of the staff had first class degrees, but nearly all had a professional qualification or a postgraduate degree or both. The three older professors had extensive experience of practice early in their careers, one had studied and taught in the United States and one had spent several years teaching in West Africa and Australia. About 60 per cent. of the non-professorial faculty have professional qualifications (a few with two or more years post-qualification experience); all but six hold postgraduate degrees, including four doctorates, one in sociology and another in philosophy. Three of the lecturers (including an American) obtained degrees in other disciplines before they turned to law. As one might expect, given expansion and the relative mobility of law teachers,[37] over half of the Rutland faculty is under 40 years old, but a bulge is beginning to develop in the mid to late thirties. Only one current member of staff has been at Rutland for more than 15 years.

Rutland has an admirable tradition of taking teaching seriously and there is a good deal of variety and experiment in respect of methods and approaches. The average official teaching load is 10–12 hours a week over 22–24 weeks, but no credit is given for supervision of research students nor for "outside teaching" on, for example, access courses, continuing legal education, and short courses for government departments or agencies, such as the Crown Prosecution Service. One professor acts as a part-time "in-house trainer" for a large provincial law firm and another is involved in the training of magistrates. Over half of the staff are involved in such activities, some of which are reasonably remunerated. In fact several individuals devote a good deal of time to this kind of work, sometimes at the expense of their research.

Until quite recently Rutland did not have a corresponding general commitment to research. There were a few productive scholars on the faculty and some distinguished work was done, but for a long time teaching clearly took precedence over research, which was largely left to the individual. Since the 1970s several factors have contributed to the development of a stronger "research culture": promotions criteria placed more emphasis on research, a professional qualification was no longer considered almost as a *sine qua non* for law teaching, research training in law began to develop slowly, and recently external pressure to produce has been exerted through the national research assessment exercises. Despite the pressures of bureaucratisation and reduced funding, "productivity" measured in terms both of publication rates and sophistication of research has steadily increased over the past 20 years. And, as we shall see, conceptions of legal scholarship have recently diversified.[38]

More fundamentally there has been a gradual redefinition of the identity of the academic lawyer, as part of a process of closer integration of the law school into the university.[39] Until the 1960s law teachers at Rutland were expected to be able to teach any of seven or eight subjects and, indeed, took a pride in being generalists. Today, almost all of the faculty, especially those under forty, consider themselves to be specialists and rarely teach more than two subjects. As in other disciplines, this has created a different kind of tension between loyalty to the institution and commitment to one's specialism.[40] Law schools like Rutland are generally too small to be able to afford groups of specialists and this tension is mitigated for some and exacerbated for others by the fact that the institution is located near the middle of a quite compact country. Increasingly, one's peers and collaborators are, or are thought to be, in other law schools. Locally based cross-disciplinary work is still quite exceptional, although that too may be changing.

At one level the Rutland faculty is committed to the academic ethic. They conceive of their role as the advancement of learning through teaching and research and most of them consider academic administration to be a chore. However, this bland statement conceals continuing conflicts and ambiguities. Individuals are given space to develop as scholars in diverse ways, because research is considered to be an individual matter. But in respect of education the familiar conflicts persist. Although undergraduate law student culture is still almost unequivocally oriented towards the legal profession, the faculty is deeply ambivalent. There are, of course, many opinions and strong vested interests. But the ambivalences run deeper. Even the most professionally-oriented teachers subscribe to the academic ethic, with varying degrees of commitment and understanding; some former practitioners made financial sacrifices in order to work in a university; but nearly all those who define themselves as intellectuals or theorists or scholars value the connection with legal practice. Some may be critical of the legal profession, but Rutland has no true legal masochists, either those who hate law or its study or who feel that they have a mission to deter their students from serving Mammon.[41] If there is one thing that unites the Rutland Faculty it is the professed belief that there is no necessary incompatibility between viewing academic law as part of the humanities and as a good, perhaps necessary, foundation for professional formation.[42] However, it is a lack of consensus on the part of the faculty about objectives, priorities and methods in the LLB that gives so much power to student culture, while leaving so little space for individual student choice.

EVENTS

One way of evoking a culture is through fiction. We have noted already that law schools are almost invisible in English campus novels. But if one were to shift the scene from a department of English or Sociology to an English law school, the possibilities would not be very different: Jim Dixon's public lecture in *Lucky Jim*[43]; a British Council tour or a spoof on post modernism in the mode of Malcolm Bradbury[44]; an academic conference, an exchange with an American institution or with "a real world", as evoked by David Lodge,[45] micro-politics along the lines of *The Masters*[46] or *The Abbess of Crewe*,[47] sexual romps in a Tom Sharpe polytechnic[48]—all of these could be accommodated in a law school without too many adjustments. There is no reason that I can tell why murder, love or intrigue is less likely in a law school than an English Department. Even some of the types satirised in *The History Man*, which helped to bring sociology into disrepute, had legal counterparts in the late 1960s and early seventies.[49] One could not compete with the wealth of literary allusions in the works of Malcolm Bradbury or J. I. M. Stewart or Amanda Cross, but law could probably produce some functional substitutes. American law school novels emphasise the Socratic case class, the hard work and stress for the students and the intensely competitive atmosphere. But these are features that to some extent differentiate American from English law schools; that is a matter of degree, however, and in England they suggest fewer fictional possibilities, at least on campus.

So what, if anything, might this change of setting have to offer? There is potential in a moot, or a visit to a court or prison that goes wrong; law centres and clinics provide a promising point of contact with live clients and real problems, even though regrettably few law students actually participate in them. Besides the traditional moot, the increasing use of simulations in teaching basic professional skills such as interviewing, negotiation, and first instance advocacy has dramatic possibilities, but these take place mainly at the second or vocational stage which has not yet reached Rutland. One could surely have fun with thirty or so lawyers bickering over the interpretation of the rules and conventions at an examiners' meeting; and visits by legal dignitaries offer scope for satire. But by and large this thought experiment leads one to conclude that switching the campus novel from Arts to Law would not lead to a major breakthrough in the genre. The similarities are much greater than the differences.

My American mentor, Karl Llewellyn, maintained that the best way into studying any group or institution was to focus on the details of routine processes and actual disputes. "If I were a cheque and I arrived at your bank, where would I go?", he would ask bankers.[50] And the Llewellyn case-method, which became standard in legal anthropology, dictates that the visitor to an institution should start by enquiring, though in more diplomatic terms, "Had any good disputes lately?"[51]

So far as I know, this method has never been applied systematically to any law school in England.[52] This is to be regretted, because conflict is endemic in law schools, perhaps even more than most other academic cultures. This is not, I think, only or mainly because lawyers are professionally involved with disputes and argumentation. If this were so, the arguments would be ritualised and the protagonists ought to be skilled in all aspects of disputing from prevention to resolution and settlement. Rather, I would advance the hypothesis that there are perennial, unresolved differences about the purposes of the enterprise as well as about priorities and methods. Some of these tensions are expressed in familiar, but dubious, dichotomies: theory/ practice; liberal/ vocational; knowledge/ skills; broad/ narrow; critical/ conservative; teaching/ research—most of which we have already encountered.[53]

Rutland is no exception. Conflicts, disagreements, and clashes of interest have been endemic throughout its history. More often than not they have been kept beneath the surface, partly out of a sense of collegiality, partly by standard means of containment and avoidance. One of the most common means of containment of conflict between colleagues has been giving every individual teacher some territory that they can call their own in respect of teaching and, more easily, of research. With relatively large classes this is often difficult because the teachers tend to work in teams, often with strong leadership, or else they further balkanise the curriculum. From time to time sharp disagreements have surfaced, typically over standard issues relating to curriculum, admissions, assessment and, above all, staff appointments. There have been feuds with the administration and occasional, usually short, conflicts with groups of students. There is a continual tension between what students want and expect, what their teachers think that they should want, and what law teachers want to give them. The students exercise power through choice of options, but on many other fronts the faculty can outmanoeuvre them through standard techniques of academic politics such as delay and avoidance. Today's students do not have a counterpart to Cornford's *Microcosmographia Academica*.[54]

How such problems have been handled at Rutland would be the subject of a fascinating study, not least because this is deemed to be a rather successful institution: it attracts good students, nearly all of whom graduate with second class honours and find employment; the teaching was assessed as excellent and the research as good in recent external evaluations. But to do justice to this theme would require a substantial book by a sociologist or ethnographer.[55]

Pressure of space precludes detailed case-studies of any particular events at Rutland. However, it is worth looking briefly at two prime subjects for treatment: faculty appointments and Open Days.

Selection of future colleagues is, of course, one point at which conflicts of values, vested interests and clashes of personality surface in any organisation. I have no evidence that law is strikingly different from other academic departments in this respect, but that is a matter of speculation. One can, of course, expect some local variants—disagreements about "black letter" versus "broader" approaches to legal scholarship or education or the relative weight to be given to practical legal experience as against publications or teaching reputation, for example.

At Rutland, during the 1970s the process of faculty appointments became so highly politicised that an unofficial, elected departmental appointments committee was set up to consider and filter out candidates before the University Appointments Committee made any decisions. This institution involved contested elections, lengthy meetings, and political intrigue, including factions and shifting coalitions that reflected a complex mix of ideological and academic differences. It was a rather clear example of an "interposed institution",[56] that was both "informal", in that it was not officially authorised, and highly formalistic in its procedures. The University administration only learned of its existence by chance when a candidate sent in a claim for travel expenses to the Academic Registrar after attending an unofficial "interview" by this departmental committee. Eventually, after lengthy wrangling, the University reasserted the exclusive jurisdiction of its official Appointments Committee and in the more authoritarian 1980s the unofficial elected body faded away. A case-study of a number of contested appointments at Rutland, or elsewhere, would tell one a good deal about the governance of the institution.

There tends to be less overt controversy at Rutland about the recruitment and selection of undergraduates, but here some of the deep ambivalences permeating law school culture are rather clearly revealed. The pluralism of our system of higher education involves applicants in a bewildering, time-consuming and anxiety-ridden process of choice of subjects and institutions. Some have decided on a career, most have not. A law school presents itself to school-leavers and other potential applicants for undergraduate places through glossy prospectuses, other written materials, Open Days and various kinds of informal contacts. Almost all law school prospectuses stress the twin themes that constitute the fundamental ambivalence of academic legal culture: on the one hand, we offer a general academic education which is a good preparation for a variety of occupations; on the other hand, our law degree satisfies the requirements of the initial stage of qualification as a barrister or solicitor and provides a good foundation for preparation for practice. There are considerable differences of emphasis in the publicity literature emanating from law schools. In many prospectuses the order of the two points is reversed or the vocational nature of the degree is deliberately emphasised. In some, flexibility and choice are the dominant themes. In a few, such as Warwick and Kent, the institution sets out to project a distinctive *persona*. This is most commonly done when the ethos is avowedly "academic", for example where there is a strong emphasis on interdisciplinary work or critical perspectives or transferable intellectual skills, but some are unequivocally concerned with preparation for legal practice. Not surprisingly, almost without exception law school prospectuses try to ride both horses, and in the process many fail to communicate a clear sense of direction or a distinctive image. Rutland fits the pattern.

While an analysis of undergraduate prospectuses in law indicates some divergent patterns,[57] this form of literature conceals as much as it reveals. It needs to be read with the scepticism appropriate to any form of advertising, especially in the current market-oriented atmosphere. Open Days may be more illuminating, not only because visitors can sniff the atmosphere, observe and ask questions, but also because they usually have direct access to students as well as staff.

When I was responsible for "Open Days" at Warwick, my main task was to try to communicate to an anxious audience the nature and significance of what we considered to be a quite distinctive ethos. This involved a deliberately "soft sell", an attempt to deter as well as to attract potential entrants and to advise those who failed to get a place about other possibilities. At that time, competition for places in law was strong, the employment prospects of law graduates were good and public financing of students was much more generous than it became later, including discretionary awards for vocational training. My task was a relatively easy one, not least because most of our students had a strong sense of the distinctiveness of the institution, and one could rely on student guides on Open Days to reinforce rather than contradict the message.

The situation in Rutland in the early 1990s was quite different. First, as we have seen, there is less of a consensus among the faculty about the objectives and ethos of the undergraduate degree. Secondly, the students are generally more vocationally oriented than their teachers and have more financial pressures than their predecessors.[58] In the absence of a clear lead from the faculty, student attitudes and expectations have a profound effect on the general atmosphere and morale of the institution. Thirdly, it is only recently that it has become apparent that a law degree is no longer an almost automatic passport to a professional qualification, if one can afford it. The combination of a recession, more stringent requirements for training, and other factors has led to a sharp decline in the number of training places relative to the number of aspirant practitioners. By 1993 it was estimated that perhaps as few as one third of law graduates could expect in future even to have the opportunity to qualify. For a place like Rutland this could have a dual effect: on the one hand, those who were determined to qualify would be likely to try to enhance their chances by applying to the more prestigious institutions, or they might try harder to get a good degree and be strongly influenced by their conceptions of "relevance".[59] On the other hand, those who had no firm career intentions or who were less well-placed to compete, for academic or social reasons, might be expected to be more sympathetic to the idea of a law degree as providing them with a good general education that would enable them to compete with other graduates in the general job market.

The situation was further complicated by other factors: there seems to be a fairly regular divergence between the conceptions of teachers, students and employers about what is "vocationally relevant" at undergraduate level. Academic lawyers, no doubt with varying degrees of conviction and credibility, may echo Karl Llewellyn's claim that the best practical training, as well as the best human training, that a law school can give is the study of law as a liberal art.[60] Students, however, tend to think that courses in areas like commercial law, procedure and evidence are "practical" and subjects like jurisprudence, legal history and even human rights are "theoretical". Some practitioners genuinely believe that the academic stage should be academic, but collectively the practising profession has so far failed to communicate to law students messages about their expectations that are clear, unambiguous and believable.[61] In considering this situation, Halpern concludes:

"What law schools may wish to consider is not so much the reduction of the more 'theoretical' or academic aspects of law but the more careful establishing of its relevance in the minds of students."[62]

This is sensible advice, but it has not yet penetrated to Rutland. The undergraduate prospectus is unequivocal in proclaiming that the three year LLB is "designed as an academic discipline incorporating the theoretical and comparative treatment of law." But this claim is contradicted even within the prospectus both by the emphasis on exemptions and the fact that all the professional core subjects are compulsory, with jurisprudence tagged on in the third year as a symbolic afterthought. In his speeches on Open Day, the Dean tends to ride both horses and his plea for theory is immediately subverted by the student guides who in a well-intentioned attempt to promote the institution emphasise the vocational strengths of law at Rutland as they perceive them. Their message is reinforced by the building and its decor, by the notices about careers advice, and by the natural concerns of the students about their prospects after they graduate. How far the changing job market will affect student choices and attitudes remains to be seen.

Rutland is in a process of transition without very clear ideas about how to cope with a rapidly changing situation. In recent years it has started to diversify its teaching and other activities, but with no definite sense of direction. To some extent its practice has outrun its self-image as essentially an undergraduate institution. It has not committed itself wholeheartedly either to being mainly a professional school, involved at all levels of professional formation and development, nor to diversifying its activities along the lines of the I.L.C. model.[63] Almost all non-degree teaching and other outside activities are done on an individual rather than an institutional basis. At undergraduate level, so long as the faculty is too ambivalent and divided to provide a clear lead and messages from the profession are ambiguous, it seems that a narrow and probably deluded set of vocational attitudes is likely to continue to dominate student culture and to condemn the institution to be and to be treated as little more than a mediocre nursery school for the profession.

Notes

[1] Cited by Milton Mayer, in *Robert Maynard Hutchins: A Memoir* (1993) at pp. 97–98.

[2] Becher, *Academic Tribes and Territories, op. cit.*

[3] *ibid* at p. 79.

[4] Becher suggests that an academic culture should be interpreted in terms of the nature of knowledge and the workings of the academic community and their interaction (Chap. 1). I am following his lead and I shall later be considering in turn the law library, the nature of contemporary legal scholarship, whether the discipline of law has a stable core, and what, if anything, it has to offer in the way of understanding law itself and more general understandings. Other, rather different, "ethnographic" studies of academic life include F. Bailey, *Morality and Expediency: The Folklore of Academic Politics* (1977); Colin Evans, *Language People: the experience of teaching and learning modern languages in British universities* (1988).

[5] Rutland is a composite. As in other works of fiction any resemblance that it bears to any particular institutions is incidental.

[6] Between 1986 and 1993 the staff-student ratio officially declined from 1:12 to 1:18, but this was partly mitigated by the increased amount of teaching provided by part-timers, about half of whom were practising solicitors. "Student load" refers to "full-time equivalents" rather than "warm bodies", of which, at a guess, there are over 1000, including part-time and modular students.

[7] Below, Chap. 5.

[8] KLRM pp. 63–65 (Underhill Moore's parking studies).

[9] Arthur Sutherland, *The Law at Harvard,* (1967) at p. 243. The elite American law school is generally considered to be a total institution, more demanding, terrifying, and competitive than its younger English cousin. cf. the hostile reaction of a student to Langdell Hall in Scott Turow, *One L* (1977) at p. 36. The exterior of the Senate House of the University of London is decorated with images of famous sages and scholars; there is a rumour (unconfirmed) that the Faculty of Law of one Latin American university has a mural depicting Justice with loaded scales and one eye peeping out of her blindfold. The exterior of my own law school at University College, much smaller than these, but still quite grand, has some unobtrusive reliefs depicting artisans and workers, hinting that, contrary

to its declared pretensions, this may, after all, be a trade school or mechanics institute.

[10] This is an example of the fallacy of the Way of the Baffled Medic: Prescribe First, Diagnose Later, If At All; in legal education this takes the form of believing that one can study rules before, or even without, studying the problems to which they are purported responses. That is rather like studying medicines or other cures without reference to diseases. HDTWR pp. 215–216, RE Chap. 10.

[11] On the core subjects see below, Chap. 7.

[12] On a scale of five grades, three represented "Research equating to national excellence in a majority of areas, or to international in some."

[13] See below n. 20.

[14] RE p. 368.

[15] There are now National, European, Commonwealth and International Law (Jessup) mooting competitions, almost exclusively for undergraduates.

[16] One notable exception is Northwestern University Law School, described TEBW pp. 109–111. The most interesting modern book on legal architecture is Yosef Sharon, *The Supreme Court Building, Jerusalem* (1993).

[17] Under the old UCCA system the national ratio of applicants for each available LLB place was fairly steady, averaging just over 14:1 between 1965 and 1991 (Wilson, *op. cit.* p. 148). Rutland's ratio in 1991 was 13.5:1. The standard offer was ABB in A levels (or equivalent) and, except for "mature" students, interviews were used sparingly. Under this system each candidate had five choices of department, so a more realistic indicator of the competition for a law school of this kind is between two and three to one, with allowance being made for self-selection. An experiment at Rutland using an English adaptation of the American Law School Admission Test (a form of critical reasoning test) was abandoned after two years in the mid-1980s. Rutland applies the same entry criteria to overseas as to home students and has had no difficulty so far in filling its university-imposed quota of "high fee" places. The ratio has remained steady over the years, but the standard minimum offer has increased as has the number of places. About 500 applicants attend open days.

[18] Nearly all of these were from outside the European Union and were, therefore, classified as paying "high fees"; in fact, over half were on scholarships or bursaries.

[19] The diversity of English law schools is brought out clearly in the 1993 surveys by Wilson, *op. cit.* above, and Harris and Bellerby (1993) *op. cit.* above Chap. 2, n. 41.

[20] See the vivid and disturbing picture presented by recent reports on the problems of ethnic minorities seeking to enter legal practice: *Equal Opportunities at the Inns of Court School of Law* (Barrow enquiry final report, 1994) and for the Law Society by David Halpern, *Entry into the Legal Professions: The Law Student Cohort Study Years 1 and 2* (1994), Chap. 8. This interim report by the Policy Studies Institute on behalf of the Law Society contains by far the most thorough profile and analysis of undergraduate and professional law students (including those taking the CPE) in England and Wales published to date. It deals with a wide range of issues affecting intending solicitors, and includes some disturbing findings on "Unfair advantages and discrimination in the selection processes for the LPC and articles."

[21] For the historical and comparative background up to the late 1980s see R. Dhavan, N. Kibble and W. Twining (eds.) *Access to Legal Education and the Legal Profession* (1989).

[22] Halpern, *op. cit.* at p. 42.

[23] This form of literature is relatively underdeveloped in this country and seems to be generally more benign than some North American examples.

[24] The figures vary from year to year and are almost as unreliable as they are uninformative.

[25] There is some anecdotal evidence that a quite high proportion of overseas law graduates proceeded to practice law in the private sector or the public service.

[26] Most home students were reasonably satisfied about careers information, but Halpern notes: "The most frequent complaints were about lack of information about careers other than the solicitors' profession (especially among law undergraduates) and about the need for better information on when, how and where to apply to for jobs and professional training (especially among CPE students)." *op. cit.* at p. 94.

[27] Wilson, *op. cit.*, at p. 168 reports that only 14 out of 34 "traditional" university undergraduate programmes had retained compulsory Jurisprudence. However, this may be an underestimate as some curricula include general theoretical courses under some other name. A survey by Hilaire Barnett (forthcoming) suggests that the figure is closer to 50 per cent. Interestingly, on the last occasion a majority of the undergraduates present at a debate on the issue voted for its retention as a compulsory subject. This was possibly because of the blatant anti-intellectualism of the proponents of change, an example of a moderately weak case being spoiled by terrible advocacy. Even more significant is the fact that students have never argued for making optional any of the "core" subjects required for professional exemption.

[28] Even Trusts, which is quite technical, is not necessarily inherently less interesting or important than Human Rights, Family Law, Labour Law, Intellectual Property or Legal History, which are all also capable of being made to seem dull. Some equitable principles and concepts are important foundations for other subjects, but this does not need a whole course.

[29] Note the two non-sequiturs: this subject is popular, therefore it should be compulsory; I might need this subject for professional purposes some time in the future, therefore I should take it now. Graduates who need to make up one or more core subjects can do so by one of a number of methods; this is particularly significant for those taking mixed degrees, but could be used to greater advantage by those who have not made definite career choices by their second year of the LLB.

[30] In a recent survey (unpublished), Esther Johnson, reports that only 5 out of 39 UK law schools studied made all the core subjects compulsory, see below n. 57.

[31] R. J. Borthwick and J. R. Schau, "Gatekeepers of the profession: an empirical profile of the nation's law professors", (1991) 25 *U. Michigan Jo. of Law Reform* 191.

[32] On the recent study of law students by David Halpern, see above n. 20.

[33] Professor David Sugarman is conducting a series of interviews of law teachers in England as part of a history of legal education and Professor Patricia Leighton is directing a survey for the Association of Law Teachers. For a more impressionistic account of the law teaching profession in the late 1970s see ALLD ("The Law Teacher as Superstar".)

[34] For example, the three volume comparative study of legal professions, edited by Richard Abel and Philip Lewis, *op. cit.* Chap. 2, n. 21 above, deals rather cursorily with law teachers. Notable exceptions include R. Abel, *The Legal Profession in England and Wales* (1988) which contains some useful statistics and Abel-Smith and Stevens (1967), *op. cit.* above, Chap. 2.

[35] Above Chap. 2 at n. 2.

Law School Culture: A Visit to Rutland

³⁶ For details see Appendix.

³⁷ Academic lawyers have the opportunity to be mobile in three main ways: to move into or from full-time practice; to move laterally or on promotion to other universities in the United Kingdom; and to teach abroad, mainly in other common law jurisdictions. Since the Second World War there has been a remarkably strong network of academic lawyers throughout the English-speaking world; recently contacts with Continental Europe have increased, but the barriers of language and different legal traditions make transfer much harder.

³⁸ Below Chap. 6.

³⁹ The ILC report on *Legal Education in a Changing World, op. cit.* Chap. 3. states that a full-time scholar teacher of law needs to be equipped as a professional lawyer, a professional researcher and as a professional educator (para. 227). One might add, also as an administrator-politician. Clearly there is sometimes conflict between these roles, but the job is no more varied than many other occupations and, on its own, does not explain academic lawyers' recurrent problems of identity. See further ALLD, Chap. 3.

⁴⁰ Colin Evans (1988), *op. cit.*, Chap. 8 contains a good discussion of such multiple allegiances and of the fragmentation within university departments as a result of increasing specialisation.

⁴¹ Legal masochism is a complex phenomenon that deserves exploration on another occasion.

⁴² Legal literature is full of assertions of this credo. My favourite is Karl Llewellyn's "The Study of Law as a Liberal Art" (1960) reprinted in *Jurisprudence: Realism in Theory and Practice,* (1962) at p. 376: "The truth, the truth which cries out, is that the good work, the most effective work, of the lawyer in practice roots in and depends on vision, range, depth, balance and rich humanity—those things which it is the function, and frequently the fortune, of the liberal arts to introduce and indeed to induce. The truth is, therefore, that the best practical training a university can give to any lawyer who is not by choice or unendowment doomed to be a hack or a shyster—the best practical training, along with the best human training—is the study of law, within the professional school itself, as a liberal art." The thesis of this book reaffirms the potential, but questions some of the performance.

⁴³ Kingsley Amis, *Lucky Jim* (1954).

⁴⁴ Malcolm Bradbury, *Rates of Exchange* (1983), *Mensonge* (trs. David Lodge) (1987).

⁴⁵ David Lodge, *Small World* (1984), *Changing Places* (1975), *Nice Work* (1988).

⁴⁶ C. P. Snow, *The Masters* (1951).

⁴⁷ Muriel Spark, *The Abbess of Crewe* (1974).

⁴⁸ Tom Sharpe, *Wilt* (1976).

⁴⁹ Malcolm Bradbury, *The History Man* (1975).

⁵⁰ KLRM at p. 316.

⁵¹ Llewellyn and Hoebel, *The Cheyenne Way* (1941).

⁵² I have twice persuaded friends with a PhD in anthropology who were about to start on a law degree in an American law school that they should treat this as fieldwork and keep a diary. Both agreed, but found the other pressures too great to be able to keep it up. See, however, J. Seligman, *The High Citadel* (1978) and Scott Turow, *One L, op. cit.*

⁵³ There are, I think, additional factors at work. Many disagreements within law schools are strongly political or ideological, however much that is glossed over on the surface. Both the subject-matter and the enterprise of studying it are so imbricated with values that practically every choice made by law teachers is

related quite directly to their commitments, ambivalences or evasions. This is, of course, a matter of degree and is also true to a greater or lesser extent in all disciplines, especially the Humanities and Social Sciences. Law tends towards the political end of the spectrum and critical theorists have drawn blood when they have attacked as mere pretences claims to be scientific or neutral or object-ive. Catch phrases like "all law is politics" or "law is ideology" are in a sense trivial because they are so patently true. The difficult question is how to maintain relative detachment and be true to the academic ethic when dealing with such contentious subject-matter.

54 F. M. Cornford, *Microcosmographia Academica: Being a guide for the young academic politician* (1908).

55 M. R. Kadish and S. H. Kadish, *Discretion to Disobey* (1973).

56 Such a book would do well to treat of non-events as well as visible conflicts, scandals, and triumphs. A detailed case-study of Rutland would need to take account of how little it has been associated with public conflict. The law school has not been involved in actual or threatened litigation over wrongful dismissal or tenure or race or sex discrimination, or sexual harrassment or examinations or student discipline or unfair admissions procedures, all of which have been the subject of legal proceedings elsewhere in recent years. This is not bad for a community of lawyers. Of course, the institution has had its share of students in trouble with the police, sit-ins, library thefts and vandalism, sexual shenanigans, complaints about teachers, political intrigues and other standard features of aca-demic life. But these have been exceptional and have almost never attracted media attention. Our sociologist would do well to test the hypothesis that this is by and large an orderly, efficient, quite professional institution which, despite endemic potential for conflict, has generally settled its affairs internally and done what is expected of it without much fuss. How far this is typical of other academic departments or other law schools would require further investigation.

57 I am indebted to an unpublished report by Esther Johnson entitled "A Comparat-ive Study of Law courses in the UK." (1993), based largely on an analysis of 1994 university prospectuses. This found significant differences in curricula in respect of (1) relative emphasis on breadth and depth of study; (2) the claimed orientation of the course (categorised as "academic" or "practical"); (3) Flexibil-ity given to students to pursue their own interests, especially in regard to the number of required courses in single honours degrees in law, which ranged from 4 to 10 compulsory subjects. Johnson constructed a Composite Model of the contemporary LLB degree which involved twelve full subjects, spread evenly over three years, eight compulsory (including two half-subjects) and five optional sub-jects (one in the second year, four in the third year). The traditional written exam-ination is the principal method of assessment, with various forms of "continuous" (almost invariably written) assessment used to supplement it. There are quite wide deviations from this model by individual LLB programmes; Rutland's curriculum is quite close to this composite model.

58 See Halpern, *op. cit.*, Chap. 6.

59 As Halpern's research has confirmed, "employers tend to be far more concerned with the prestige of institutions than with the content of their courses." (*op. cit.* at p. 98) Yet the most prestigious institutions, especially Oxford and Cambridge, are considered by students to have the most "theoretical" courses. Halpern reports a higher degree of discontent with their courses but not with their social life among such students. One outcome of increased competition to qualify is that the most vocationally oriented students may be attracted to the most "theor-etically" oriented institutions and that such institutions, whatever their academic

commitments, will become arenas for competition for entry into the profession.

[60] Llewellyn, *Jurisprudence* (1962) at p. 376. For the full passage see above n. 42.

[61] W. Twining, "Preparing lawyers for the Twenty-first Century", (1992) 3 *Legal Education Rev.* 1.

[62] *op. cit.* at p. 38.

[63] Above Chap. 3.

5. The Law Library

"[L]aw is a science, and . . . all the available materials of that science are contained in printed books. If law be not a science, a university will consult its own dignity in declining to teach it. We have . . . inculcated the idea that the library is the proper workshop of professors and students alike; that it is to us all that the laboratories of the university are to the chemists and physicists, the museum of natural history to the zoologists, the botanical garden to the botanists."

Christopher Columbus Langdell.[1]

Adjudicated quarrels of mankind,
Brown row on row!—how well these lawyers bind
Their records of dead sin,—as if they feared
The hate might spill and their long shelves be smeared
With slime of human souls,—brown row on row
Span on Philistine span, a greasy show
Of lust and lies and cruelty, dried grime
Streaked from the finger of the beggar, Time.

Archibald MacLeish.[2]

For those who use it regularly, Denning House may signify many things: the office, a home from home, a base, a club, a trysting place, a womb, a sanctuary, a bastion of male privileges, or a prison. Visitors may find it intimidating or congenial or over-regulated or ugly or cosy or just dull. Whatever else it may signify, it is recognisably part of the family of educational institutions, closely resembling its nearest relatives, that is other university law schools and other departments on the same campus. Dean Langdell has often been criticised for calling law a science and for claiming that all its available materials are in printed books. We shall examine both improbable claims in due course. But Langdell was surely right in emphasising that most learning about law centres on books and that the centre of the law school is the library. The man who

91

is credited with revolutionising the methods of law teaching can be produced as a witness against the fallacious belief that learning mostly takes place in classrooms.

In 1992 the Harvard Law School Library, probably the best collection in the world, was reported to contain almost one and three quarter million volumes. The estimated holdings of the two principal legal academic research libraries in the British Isles were for the Bodleian Law Library at Oxford about 250,000 volumes and for the Institute of Advanced Legal Studies in London about 215,000.[3] The most recent prescription for recommended holdings for academic law libraries in England and Wales specified an initial capital expenditure of about £500,000 and an annual upkeep of £30,000 for reference works and a further £6000 for "textbooks".[4]

These figures become more impressive if considered in the light of three apparent paradoxes. First, law books are notoriously long, heavy and expensive; yet the interpretation of legal texts—one kind of legal reading—can involve as careful analysis of every phrase, word or punctuation mark as any form of textual analysis. Sir Roger Casement, it is said, was "hanged by a comma".[5]

A second apparent paradox is that there is likely to be hardly any overlap between the contents of an orthodox law library and the stock of a general book shop. Most law libraries contain mainly law books in a narrow sense. You are unlikely to find in many law libraries *Crime and Punishment* or legal novels or popular accounts of famous trials or the works of Kant or most other kinds of "books about law" that were mentioned in the first chapter. A law student who wishes to gain a broad general education about law will, no doubt healthily, have to visit other sections of the university collection or a good public library. Almost the only overlap between the stock of a good general book shop and an average university law library is likely to be students' textbooks and casebooks. But the former tend to be a bastard form of law book; the latter are mainly a substitute for using the library. Thus law libraries are among the most extensive and expensive kind of library despite the fact that they tend to adopt rather narrow definitions of what constitutes legal literature.

There is one further apparent paradox. It is often said that books are the lawyers' tools; the library, their laboratory. Yet ancient legend and recent research both suggest that the great majority of practising lawyers devote very little time to consulting, let alone, reading law books. Thus one survey suggested that partners in solicitors' firms in a major Scottish city spent less than fifteen minutes per week referring to books and that a remarkable amount of information about law is acquired by telephone, often from non-lawyers.[6] A similar picture is suggested by the well-known anecdote of the solicitor who always got his clerk to climb up and pull down the same volume of the *English Reports*, which on inspection turned out to be *Everyman His Own Lawyer*, impressively disguised in a leather binding.

At Rutland the law school is physically separate from other departments and seems aloof and self-contained. Yet the law library is part of the main library, right in the middle of the campus. In 1991 it reported holdings of 32,000 volumes, which puts it in the middle range of "traditional" university law schools, but better off than most former polytechnics. Physically, the space it occupies is not strikingly different from other parts of the library, but some concessions have been made to its claims to be special: there is a separate catalogue (not yet computerised) in the main law reading-room in addition to the general catalogue; there are terminals for LEXIS and other databases, but CD ROM is in the future[7]; there is relatively generous seating provision for students; and there is a specialist Law Librarian, who is also responsible for Government Publications and Politics. The rules governing borrowing are more restrictive than for most other disciplines. It is symptomatic of the continual tug-of-war between librarians and the law school that the former refer to "the law section", while teachers and students call it "the law library".

As one enters Rutland's main Law Reading Room, one senses that there is something different about it, but it is not easy to pinpoint what that is. On an average day during term nearly all the seats are taken, and the law students have spilled over into adjacent areas; the law library is the law students' special territory, but not vice versa. Observing the behaviour of the readers may provide some further clues: they seem to walk about a lot, to the shelves, to the xerox machines and to the central desk, where there is an extensive reserve collection; rarely does a reader have only a single book in front of them; often a desk will have acquired a row of a dozen or more volumes arranged vertically rather than in a pile. Undergraduates immediately recognise the point when they are told that the Rutland faculty prescribes one classic text in Jurisprudence to be studied in the original, because they believe that all Rutland law graduates should have read at least one whole book during their three years. In a law library one consults and uses, rather than reads books—it is primarily a place of reference.

The Law Library

A guide to the Bodleian Law Library, written in 1974, starts as follows:

"LEGAL LITERATURE OF THE UNITED KINGDOM
Lawyers rely absolutely on the written word, because law follows a precise path. It is for this reason that law is a well-documented subject with highly developed and specialised bibliographical aids".[8]
After briefly describing some of these aids—which are not referred to as books[9]—the guide continues:
"Legal literature is vast but it almost universally consists of four main classes: (1) Legislation, (2) Law Reports, (3) Legal Periodicals, (4) Textbooks".[10]

In 1994 this would generally be considered an unduly narrow view of both law and legal literature, even for an introduction. Nevertheless this is a convenient summary of the traditional view of a law library. Three points about this account are worth emphasising. First, primary materials predominate; legislation and reported cases are authoritative primary sources of law; so, to a limited extent, are some treatises. At Rutland legislation and law reports occupy over half the shelf-space in the law library. If one includes other official documents (such as Hansard, and official reports) and bibliographical aids, the proportion approaches 75 per cent. Moreover, within the textbook section will be found a fair number of casebooks and collections of statutes. These anthologies, largely of primary materials, are "portable libraries" designed both to take pressure off the main collection and to ensure that important original texts are available in class. Secondly, the list of categories refers almost exclusively to law books in a strict sense, that is works which focus on legal doctrine—what the law says—rather than "books about law" concerned with critical, descriptive or explanatory accounts of what the law does.[11] Legal periodicals range more widely, but most of the rather modest collection in the Rutland library are also mainly concerned with legal doctrine. Thirdly, the most striking feature about this list is what it excludes—a point to which I shall return.

Law libraries not only exclude books, they also appear to exclude people. Even where the law library is not physically separate, as it is in many universities, it must seem daunting to most outsiders: the titles, the system of classification and citation, the military orderliness, even the physical size of most volumes seem calculated to deter the visitor and the neophyte. And are they not

94

written in a foreign language? There is probably no branch of the humanities and social sciences that at first sight seems less user-friendly to the non-specialist. The law library can be taken as a prime symbol, and as part cause and part effect, of the marginalis-ation of law in our general intellectual culture.

Yet, I would suggest, this is a false impression. For it is probably also true that no other discipline is so well-served by "finding aids". These include not only bibliographies and dictionaries, but also encyclopaedias, digests, citators, guides and some of the most advanced kinds of computerised information retrieval systems yet developed. Above all, there is the law librarian, who in my experi-ence typically feels under-used as a source of help and advice. The reason for this wealth of research tools is simply that there is a need for help with finding answers and authorities relevant to spe-cific practical problems and therefore there is a market which extends far beyond academia. Many of the aids and guides are geared to that special kind of need, but books on "legal research" also cater for the academic market.[12]

Similarly, while it is true that some knowledge, skill and specific techniques are necessary to find one's way round a law library, the difficulties can easily be exaggerated. The most important initi-ation rite for the new law student is "introduction to the law lib-rary". This normally takes at most a few hours and one or two simple exercises, reinforced in later years by more advanced, but essentially simple, instruction.[13] Once one is over the initial hurdles, the law library really is extraordinarily user friendly.

To paraphrase Mrs Beeton: "it is one thing to catch your hare, another to jug it". Of course, finding one's way around a law lib-rary and locating material is only the first step. The next obstacle is language: there is a massive literature on legal language, jargon and mystification.[14] Undoubtedly lawyers use unfamiliar terms and familiar terms in unfamiliar ways; as with other disciplines, learning law includes mastering certain basic, often complex, concepts; but the difficulties of acquiring a basic vocabulary are often much exaggerated. I send first year students a list of 100 words, some peculiarly legal (such as bailment or tort or *obiter dictum*), some that have special technical meanings in legal contexts (such as trust or licence). I advise them to buy a small law dictionary, to master this basic vocabulary, and to make a habit of looking up any unfa-miliar or puzzling term in their dictionary as they come across it. There is an initial barrier, but it too is quite easily surmountable by a bit of effort. A more nuanced understanding of the legal vernacular obviously requires study, experience and local knowledge, but as with the skilled traveller, one can get remarkably far with a few dozen words and phrases. Demystifying the law is as much as anything a matter of confidence.

Interpretation is a more weighty affair. Learning how to read, interpret, and use different kinds of legal texts efficiently and intelligently is a complex art which, in the eyes of many, is central to a good legal education.[15] However, insofar as academic legal education is an exercise in learning how to read intelligently, it is not very different from, for example, English or History or Music. It is part of my thesis that how to use a law library intelligently and how to read and use cases, statutes and other materials of law study deserve to be as much a part of "general education" as how to read a Shakespeare play, a poem by Auden, *The Financial Times*, a post-modern novel or a company balance sheet. It is also my contention that law libraries are a rich resource that have been radically under-exploited by scholars in other disciplines. In order to develop these twin themes, let us take a brief conducted tour of the rather modest Rutland law library, considering in particular its accessibility and what it might offer to "non-lawyers"—that is students and scholars from other disciplines. Let us consider in turn the four categories highlighted in the Bodleian guide.

LEGISLATION

"Legislation" in this context is used to cover Acts of Parliament, Public Bills, Subordinate or Delegated Legislation, Private Acts, local by-laws and the various law-making instruments of the European Union, including Regulations, Directives and Decisions.[16]

Stendhal is reported to have read the Code Napoleon regularly in order to improve his prose style. It is difficult to imagine any English novelist or poet attempting the same with any type of United Kingdom legislation. Our traditional style of legislative drafting is notorious for its unreadability; and there has been persistent criticism of the disorderly and inconvenient way in which legislation is promulgated, amended and communicated to those who are subject to it. Some enthusiasts talk of the architecture of statutes, but one cannot pretend that our statute book has aesthetic appeal or is easy to use.

The reason why every educated person needs to develop at least some basic skills in handling legislation is that it is so important:

everyone is affected by legislation, directly and indirectly, every day. Most people have to read, interpret, apply, follow, avoid, evade, and manipulate formal legal rules—such as those governing V.A.T., social security benefits and road traffic.[17] Many people are also involved in rule-making—for example, in discussing and formulating rules of discipline or the constitution of a club or office procedures. The techniques of handling rules in fixed verbal form are much the same whether or not they are part of the law emanating from the state. Acts of Parliament and, increasingly, European Union legislation, international conventions on human rights, and international regulation of economic matters are the most important in respect of both status and scope, but they are only the tip of the iceberg. Our destinies and our lives are to a large extent regulated by rules in fixed verbal form. Being able to find, understand and cope with formal rules is an important part of being a citizen or a subject. Rule-handling is a basic social skill.[18]

A law library is the place in which one will find the most advanced literature on the making, interpretation and use of legislation in this broad sense. It is also the repository of rich collections of examples of different kinds of legislative texts. The literature on law-making processes is fairly evenly divided between politics and law. The secondary and theoretical literature is not as developed as one might expect or hope, given the importance of the subject, but there is enough available to serve as an adequate vehicle for studying it from different perspectives and at different levels of sophistication. Whether or not one continues to be repelled or whether, as some do, one finds that the subject improves on acquaintance and can even be a source of delight, the fact remains that basic rule-handling skills are part of the equipment needed to understand and cope with living and working in modern society.

It is not only non-lawyers who have shied away from the subject. Traditionally common lawyers have preferred judge-made law to legislation. Blackstone complained about the messy intrusions of the legislature into the common law[19]; two of the best-known evangelists for the Harvard case-method, Joseph Henry Beale and James Barr Ames, resisted the introduction of courses on legislation into the curriculum.[20] Such courses are still relatively underdeveloped. Insofar as they cannot avoid dealing with statutes, many law teachers still tend to introduce legislative material mainly through the medium of cases interpreting them. This is not difficult, for the great majority of modern reported cases involve interpretation of legislative texts. In 1982, Professor Guido Calabresi of Yale argued,

97

in a book entitled *A Common law for the Age of Statutes*, that American courts ought to have the power to modify legislative rules, especially older statutes, as they do to modify the common law.[21] Whether or not one interprets this as a rearguard action by a representative of the common law tradition, it is symptomatic of recent belated attempts by case-trained academic lawyers to come to terms with the predominant legal form of our age.

LAW REPORTS

"The reports of cases since the middle of the last century ought, in most instances, to be read in course, and they will conduct the student over an immense field of forensic discussion. They contain that great body of the commercial law, and of the law of contracts, and of trusts, which governs at this day. They are worthy of being studied even by scholars of taste and general literature, as being authentic memorials of the business and manners of the age in which they are composed. Law reports are dramatic in their plan and structure. They abound in pathetic incident, and displays of deep feeling. They are faithful records of those 'little competitions, factions, and debates of mankind' that fill up the principal drama of human life; and which are engendered by the love of power, the appetite for wealth, the allurements of pleasure, the delusions of self-interest, the melancholy perversion of talent, and the machinations of fraud. They give us the skilful debates at the bar, and the elaborate opinions on the bench, delivered with the authority of oracular wisdom. They become deeply interesting because they contain true portraits of the talents and learning of the sages of the law."

James Kent.[22]

"Case law is law found in decided cases and created by judges in the process of solving particular disputes. Case law in some form and to some extent is found wherever there is law. A mere series of decisions of individual cases does not of course in itself constitute a system of law. But in any judicial system rules of law arise sooner or later out of such decisions of cases, as rules of action arise out of the solution of practical problems, whether or not such formulations are desired, intended or consciously recognized. These generalizations contained in, or built upon, past decisions, when taken as normative for future disputes, create a legal system of precedent. Precedent, however, is operative before it is recognized. Toward its operation drive all those phases of human make-up which build habit in the individual and institutions in the group: laziness as to the reworking of a problem once solved; the time and energy saved by routine, especially under any pressure of business; the values of routine as a curb on arbitrariness and as a prop of weakness, inexperience and instability; the social values of predictabil-

98

ity; the power of whatever exists to produce expectations and the power of expectations to become normative. The force of precedent in the law is heightened by an additional factor: that curious, almost universal, sense of justice which urges that all men are properly to be treated alike in like circumstances. As the social system varies we meet infinite variations as to what men or treatments or circumstances are to be classed as 'like'; but the pressure to accept the views of the time and place remains."

Karl Llewellyn.[23]

These quotations, both by American jurists, sum up the enduring appeal of the law reports for lovers of the common law. For every purple passage in their praise, it is not difficult to find one that complains about them: for example that they are garrulous, repetitious, pompous, hypocritical and self-contradictory; they make law teachers case-mad and law students case-weary; they conceal or distort as much as they reveal; above all, they are too numerous: American courts, it has been estimated, issue over 100,000 reported decisions every year.[24] The common law has nearly drowned under the never-ending flood of judgments. The case-lover has a simple response: as with any other form of literature, one needs to read the law reports selectively and with a trained eye.

It would be as foolish to try to give a comprehensive account of the law reports in a few pages as it would be to do the same with English literature. Even the Rutland law library, which has rather thin American and Commonwealth holdings, probably has a more extensive collection of short stories than all of the literature sections of the library combined. In the time available, after a brief look at a single volume of the *All England Reports*, I wish to develop a single theme: that the law reports are both over-used and shamefully neglected as a resource.[25]

THE NATURE OF THE LAW REPORTS

Law reporting has a long history and has experienced a number of mutations. But modern law reports conform to a fairly standard form throughout the common law world. When lawyers talk of finding, reading or citing cases they are referring to the kind of document or text that is typically collected, edited and published in the law reports. Here, one can usefully adopt, with slight modification, a well-known American definition:

"A case is the written memorandum of a dispute or controversy between persons, telling with varying degrees of completeness and of accuracy, what happened, what each of the parties did about it, what some supposedly impartial judge or other tribunal did in the way of bringing the dispute or controversy to an end, and the avowed reasons of the judge or tribunal for doing what was done."[26]

The great majority of cases to be found in modern English law reports emanate from superior courts; some specialised series report decisions of tribunals, arbitrations and other adjudicators. Cases have been selected for inclusion for one main reason: the facts raised and the court purported to resolve one or more contested issues of law. There was a doubt about the law and the court's decision represents an authoritative answer to the question(s) of law involved. That is what is meant by a precedent.

Let us pause to look briefly at just one volume from this massive collection. The volume I have chosen, almost at random, is the fourth volume of the *All England Law Reports* for 1991. It is bound in Royal Blue with gold lettering on the spine. It is published by Butterworths, who provide regular services to subscribers, including weekly unbound parts, tables and indexes and an annual review. This volume contains 16 pages of preliminary material and 992 pages of reports of cases.[27] The preliminary material includes an alphabetical "digest" of the cases reported, classified according to legal categories, from Action to Writ. From this we can see that just under 100 cases are reported in this volume; about 60 per cent. are decisions of the highest courts, the House of Lords, the Court of Appeal, and the Judicial Committee of the Privy Council. Those of the Court of Appeal are, as usual, the most numerous. The spread of topics is broad: there are nearly 60 headings in the digest, with Criminal Law (11), Practice (14) and Ecclesiastical Law (4) having the most entries. One case can appear under several headings. The parties are also varied, including multi-national companies, ministers, local authorities, universities, newspapers, individuals charged with a variety of offences and ordinary citizens. The amount at stake, in both human and financial terms, is also varied: they range from disputes involving millions of pounds to a question about the right of a parishioner to reserve a grave space in a churchyard; from cases involving homicide and rape to a prosecution for outraging public decency through lewd, obscene or disgusting behaviour, in this instance leaving notes in public places seeking preliminary meetings with boys. The spread, at first sight, seems to be almost as broad and as random as the contents of a newspaper; there is, of course, some overlap, but a significant difference of emphasis. It would be interesting to contrast the picture and treatment of "public life" in the law reports and the news media, using modern methods of analysing and interpreting the content and form of the various kinds of publication.[28] One might conclude that they represent rather different kinds of distorting lenses on our social life.

Here we have to be content with a few quick impressions. By chance, perhaps the most important case from a legal point of view that is reported in this volume relates to a spectacular national tragedy. Its presence is signalled rather cryptically (and not entirely accurately) in the Digest as follows:

DAMAGES—Personal injury—Nervous shock—Disaster at football stadium—Persons with relatives at stadium seeing live broadcast of events
Alcock v Chief Constable of South Yorkshire Police   HL 907

The case dealt with one aspect of the Hillsborough Stadium disaster in which 95 spectators were crushed to death and 400 were injured during the semi-final of the F.A. Cup on 15 April 1989. This report dealt with the culmination in the House of Lords of proceedings by 15 plaintiffs who had been in a different part of the stadium or who had heard about the disaster on television or radio and as a result had suffered nervous shock which caused psychiatric illness because they believed that a close relative or fiancé(e) might have been one of the victims. The South Yorkshire Police had admitted liability in negligence to those who had suffered physical injury in the crowd, but denied that they owed a duty of care in negligence to onlookers (whether at the ground or through the media) who had suffered nervous shock resulting in illness. The plaintiffs claimed that the defendants were liable if the resulting illness was reasonably foreseeable. The House of Lords unanimously rejected all of the plaintiffs' appeals.

From a social point of view the report is of interest because it focuses a very bright light on just one aspect of a tragic event that not only affected the victims, their families and the whole country, but also had considerable repercussions on such matters as the design of football stadiums and police practices of crowd control.[29] From a legal point of view *Alcock* is a leading case because it put in issue a variety of issues about the duty of care in negligence that have long troubled the courts: can a distinction be drawn between psychiatric and physical injury in personal injuries cases? Can anyone recover damages for "nervous shock" on learning of the death or injury caused to another by negligence? Or is liability limited to very close relatives and, if so, does that include a brother, grandparent, fiancé(e), brother-in-law? Does it make a difference how the person learned of the news or how close they were in time and space to the event? The general problem is familiar to students of negligence. The *Alcock* case illustrated in a dramatic way some of the many complex permutations and combinations of circumstances that have to be dealt with by law. The five Law Lords unanimously denied all of these claims, but they have since been criticised both for artificially limiting liability in negligence and, by justifying their decision in four different discursive judgments, leaving the law almost as uncertain as it was before.[30]

The law reports and precedents are far too varied to be represented by a sample of one. The *Alcock* case, although dealing with a much-debated problem, is hardly representative of cases in this volume let alone in the law reports generally. However, it is a quite good illustration of the form and content of modern law reports, and it shows rather clearly how judges have to be concerned with justice in the individual case (the affect of the speeches is generally sympathetic) and yet be clinically intellectual in their treatment of legal doctrine at a general level. The judges were involved with only one aspect of the Hillsborough tragedy and this precedent has implications for a wide variety of situations involving negligence.

THE FASCINATION OF THE LAW REPORTS

Given their nature, it is not surprising that the law reports have fascinated both practising and academic lawyers to the point of obsession. But, at risk of belabouring the obvious, it is worth analysing the ingredients that make them so alluring. Let us start with an analogy: imagine a vast anthology of stories, each one of which raised a moral or social dilemma or problem. In order to be included in the anthology the problem was such that people genuinely disagreed about the best solution. In addition to each story closing with an ending, denouement or other resolution, it also contained a sub-plot in which arguments for and against competing endings were advanced and then one or more wise persons announced their solution and their reasons for adopting it. Many also contain secondary stories—of the particular proceedings or of the development of prior solutions or, occasionally, the life-stories of one or more participants.[31] Imagine that every week, in this country alone, dozens of such morality tales were added to the collection, each one telling a new story which raised hitherto unresolved questions or doubts—and that around the English-speaking world the same process is going on, so that in any one year thousands of fresh items are added to the collection. Imagine, then, that there is a whole industry of specialist editors and publishers who select, package, index, cross-reference, produce and distribute these anthologies systematically and regularly, and that there are also secondary industries of critics, commentators, synthesisers and summarisers making the collection accessible and convenient to use for a variety of purposes. Nowhere in literature, folklore, mythology, or even medicine or social work, does such a collection exist. But it exists in law.

There are, at least, three other characteristics of the law reports that deserve special emphasis: they are authentic; they are detailed; they are interconnected.

(a) Authenticity. The law reports are authentic in the sense that the facts arose out of actual disputes rather than out of the imagination of an individual or a community: unlike myths, legends, fiction or hypotheticals dreamed up by academics such as the prisoner's dilemma, the Cretan liar paradox, or the rodeo problem[32], they come fairly directly from "the real world". One does not need to adopt a correspondence theory of truth to see that this is highly significant. One may readily agree that the stories in the law reports have been constructed, processed, and packaged in ways that often take them a long way from the original events and that "the facts" are often homogenised or distorted or translated into lawyers' categories that may make them almost unrecognisable to the original participants. Some facts, as in the famous case of *Donoghue v. Stevenson*, were merely allegations that were never proved by evidence.[33] Even if one concedes all of these points, which can easily be overstated, the stories presented to the judges, the commentators, and other readers came from outside. Also, very few cases reach the law reports in which the facts were not backed by carefully sifted evidence—which is not to say that "the facts" are always true. Modern law reports are also authentic in another sense: they are professionally edited by barristers and the texts of the judgments contain the judges' own words. In that sense they

are really primary. The integrity of these documents is enhanced by the fact that there is a further source against which an appellate court's rendering of the facts can be checked—the records of the trial court.

(b) They are well-documented. Not only are the texts reasonably reliable, they are also quite detailed. The statement of the facts in a typical reported judgment is more detailed than is strictly necessary for the purposes of precedent. Judges state the facts in a way which is conditioned by lawyers' strict notions of relevance—here relevance to the issues of law—but they include a good deal of detail, partly to establish a comprehensible background, partly to describe the particular situation as they see it, not least to communicate this understanding to the parties and their legal representatives. Equally important, the reasons given in justification for a decision are also detailed—sometimes taking up a dozen or more pages, occasionally over a hundred. The judges of our highest courts are learned; they do not always wear their learning lightly; and succinctness is not their forte. The length and discursive nature of common law judgments are often singled out as key features of differences in style between the common law and civil law traditions. In no other sphere of social life are decisions by state officials so regularly documented publicly and in detail. The full and precise treatment of both facts and arguments makes the law reports a particularly rich source to be used for purposes other than those for which they were intended.

(c) They are interconnected. Few lawyers read single cases in isolation. They read cases grouped in different ways for different purposes. For example, cases can be related to each other because they bear directly on a single precise point of law, or because they represent a historical sequence, a story of legal development, or because they illustrate a diversity of problems within an area or because taken together they form the basis of a systematic account of a topic or field of law. Modern literary theorists talk of "inter-textuality". This repulsive term accurately describes one of the chief characteristics of the law reports. Cases feed off, build on, confirm, extend, erode, displace or overturn other cases. The inter-relations are complex. The secondary aids classify, index and cross-refer in a number of standard ways; with new technology, such as full-text retrieval, inter-textuality is greatly extended. The common

law mixes its metaphors quite graphically: the law reports are more like a seamless web than a wilderness of single instances.

THE DISTORTING MIRROR: OVER-USE OF THE LAW REPORTS

It is easy to see why the law reports can be depicted as a rich treasury of inter-related stories, arguments and decisions, extending over time and space and many spheres of social life; public, concrete, detailed, authentic and accessible. Common lawyers have quite understandably cherished and loved the law reports; the trouble is that they have too often loved them to distraction and have become case-mad.

For the law reports have very distinct limitations and to use them as the main route to understanding law, let alone social life, is to become over-reliant on a kind of lens that distorts as much as it illuminates. Let me just pick out a few points from a long litany.

First, the law reports are unrepresentative in several important ways. Imagine, as if on a map, a total picture of all disputes and conflicts in society. Only a minute percentage of these ever comes near a lawyer or law enforcement official. Focus, for the sake of argument, on civil claims on which a solicitor is consulted: the vast majority of these will be settled or dropped without any formal process of litigation being started; of the tiny number in which a writ is issued or formal proceedings are begun, nearly all will be settled out of court. Of those cases which reach court, it is most commonly the facts that are mainly in dispute, or possibly disposition or sentencing, rather than questions of law. In the relatively small number in which the court of first instance has to determine an issue of law, there is usually no appeal. By no means all appellate cases involving a question of law reach the law reports—for our system of law reporting is much more selective than in the United States.[34] The statistics vary according to the subject-matter and the type of proceeding—but in almost all spheres of litigation reported cases are exceptional. At every stage, cases get filtered out, by no means randomly: some litigants cannot afford to continue; many disputes are not worth the costs, economic and otherwise, of litigation; some repeat-players—insurance companies, for example—will settle, rather than provide courts with an opportunity to create an unwelcome precedent. And so on.

Some of the main reasons for treating the law reports with caution were summarised well by Sir Otto Kahn-Freund:

"Is it not in the nature of the lawyer's work that his mind concentrates on phenomena which are socially marginal? Legal thinking must, I think, be constituted that way—this is perhaps the principal difference between law as an academic discipline and the other social sciences which are concerned with typical and not with marginal situations. Above all: litigation is a pathological phenomenon in the body politic. The reported cases are the cases of the most serious diseases, and the leading cases are often the worst, and least typical of all. . . . Is legal education based on case law not like a medical education which would plunge the student into morbid anatomy and pathology without having taught him the anatomy and physiology of the healthy body? More than that, is the concentration on decided, and especially on reported, cases not like a clinical education which would enable the doctor to diagnose and to treat some complicated brain tumor without ever telling him how to help a patient suffering from a simple stomach upset?"[35]

The law reports are selective in another sense. They only give one, rather peculiar, perspective on an individual dispute. They tend to treat it in isolation from wider issues; they process the facts and frame the issues for a quite narrow and specific purpose. They typically leave out large parts of the wider context and the human dimensions of the process. They treat what are often complex dilemmas and tragic choices in an artificially rigid, all-or-nothing, winner-takes-all dichotomy[36]: guilty/not guilty; liable/not liable. Only exceptionally do they provide for compromise or for an admission that a problem is insoluble.[37] The duty of the judge is to decide and there are elaborate rules and devices—such as presumptions—for assisting in the process of producing a final resolution to often insoluble dilemmas.

Stranger still, the law reports often to do not tell us the end of the particular story. They do not tell us what happened to the police officers and the Hillsborough plaintiffs and football stadiums after the House of Lords' decision in *Alcock*.[38] The law reports contain a massive collection of artificially selected and truncated slices of legal life which conceal and omit as well as inform.

Recently a new genre of literature has developed of which Professor Brian Simpson is the principal exponent. Contextual studies of leading cases explore their broader social context and the human dimensions and political significance in depth. For example, Simpson's enthralling *Cannibalism and the Common Law* explores the background to the case of *R v. Dudley and Stevens*, in which it was held that killing and eating a fellow crew member in order to save one's own life cannot be justified by a defence of necessity.[39]

Simpson's *In the Highest Degree Odious* and other works in this genre are important counterpoints to the law reports.[40] They are also very readable. They point to one possible route for helping the discipline of law to reach its potential to be one of the great humanistic disciplines, but so far, for reasons which I have explored elsewhere, no regular niche for them has been found in formal legal education.[41]

The same is true of many other neglected materials of law study. Despite its obvious importance in our political, social and legal life, legislation comes a poor second to the law reports in legal studies. Many other kinds of sources, primary and secondary, fare even worse. This is partly because the law reports are more congenial, partly because of the prejudices of common lawyers, but— more important—because we have yet to develop suitable theories and techniques for using this kind of material for educational purposes. Academic legal culture is extraordinarily sophisticated in its use of cases and still quite primitive in its use of other materials.[42]

LAW REPORTS AS A NEGLECTED RESOURCE

There are several standard and quite different ways in which the law reports are used, each of which requires different methods of reading. For instance, cases can be used simply as concrete illustrations of a general rule or principle; they can be used for their bearing on a specific issue or analogous fact-situation; they can be studied in sequence to trace the development of a concept or doctrine; they can be synthesised into a single coherent expository statement of the law on a given topic; and, of course, they provide raw material for arguments for each side on a disputed question of law. Each of these types of reading requires somewhat different lenses. In some cases, for instance in dealing with potentially adverse or favourable precedents in the context of legal argument, a wide range of relatively sophisticated techniques can be learned and deployed.[43]

Within the discipline of law a number of less standard ways of reading cases has been developed in recent times: Karl Llewellyn advanced a theory of judicial styles—meaning here styles of argumentation by judges—and required his students to read cases from a single court in chronological sequence rather than in terms of orthodox legal classification by subject[44]; John Griffith has analysed how senior English judges have dealt with students, trade unionists,

women and minorities—again independently of legal categories—
and has suggested that this kind of reading reveals systematic political biases on the part of the judiciary[45]; in the United States a
specialism known as jurimetrics, a branch of cybernetics, involves
the application of statistical techniques to appellate opinions; for
example, with a view to assisting prediction of how American
Supreme Court Justices or other appellate judges are likely to vote
in future cases[46]; at the core of the Law and Economics movement
is the application of certain standard techniques of micro-
economic analysis to reported cases; on the left, critical legal
scholars, using techniques developed in literary theory, deconstruct
judicial opinions and purport to show them to be self-
contradictory, incoherent or meaningless.[47] James Boyd White, a
Professor of both literature and law, has applied methods of reading
literary texts to illuminate the law reports more sympathetically.[48]
It has recently become quite fashionable to read the law reports in
terms of story-telling, rhetoric and semiotics.[49]

Most of these alternative methods of reading have been
developed within law schools but, with the exception of economic
analysis, none has really been integrated into the mainstream.
Many of the techniques have been borrowed from other disciplines
and some have been applied rather crudely. Almost without exception, these various readings have been applied to the law reports
for legal purposes, mainly to explain and interpret legal phenomena: the role of judges; styles and techniques of argumentation; the
business of appellate courts as well as legal doctrine. I have argued
elsewhere that law students should be taught to read and use the
law reports more systematically, consciously developing more than
a dozen ways of looking at and handling this kind of text, rather
than the standard three or four.[50] To that extent the law reports are
an under-used resource even within the discipline of law.

The main reason for claiming that they are neglected, however,
is that they are hardly exploited at all by non-lawyers. Enough has
been said to make the point that this is an enormously rich body
of material in respect of extent, scope, accessibility, authenticity
and detail. The cases are there, asking to be studied. In order to
tap into this potential gold-mine it is of course useful to know what
is in them, how and why they are selected and constructed, and
some of the terminology and the institutional and procedural context. In short, some local knowledge is needed before one starts
digging. The possibilities are potentially endless. Let me just give
a few examples of uses to which they have been put, though so

far only on a modest scale: moral philosophers, probability theorists and statisticians have found them to be a fruitful source of concrete examples of puzzles or problems—often more realistic and sometimes more complex than standard hypotheticals; students of logic and rhetoric have occasionally subjected examples of legal arguments to detailed analysis; political scientists, especially in the United States, have made fairly extensive use of Supreme Court Reports, especially on constitutional matters. A few non-lawyer historians, psychologists, discourse analysts, and literary theorists have used examples from the law reports, sometimes rather selectively and not always with due regard to context.[51] But this is rather like picking up a few diamonds on the surface of an extremely rich lode. In order to start it is sensible to read two or three books on using a law library and legal method, and then to dig in.[52]

LEGAL PERIODICALS

Law journals and other periodicals occupy almost one fifth of the shelf-space in the Rutland law library. However, we shall not pause here very long; for, although segregated from the general periodicals section of the main library, academic law journals share many of the features of their counterparts in other disciplines: there is an informal hierarchy of prestige; they are indexed in much the same ways; they are the main outlet for specialist writing and, to a lesser extent, for polemics and book reviews; they continue to proliferate in ways that suggest that they are more producer-driven than demand-led; and, perhaps for that reason, they command a small audience. They are rarely the best starting-point for visitors from other disciplines.

Legal periodicals are more varied than the law reports. In England they include general journals of mainly academic interest, such as *The Cambridge Law Journal, The Modern Law Review,* and *Legal Studies.* There are several kinds of specialist periodicals, some of which serve both practitioners and academics, or like *The Criminal Law Review,* a wider professional audience; as in other disciplines this is an expanding sector, involving high prices and low print-runs. There are general practitioners' journals, such as *The Law Society's Gazette, The Solicitors' Journal, Counsel* and the more general weekly *New Law Journal.* There are proliferating newsletters, information services and broadsheets. These categories are replicated on a modest scale in the smaller jurisdictions of the

British Isles. There are reasonably good bibliographical aids, but these are not as highly developed as for primary sources. The periodicals section is the most cosmopolitan part of the law library and the one that causes the most headaches.

The Rutland collection concentrates on academic journals from the English-speaking world. Even in a quite small law library, American journals tend to predominate. Nearly every American law school produces at least one law journal, which serves public relations and educational as well as scholarly functions. The distinctive feature of this form of literature, if it deserves the name, is that most are edited and largely controlled by students for whom it is a prestigious and extremely tedious activity. Being "on law review" at one of the leading law schools is at once a route to and an apprenticeship for well-paid helotry in a large law firm. The system results in serendipity in selection and extreme formalism in editorial style. Whether the educational benefits outweigh the scholarly costs is an open question that has been much debated.[53] Some of the content of American law reviews influences the judiciary and leaders of the profession indirectly, largely through written briefs and the system of judicial clerkships. Perhaps the most important consequence of this bizarre system is that nearly all of the more prestigious American law journals have traditionally been general rather than specialised and, although this may be changing, researchers have to range remarkably widely to find relevant specialist material.

English academic legal periodicals are somewhat overshadowed by their American cousins. They are fewer in number, more succinct and are nearly all edited by academics. At least until recently, most of the leading ones had a close connection with one institution: *The Cambridge Law Journal*, *The Modern Law Review* (LSE), *Current Legal Problems* (UCL), and *The Oxford Journal of Legal Studies*. Traditionally the most prestigious, *The Law Quarterly Review*, had a close connection with Oxford as well as being an important line of communication to the legal establishment; but it might now be said to be semi-detached. The expansion of law schools, academic specialisation, and trends in publishing have combined to increase the number, and to a lesser extent, the standing of specialist journals. In so far as one can generalise, law journals in England tend to have been less rigorously refereed, less well-served by abstracts and relatively informal, compared to other disciplines.

At a seminar held in 1977 for editors and publishers of law journals, someone asked: "What are law journals for?"

"The answer, from the Editor of *The Law Quarterly Review*, accepted in general by those present, was that a journal should not only be a medium of reportage but had a wider duty to legal scholarship and to the development of the law itself. It should provide a body of comment, analysis and criticism of the law, pointing out flaws, anomalies and longstanding misapprehensions. This criticism should embrace not only statutes and decisions but also books and even other journals."[54]

It would be tempting to analyse the assumptions about legal scholarship and writing underlying this view, and to speculate whether this would reflect a consensus today. The *Law Quarterly Review* is one of the few academic journals that is regularly read by judges and other senior members of the legal establishment. It seeks to influence legal opinion as well as to be a vehicle for high quality scholarly writing, mainly of a fairly traditional kind. Volume 109 for 1993 conforms fairly closely to the model of comment, analysis and criticism of law, suggested by the former editor. There were 19 articles, about 14 of which could be said to be scholarly analyses of contemporary legal doctrine. Two articles were by senior judges. There were over 60 notes, almost all of which were analytical, reflective, sometimes critical comments on recent reported cases. The *Law Quarterly Review* and other similar journals also comment fairly regularly on recent legislation and on important public reports, especially those relating to law reform. This volume also included reviews of 26 books. Most of the reviewers and authors were legal academics.

While the *Law Quarterly* has been influential on the form and style of other leading academic law journals, each has its own editorial policy and distinguishing characteristics. Few so consistently seek to bridge the academic/professional divide. Some are more commitedly theoretical, some are more polemical, and a few are consciously outlets for sociolegal or "critical" or other non-traditional perspectives. By and large, despite the economic climate, they have kept pace with the increase in the number of producers and the diversification of legal scholarship. In law, it is not too difficult to get published; it may not be so easy to get read.

OTHER LEGAL LITERATURE: INCLUSIONS AND OMISSIONS

It is revealing that the Bodleian Law Library guide of 20 years ago only included textbooks and periodicals as the main categories of secondary literature of the United Kingdom. In 1974, Jurisprudence, Legal History and even Criminology were included in the Bodleian law library, although they were placed to one side. This is not to criticise the guide, which reflected prevailing attitudes. At that time the study of law was largely equated with the study of legal doctrine: Roman Law through classical institutional works, and English Law through cases, statutes and, textbooks and more specialised commentaries in the law reviews. Except for Jurisprudence, almost everything else was secondary or marginal. It is rumoured that one of the leading law libraries in the country refused to stock books in series with names like "Law in Society" and "Law in Context" on the ground that they were not really law books.

Such attitudes seem almost unthinkable today. Legal literature has diversified in many directions: a much wider range of subjects; different approaches: and, especially significant in this context, more varied literary forms: for students, "cases, materials and text" have joined the traditional case-book; critical introductions and contextual works compete with the black-letter textbook; there are critical introductions, skills manuals and workbooks, interactive and ordinary videos and computer programmes. There are also many more monographs and symposia and, a headache for librarians, many more works that cross disciplines: law and economics, law and psychology, and other branches of socio-legal studies; the sociology of the legal profession, constitutional theory, law and administration, law and medicine, and law and literature are just some examples

Clearly this proliferation is a function of expansion—more producers fanning out into hitherto unoccupied territories. Such taxonomic puzzles and problems of allocation suggest that at least some progress has been made in the direction of crossing disciplinary boundaries.[55] Most academic lawyers probably read more widely as part of their work than their predecessors did. Sometimes their writings are read by colleagues in other disciplines—but my impression is that this is still exceptional. What has happened falls far short of a revolution, and traditional exposition of doctrine in textbooks and treatises is still the dominant literary mode.

Contemporary legal scholarship and some of its unresolved problems and tensions are the subject of the next chapter. So I shall postpone detailed consideration of the nature of legal exposition and of some of the emergent forms of legal scholarship. However, it is convenient to pause here and consider a few general points about secondary legal literature as it is found in law libraries today and to visit one section, Jurisprudence, which by its very nature transcends boundaries between disciplines.

Secondary legal literature is secondary. It is parasitic upon institutions, practices, and phenomena that exist independently of their academic study. This is, of course, true of most disciplines—though in different ways and degrees. The discipline of law stands in an analogous, but not identical, relation to legal practice and the law in action, as military history stands to military practice or political science to actual politics. Such relationships are subtle and complex and vary not only according to the nature of the subject of study, but also in respect of time, place, tradition and fashion. For instance, as we shall see, the extent to which legal scholars are participants in and influence their own legal system varies considerably. How far they should do so is much discussed.

Law is not unique in this respect. But an orthodox law library suggests that there may be some special features of this kind of relationship in our tradition. Let me suggest some tentative hypotheses: first, the secondary literature in a law library is dwarfed by the primary material. The main primary sources, legislation and statutes, are far more extensive and continually proliferating; they also are authoritative texts, which trump even the most respected juristic writings: Coke, Blackstone, Salmond, and Cross are writers of authority, but they can be overridden on a specific point by the decision of even an inferior court. Law students and legal scholars have a special and intimate relationship to these primary sources: the authoritative texts of religions and theology are not as extensive nor do they proliferate and change so rapidly; the primary texts for students of literature, such as poems, novels and plays, may be as expansive, but they are not authoritative in this way.

A second special characteristic of legal literature is that a great deal of scholarly legal writing is not done by academics. Practising lawyers claim to belong to a learned profession, although this often needs to be treated with a pinch of salt, and some of the most important legal scholarship has been produced by judges and practitioners. This has two facets: a great deal of genuinely scholarly writing is to be found scattered throughout the law reports and, to be a lesser extent, in law reform documents and, in the United States, in written briefs.[56] Furthermore, many important textbooks and treatises have been written by practitioners, who also contribute to periodicals. Legal treatises have a long history. Before the study of English Law became established in the universities, almost all expository works, including those intended for students, were written by practitioners and judges. During the nineteenth and early twentieth century many legal authors were part-time teachers, with a foot in both camps. Since the Second World War the balance has shifted: some of the leading practitioners' treatises have been taken over by academic lawyers or by combined teams of academics and practitioners.[57] In recent years there has been a growing divide between practitioners' treatises and student works and academics tend to monopolise the latter. Nevertheless, practitioners and judges continue to make substantial contributions to legal scholarship. That is one reason why the word "jurist" transcends the academic-practical divide.

A third, related point, concerns the economics of publishing, which had some important consequences for legal scholarship. Until about 1960, commercial law publishing in England was dominated by two specialist publishers, Butterworths and Sweet and Maxwell. This had profound effects on the form, style and content of law books and, above all, on what did and did not get published. For example, those books that were published were professionally edited, efficiently distributed, and usually had an assured market, for a fair number of books were bought by both students and practitioners. However, the leading law publishers had firm, rigid, and very narrow ideas about what did and what did not constitute a law book. Law books were essentially expository works, ranging from practitioners' treatises down through student textbooks to "nutshells" and other cram books for examinations that were largely tests of memory. There were few outlets for legal scholars who wished to write books that did not fit this rigid mould. Furthermore, the specialist law publishers concentrated on the legal market, which consisted mainly of three main categories: practitioners, students, and law libraries. Publishers, booksellers, authors and purchasers were caught in a self-renewing straitjacket.

From the late 1960s this situation began to change. It is not possible here to enter into the complexities of the story. In 1977 a report on academic law publishing listed over 20 publishers with law lists; most of those had entered the field quite recently.[58] The trend has continued. Butterworths and Sweet and Maxwell still command a large share of the market, but they now face strong competition, in both academic and practitioner markets, and they have themselves broadened their range.[59]

A fourth point about academic law libraries is what they do not include. The content of a university library is closely related to what is taught. Purchasing policies naturally give priority to the needs of students and, to a lesser extent, of academic researchers. But the curriculum is itself dependent on the availability of published materials and library resources. Often in the history of legal education publishers have waited on the courses, while the development of courses has been hampered—although not completely frustrated—by the absence of suitable books. Perhaps even more surprising to the outsider is what one does not find in respect of primary sources. We have already seen that there is a wealth of published primary material in the form of law reports and statutes; almost as striking is the absence of other kinds of primary documents. It is not only legislatures and superior courts that produce masses of written material. As the Commonwealth Legal Records project has shown, these represent only a small and in many respects unrepresentative sample of legal records.[60] For every appellate judgment, there are dozens of trials; for every record of a contested trial, there are many more documents relating to disputes that were settled out of court by negotiation or by some other form of dispute processing (many of these are, of course, confidential); for every litigated contract, there are probably thousands that were not disputed; and then there are routine wills, conveyances, standard form contracts and dozens of other kinds of legal instruments. These records of transactions and operations, which are the stuff of daily practice, hardly feature in law libraries at all: the records of a few famous trials, which are rarely systematically collected; some collections of standard forms for contracts, wills, and conveyances; and not much else. These potentially rich materials for study by law students, by legal scholars and by scholars from other disciplines are almost systematically neglected. They are as strong evidence as any of the extraordinary bias of the tradition of academic law towards the upper reaches of the system and the preference for the exceptional and the pathological over the routine and the mundane.

The holdings of secondary works in the Rutland Law Library illustrate these patterns. The secondary literature (including periodicals) represents about 20 per cent. of the collection. There is a reasonably well-developed academic literature in the eight or so standard undergraduate subjects and for some of the more popular or long-established options, such as Family Law and Public International Law. European Community Law is burgeoning, and there is a small literature of exceptionally high quality on Restitution. Commercial Law, Conveyancing, Valuation, Agricultural Law, Planning, Landlord and Tenant are largely dominated by practitioners' works, although in recent years some of these areas have been increasingly serviced by academics. Some fields have a long tradition of academic study and writings which reflect this: Jurisprudence, Legal History, Roman Law and, to lesser extent, Comparative Law are obvious examples. To adopt Becher's terminology: specialist secondary academic literature ranges from the urban to the rural, with evidence of shifts of population and other demographic changes from time to time. Overall the population is growing. It is increasingly diverse and cosmopolitan, reflecting the enormous growth in academic law over 30 or so years, and hence the increase in producers as well as consumers.

Professor Julius Stone called Jurisprudence (or Legal Theory) "the lawyer's extraversion",[61] and the Jurisprudence section at Rutland is the one that is closest to being genuinely multidisciplinary and belonging to the intellectual mainstream. It contains a selection of works from philosophy, political theory, social theory, psychology and theology, with recent additions from areas as diverse as women's studies, statistics, literary theory, and linguistics. For example, one finds there works by many "non-lawyers",[62] including Aquinas, Aristotle, Derrida, Durkheim, Foucault, Freud, Hayek, Hegel, Hobbes, Kant, Lacan, Locke, Marx, Mill, Rawls, Rousseau, Weber and Wittgenstein.[63] There are some jurists whose work may be quite widely known beyond law, Bacon, Bentham, Dworkin, Hart, and Maine, for example; but the number is disappointingly small. The rest of the collection is mainly taken up either by secondary writings about jurisprudence, (textbooks, histories, intellectual biographies) and by works by those who might be termed "jurists' jurists", such as John Austin, Lord Devlin, Fineman, Frank, Fuller, Gilligan, Hohfeld, Kelsen, Holmes, Llewellyn, MacCormick, Olivecrona, Posner, Pound, Raz, Savigny, Stone and Unger, few if any of whom are likely to feature in series devoted "to ideas that have changed the life and thought of our age".[64] The Rutland collection reflects some changes in fashions of Jurisprudence teaching over the years and a heavy emphasis on twentieth century Anglo-American legal thought.

Jurisprudence is my subject and I am tempted to linger here and dwell on such topics as the history of Anglo-American Jurisprudence, the eclecticism and diversity of contemporary legal theory, the poverty of much teaching in the area, and the tendency for Jurisprudence, and especially Legal Philosophy, to become highly specialised and to be seen as a subject apart both within and outside law schools.[65] However, a guide should not ride his personal hobby horses and we must press on. Some of these themes and the names I have dropped will feature briefly in the next chapters.

CONCLUSION

The law library is at the heart of academic legal culture. We have seen that the buildings, people, events and conflicts of a law school are not strikingly different from what one might find in other departments in the social sciences and humanities, but that there are a few special features. The tension between the relatively detached study of law as a whole and a more narrowly focused vocationalism reflects endemic disagreements about objectives and priorities. Aspects of the culture of legal practice have infiltrated law schools, some more than others. Law students and law teachers may be slightly peculiar. Nevertheless, the one really distinctive feature is the law library, which both reflects and defines law school culture.

The orthodox library represents central aspects of the common law tradition, notably the pre-eminence of primary over secondary sources; a preference for case law over legislation; a tendency to focus selectively on litigation rather than other forms of legal action, on questions of law more than questions of fact, on higher courts rather than trial courts, on the pathological rather than the routine.

Perhaps the most striking feature of the law library is its exclusions: it has adopted a narrow conception of legal literature, which itself is highly selective in its treatment of law as a phenomenon, especially the law in action. Despite this narrow selectivity, the law library contains a rich repository of materials which until now have been almost exclusively the domain of the initiated. It has projected an image of dry technicality, obscure jargon and difficulty of access that has deterred all but a few non-lawyers.

That image is largely misleading. Moreover, like Blackstone's Tower, the law library is in a process of quite rapid transition. As legal education broadens its scope and clientele, legal literature is quietly becoming more varied. In the next chapter we shall look in more detail at one aspect of this process, the diversification of legal scholarship. At least as important are developments in information technology, which will soon make the traditional law library obsolete. The "virtual library" will soon be upon us.[66] There are already quite advanced systems for finding and providing

117

information and full texts of materials geared to standard needs of practitioners and traditional kinds of legal research.[67] Quite soon most law students, as well as practitioners, will have "home access" to most of the information that they are thought to need. Collections of printed material will get smaller rather than larger and will undergo changes of use. Disparities between rich and poor collections may be less marked than at present, at least in richer countries.

There is a good prospect that technological developments will break down some barriers between disciplines: "non-lawyers" may find access to legal texts easier and less daunting; conversely, law students and researchers should in principle be able to reach and use a much wider range of materials of law study, including neglected legal materials, such as trial records and documents connected with non-litigious practice, and materials generated by other disciplines and spheres of activity. One will be able to call up *Crime and Punishment* or *Antigone* on the screen, although what one will do about horizontal reading is not yet clear. The transition may be painful for those of us who were brought up to love books and the media will almost certainly change the messages. Some developments may also be regressive if, for example, the enthusiasts for information technology are informed by simplistic or out-dated conceptions of law. The mechanisation of legal literature could involve the revival of mechanical jurisprudence. That is one more reason for spelling out to non-lawyers the diversity and subtlety of our intellectual heritage.

Notes

[1] C. C. Langdell, Speech at Harvard University (1887) 3 L.Q.R. 123, at p. 124.

[2] Archibald MacLeish, "A Library of Law", in *Tower of Ivory* (1917), at p. 46.

[3] These figures include microforms (volume equivalents). They are only approximate. Information technology will soon make such estimates almost meaningless.

[4] Clive Weston, "Statement of Minimum Holdings for Law Libraries in England and Wales (revised 1993)", (1993) 13 *Legal Studies* 332. A further revision is in progress.

[5] The legal point is discussed in H. Montgomery Hyde (ed), *Trial of Sir Roger Casement* (1960) Introduction, at pp. cvii–cxv.

[6] David Kidd, *The Information Needs of Scottish Solicitors*, unpublished thesis, University of Edinburgh, 1979; see also, Kidd "Scottish Solicitors' Use of Legal Information, Their Legal Information Needs and Legal Problem Solving Routines" in William Twining and Jennifer Uglow (eds.) *Law Publishing and Legal Information: Small Jurisdictions of the British Isles* (1981); Carole Willis "Solicitor's Legal Research and the Use of Libraries", (1992) 23 *The Law Librarian* 171. The reading habits of barristers and solicitors differ and, of course, vary according to the type of practice.

[7] A good introduction to computer information retrieval systems for law is David Stott, *Legal Research* (1993), Chap. 5.

[8] E. H. Cordeaux, *Bodleian Law Library: Legal Literature of the United Kingdom.* (1974), p. 1.

[9] *cf.* Theodore Roosevelt's distinction between books and instruments of a profession such as law books, medical books and cookery books, which "are not properly 'books' at all, they come in the category of time-tables, telephone directories, and other useful agencies of civilized life." T. Roosevelt, *An Autobiography* (1913) at p. 360.

[10] Cordeaux, *op. cit.*

[11] Above Chap. 1 at pp. 12–13.

[12] *e.g.* Jean Dane and Philip Thomas, *How to use a law library,* (2nd ed., 1987), Peter Clinch, *Using a law library: a student's guide to legal research skills* (1992).

[13] Law librarians rightly claim that a few hours are not enough to train students in research skills; but such introductions should enable the beginner to overcome initial fears and to start to use the library.

[14] The classic attack on lawyers' mystification through "jargonization" is by Bentham: *Rationale of Judicial Evidence* (1827) Book VIII, Chap. XVII.

[15] See below Chap. 7 and 8.

[16] See generally, David Miers and Alan Page, *Legislation* (2nd ed., 1990), HDTWR Chap. 9 and 10. For the sake of convenience librarians often place legislation close to official reports of law-making bodies, such as Hansard's Parliamentary Debates, Journals of the House of Commons, and Parliamentary Papers.

[17] For an illustration of the amount and range of new statutes enacted by Parliament in a five year period (1985–89) see HDTWR at pp. 323–324.

[18] See further HDTWR, *passim.*

[19] Blackstone's attitude to legislation was quite complex, see David Lieberman, "Blackstone's Science of Legislation" (1989) *Law and Justice* 61.

[20] F. Ellsworth, *Law on the Midway* (1977), pp. 68–73.

[21] G. Calabresi, *A Common Law for the Age of Statutes* (1982); for a comparison of English and American approaches to legislation see P. S. Atiyah and R. S. Summers, *Form and Substance in Anglo-American Law* (1987) Chap. 11.

[22] James Kent, 1 *Commentaries on American Law* (1830) (11th ed. 1866) para. 496.

[23] Karl Llewellyn, "Case Law", 3 *Encyclopedia of Social Sciences* (1931) p. 449.

[24] In 1987 Westlaw contained over 40,000 decisions issued by Federal Courts and over 80,000 issued by State Courts, of which about 60,000 had full opinions. "There have now been over three million cases published in [the United States], and most of these can be found in any law school library". M. Cohen, R. Berring, and C. Olson, *How To Find the Law* (9th ed., 1989) p. 2. The availability of transcripts of unreported cases on Lexis threatens to make over-supply of precedents an increasingly serious problem in the UK.

[25] For a general introduction to case law see HDTWR Chap. 7 and 8.

[26] Adapted from N. Dowling, E. Patterson and R. Powell, *Materials for Legal Method* (2nd ed., 1952), pp. 34–35.

[27] The early pages are "furniture": a list of reporters (all barristers), a list of all the judges of the superior courts of England and Wales; the correct citation of the volume ([1991] 4 All ER) and of the four major works of reference that are regularly referred to in the reports: Halsbury's Laws of England, Halsbury's Statutes of England and Wales, the Digest, and Halsbury's Statutory Instruments. There is an index of cases reported in this volume and a Digest of these cases.

The Law Library

[28] S. Chibnall, *Law and Order News* (1977); P. Schlesinger and H. Tumber, *Reporting Crime: The Media Politics of Justice* (1994).

[29] *e.g.* *The Hillsborough Stadium disaster, 15 April 1989*, final report, (Lord Justice Taylor), Cmnd. 962 (1990).

[30] *e.g.* A. Mullis, "Tort", [1991] *All E. R. Annual Review* at pp. 371–377; S. Hedley, (1992) 51 *Cambridge Law Jo.* 16.

[31] RE Chap. 7.

[32] The rodeo problem refers to an example by the philosopher Jonathan Cohen of 1,000 spectators at a rodeo of whom 501 have not paid. The question posed is whether this bare statistic is sufficient on its own to satisfy the test of "balance of probabilities" in an action for the price of entry brought against a randomly chosen spectator. The reasons why this example does not illustrate the point it was designed to are explored in *Analysis* at pp. 440–441. I assume that the other two examples in the text are sufficiently part of general culture not to need explanation.

[33] [1932] A.C. 562 (HL).

[34] However, unreported cases are increasingly available on Lexis, see n. 67, below.

[35] O. Kahn-Freund, "Reflections on Legal Education" (1966) 29 M. L. R. 121, at p. 127. Kahn-Freund then addressed some of the implications for legal education: "Each student should in the course of his studies obtain two things: a general survey of his field, and a detailed map of a few selected areas, selected by him or for him. There is, I think, such a thing as a "general legal education" and this does certainly not consist of the knowledge of dozens of memorised cases. The practising lawyer as such is always interested in a number of branches of the law which happen to be important for litigation, for conveyancing, for the things through which lawyers earn their living. The Rule against Perpetuities is more important to him than the National Assistance Act, and the details of certiorari are more important than the organisation of the police forces. But for our student who should know what law does in society it is at least as vital to know about the law of public assistance as it is to know about perpetuities, and watch committees may be more important in this context than administrative remedies. Marriage is a more important legal institution than divorce, whatever the practitioner at the Bar may think about it. That "general legal education" which I have mentioned can be transmitted only in a university and nowhere else." at p. 129.

[36] This is a characteristic of legal thought emphasised in autopoiesis, the theory that law is inescapably self-referential and, in that sense, autonomous. G. Teubner, *Autopoietic Law* (1993).

[37] See A. Ehrenzweig, *Psychoanalytic Jurisprudence* (1971) pp. 276–279. J. Jaconelli, "Solomonic Justice and the Common Law" (1992) 12 *Oxford Jo. Leg. Stud.* 480.

[38] Nor do they tell us that after the House of Lords had ruled in her favour, the pursuer (plaintiff) in *Donoghue v Stevenson, op. cit.,* settled out of court.

[39] (1884) 14 Q.B.D. 273.

[40] Other notable examples of the genre are John T. Noonan Jr. *Persons and Masks of the Law* (1976) and Richard Danzig, "Hadley v Baxendale: A study in the industrialization of the law", (1975) 4 *Jo. Leg. Studies* 249.

[41] W. Twining, "Cannibalism and Legal Literature", (1986) 6 *Oxford Jo. Legal Studies* 423.

[42] This theme is developed in W. Twining, "Reading Law" (1989) 24 *Valparaiso L. Rev.* 1.

[43] *ibid.,* HDTWR pp. 445–457.

120

[44] Karl Llewellyn, *The Common Law Tradition* (1960); KLRM, Chap. 10.

[45] John Griffith, *The Politics of the Judiciary* (4th ed., 1991).

[46] For a general discussion, see D. Lloyd and M. Freeman, *Introduction to Jurisprudence* (5th ed., 1985) at pp. 701–705.

[47] *e.g.* T. Murphy and R. Rawlings, "After the Ancien regime", (1981) 44 *M.L.R.* 617.

[48] *e.g.* James B. White, *The Legal Imagination* (1973); *Heracles' Bow* (1985).

[49] *e.g.* B. Jackson, *Law, Fact and Narrative Coherence* (1988); RE Chap. 7.

[50] *op cit.* n. 42.

[51] An outstanding exception is Paul Brand, *The Making of the Common Law* (1992).

[52] See the works by Stott, Clinch and Dane and Thomas cited above, n. 7 and 12.

[53] F. Rodell, "Good-bye to law reviews" (1936) *23 Virginia L. Rev.* 38 and (1962) 48 *ibid.* 279; Symposium, "Student-edited law reviews", (1986) 36 *Jo. Legal Educ.* 1–23.

[54] Jenny Uglow, *Law Journals* (S.P.T.L. Working Party on Law Publishing, Working Paper No. 2, 1977) at p. 12.

[55] Who is to pay and where is it to be shelved if a lawyer orders a book for the library on political philosophy or legal anthropology or cybernetics? Or a political scientist orders a work on constitutional history or the politics of the judiciary? Or a philosopher recommends books by legal philosophers on liberty or punishment or criminal responsibility? Who has the strongest claim to house the *Collected Works of Jeremy Bentham* or *Utilitas, a Journal of Utilitarian Studies*? Such issues involve inter-departmental political economy as well as problems of taxonomy.

[56] There is a good deal that could be called scholarly in lawyers' opinions, memoranda and other written work that is typically unpublished and usually confidential.

[57] See below, Chap. 6 at pp. 135–137.

[58] S.P.T.L. Working Party on Law Publishing, *Law Publishing and Legal Scholarship* (1977).

[59] However, the law market is still very much a thing apart. I have devoted a good deal of my career in trying to help break the mould. I can only report limited success: legal literature has diversified, on the whole for the better, but the structure of the market has not changed significantly. To speak from personal experience: only exceptionally has it been possible to include a book in the *Law in Context* Series unless it had a reasonable prospect of securing or creating a place in the law student market. Even more disappointing is the fact that books that were intended to be broad or inter-disciplinary have almost invariably failed to reach beyond the law market. *Law in Context* books have been accepted into the law library, but not into other sections of libraries or book shops. Thus legal scholarship has been strongly influenced by the economics and traditions of law publishing.

[60] Above, Chap. 1.

[61] Julius Stone, *Legal System and Lawyers' Reasonings* (1964) p. 16.

[62] Some of those listed, *e.g.* Marx and Weber, had a strong legal background.

[63] This list is eclectic, but not arbitrary; it is based largely on two surveys of jurisprudence teaching by H. Barnett and D. Yach, "The teaching of jurisprudence and legal theory in British universities and polytechnics", (1985) 5 *Legal Studies* 151, and H. Barnett, "Jurisprudence and Legal Theory in Legal Education: Australia, Canada and the United Kingdom "(forthcoming).

[64] The quotation is from the description of the Fontana *Modern Masters* Series, on

which see the Preface, above. This list is also largely based on the two surveys cited above n. 63.

[65] LTCL Chap. 3 and 13; RB; TAR; KLRM.

[66] Joint Funding Councils' Libraries Review Group, *Report* (Follett Report) (1993).

[67] LEXIS is described as follows: "It is a service which, if used with legal knowledge, a grasp of the legal problem being researched, an understanding of primary and secondary source materials plus a lively imagination, can help the lawyer or accountant to retrieve from its vast libraries material which, when analysed, may prove to be precisely relevant or helpful in solving the problem being worked on". *What is LEXIS?* (Butterworth Guide).

6. Legal Scholarship and the Roles of the Jurist

"The predominant notion of academic lawyers is that they are not really academic . . . Their scholarly activities are thought to be unexciting and uncreative, comprising a series of intellectual puzzles scattered among 'large areas of description.' "[1]

This summary of Becher's findings reinforces a quite common view that legal scholarship does little or nothing to advance knowledge. Lewis Eliot in C. P. Snow's *Strangers and Brothers*, although he was surrounded by dedicated researchers, was treated like a resident man-of-affairs, rather than as an academic: he was not *expected* to do research or to publish.[2] One unnamed Harvard Professor, a non-lawyer, is reported to have said that there is no Nobel Prize for law because common lawyers have no respect for original thought.[3] Professor Brian Simpson, himself a noted scholar, suggests that there have been no great legal discoveries in the past hundred years.[4] Becher reports one respondent as saying that academic law is concerned "mainly with ordering a corpus of knowledge: it is a largely descriptive pursuit".[5]

In this chapter I shall argue that this negative view is misleading in at least three respects: it is out-of-date; it oversimplifies by focusing solely on expository work; and it fundamentally misconceives the nature of legal exposition. First, legal scholarship is now a large-scale, burgeoning enterprise. If Lewis Eliot was ever a recognisable representative of an earlier generation of academic lawyers, we said good-bye to him a long time ago. Secondly, the idea of legal scholarship as essentially descriptive and authority-based refers to only one kind of activity: exposition, which has declined in prominence and prestige in recent years. Today, academic law is pluralistic, involving a bewildering diversity of subject-matters, perspectives, objectives and methods. Thirdly, even the lowest forms of exposition involve interpretation, selection and arrangement of quite elusive data. It can no more be interpreted as "merely

123

descriptive'' than the writing of history. In its higher forms expository scholarship is quite creative, more like landscape painting or divination than the collection of specimens. However, Becher is quite correct in suggesting that the discipline of law is beset by self-doubt and controversy[6]; the criticisms that he reports persist; and much of that criticism comes from within. There are important questions that are worth asking about the nature and possible future directions of legal scholarship.

Becher and others depict academic law as monochrome, descriptive and rather jaded. In contrast, I have already painted a rather more positive picture: an interesting and important subject-matter; high student demand; a lively, if confusing pluralism; and at least some evidence that it has been almost fully integrated into the university during the last twenty years. From this account it would be quite easy to construct an alternative to the old stamp-collecting image: energetic, introspective, and rebellious against authority; willing to experiment; susceptible to noisy fashions; unsure of its identity or what it wants to be or do; and caught between the temptations of respectable security and dilettanteism. In short, a relatively young discipline exhibiting all the symptoms of a lively late twentieth century adolescent.

Both images contain a core of truth, but they are essentially caricatures. A judicious overview requires a more mundane approach. Let me begin, then, by considering what academic lawyers in fact do in addition to teaching and administration.

WHAT ACADEMIC LAWYERS DO IN FACT

EXTRA-CURRICULAR ACTIVITIES

One of the functions of law schools and academic lawyers is to provide certain kinds of extra-curricular services. These include the production of educational materials; the provision of information services; law reform activities; voluntary work; journalism; commentary; criticism; and various forms of consultancy, including advice in individual cases. Academic lawyers in nearly all countries perform such functions, but the extent of their involvement, how these activities are organised and what prestige or priority they are accorded varies considerably. For example, in some jurisdictions academic lawyers play a major role in law reporting and providing regular legal information services—during the first three years of my career, editing the Sudan Law Reports was my main extra-curricular activity. In England, the bulk of such work is done outside the universities, much of it in-house by commercial law publishers. Giving specialist advice in individual cases has been largely a monopoly of the practising Bar, except in a few fields, such as Public International Law. Academic lawyers have contributed to law reform—as commentators on recent cases and legislation, as more general critics of the law, and increasingly, as members of law reform groups, Royal Commissions, official committees and the Law Commission. Law schools have their fair share of human rights activists, pro bono workers and TV dons. And, of course, law teachers are the main producers of educational works which range from mundane study aids up to substantial original works of scholarship published in a form that has a potential student market.

Most of these activities are of practical value and contribute to the dissemination of knowledge. There is, however, room for differences of opinion about which of them can be appropriately counted as original research or scholarship. Some may divert energies from more ambitious scholarly work. Here I shall adopt a broad conception of research and scholarship, but I shall focus on the upper end of the spectrum, or as the Quebecquois charmingly put it, more on *recherche sublime* than *recherches ponctuelles.*[7]

THE RANGE OF LEGAL SCHOLARSHIP

Contemporary legal research is so diverse in so many ways that individual projects and publications often defy classification. Academic specialisms can be categorised on the basis of three distinct kinds of logical category: theory, methods or subject-matter.[8] Scholarly publications also have varied audiences. The most ambitious attempt to date to construct a total picture of what academic lawyers do under the name of research in one country is to be found in the Arthurs' Report on *Law and Learning*, which was published in Canada in 1983.[9] The report divided non-ephemeral research into four main categories[10]:

(a) "conventional texts and articles—research designed to collect and organize legal data, to expound legal rules, and to explicate or offer exegesis upon authoritative legal sources[11];"—this broadly corresponds with what I shall refer to as exposition, using that term in a broad sense;

(b) "legal theory—research designed to yield a unifying theory or perspective by which legal rules may be understood, and their application in particular cases evaluated and controlled; this type would include scholarly commentary on civil law, usually referred to as *'doctrine'*"[12];

(c) "law reform research—research designed to accomplish change in the law, whether to eliminate anomalies, to enhance effectiveness, or to secure a change in direction"[13];

(d) "fundamental research—research designed to secure a deeper understanding of law as a social phenomenon, including research on the historical, philosophical, linguistic, economic, social or political implications of law."[14]

Types of legal research

Source: *Law and Learning,* Social Sciences and Humantities Research Council of Canada, Ottawa: 1984.

Any such taxonomy is inevitably crude, with many grey areas and borderline cases. But Arthurs used it intelligently to build up a revealing profile of the situation in Canada in 1980.[15] The main findings were quite striking: 90 per cent. of the research of law professors involved doctrinal analysis, sometimes mixed in with some history or theory. Similarly 90 per cent. of monographs were found to be "doctrinal and theoretical" and over 50 per cent. of journal articles were doctrinal (indicating *recherches ponctuelles?*) with a further 18 per cent. being "theoretical" but essentially expository. Roughly 25 per cent. of articles in law journals were produced by lawyers outside the universities (including judges and government lawyers). The Arthurs Committee interpreted these findings to mean that the overwhelming bulk of research effort and publications was directed to what has been called "practical doctrinal research".[16] The second largest category, "law reform research", some of which was interdisciplinary, was also directed to the professional constituency. The main conclusion of the Arthurs Report was that the combination of traditional emphasis on exposition of doctrine and the gravitational pull of the immediate demands of a practice-oriented audience (including law students) had created a serious imbalance between fundamental and applied work and between research "on" law and "in" law:

> "Scholarly legal research, and especially fundamental and theoretical research, has been consistently undervalued by the legal community, and even by legal academics, whereas it has an essential contribution to make to legal education, to the legal profession and the practice of law, and to the evolution of law and society."[17]

There is no study of legal research in England which is as comprehensive and as thorough as the Arthurs Report.[18] The available sources suggest that the situation in England in 1980 was already more diverse than it was in Canada and that the trend in both countries has, since then, been towards a greater emphasis on theoretical and interdisciplinary work and away from *recherches ponctuelles*. On the other hand, the general climate of opinion strongly favours applied research and this is reflected in funding policies for areas such as socio-legal studies, where a high priority is given to policy-oriented work and funds for "pure" or "fundamental" research are hard to come by.

There is plenty of anecdotal evidence to refute the suggestion that what passes for "legal scholarship" consists almost entirely of expository works. Indeed, Arthurs' categories do not do justice to the remarkable diversity of modern legal scholarship. Every year I read dozens of annual reports of law schools, research proposals, individual resumés, periodical indexes, book reviews and publishers' catalogues relating to my discipline. The overwhelming impression is of a somewhat bewildering pluralism. The areas of enquiry, methods, perspectives and audiences all seem to be much more diverse than they were 10, let alone 20 or 30 years ago. For example, the catalogue of new publications in law from Oxford University Press, which arrived as I was writing this, included major works in legal philosophy, new series on Criminology and Socio-legal studies, three new books on European Community Law, new editions of orthodox and not so orthodox expository texts, "an evaluative study" of the principles underlying the criminal justice system, critical studies of the English intelligence services and Australian drug laws, several works on legal history and international law, and a reissue of a major work on Roman Imperial Rescripts between A.D. 193 and 305, complete with a high density diskette containing a *Palingenesia* (reconstruction) of 2,609 rescripts.[19] This is only a sample from a much longer list that is hardly symptomatic of dull uniformity.

As to quantity and commitment to research, the available empirical evidence comparing law with other subjects generally supports the view that, except for research training, law schools have developed a research culture that in respect of commitment and productivity is not significantly different from other disciplines, especially in the humanities and social sciences. This is hardly surprising, since in most universities the criteria for appointment and promotion, especially to Readerships and Chairs, are generally uniform across disciplines.[20]

LAW AS A PARTICIPANT-ORIENTED DISCIPLINE

Law is, of course, part of the practical world of affairs and, as such, is an applied discipline. It is not surprising that a great deal of legal education is devoted to preparing people for legal practice in a narrow sense. But we have seen that the law in action is much wider than lawyers' action.[21] The Arthurs Report shows how the potential audiences for scholarly writing can exert a strong gravitational pull towards applied scholarship for the profession; it also illustrates some of the varied ways in which such work can be of practical value, for example, in policy-making and law reform, in providing useful works of reference, in imposing order on the law and in providing raw material for legal argument. Similarly academic lawyers have the opportunity to participate in the legal system in a variety of roles besides teaching and scholarship.

However, academic legal culture can be said to be participant-oriented in a stronger sense. Let me illustrate this with an anecdote. I was once asked by a senior postgraduate student of philosophy if he could sit in on some of my undergraduate seminars in legal theory. By chance he turned up when we were studying utilitarianism—in two weeks. In the second seminar, behaving as law teachers do, I used a standard role-play technique: the group was to pretend that it was an international committee established to consider revisions of the European Convention on Human Rights. Each student was asked to represent a Government that based its position on a particular kind of moral theory, such as classical act-utilitarianism, indirect utilitarianism, one or other kinds of rights theory, or moral relativism. We focused mainly on the question whether utilitarians of any kind could justify supporting an absolute prohibition on torture, inhuman and degrading treatment (Article 3). Each participant was required to vote on a number of motions and amendments, sometimes as a representative of a particular position, sometimes as a matter of individual conscience. No abstentions were allowed. I was slightly apprehensive that the philosopher would think the exercise simplistic and naive. Instead, he told me afterwards that he had suffered mild culture-shock. Although he had taken several courses on ethics, including a whole semester on utilitarianism, he had never before been asked to make a *decision* in class.

This incident illustrates the notion of law as a participant-oriented discipline. In classes, in examinations, in moots and other exercises, law students are as a matter of course asked to adopt and act out different participatory roles in specified contexts[22]—to pretend that they are an appellate judge or advocate, a solicitor advising a client on a point of law, a law-maker or law reform pressure group, or a businessman or citizen contemplating the implications and likely consequences of a course of action. The purpose of this class was to help students understand the differences between some standard moral theories and to clarify their own views in relation to them. The use of simulations and role-plays in legal education is not restricted to the development of "skills".[23]

R.G. Collingwood argued that a historian could not give an adequate account of the Battle of Trafalgar or Caesar crossing the Rubicon without understanding the situation and internal point of view of key participants in the action.[24] More generally it is widely accepted across disciplines that in order to interpret, describe and explain social action one needs to be able to take into account such internal points of view. Jurisprudence has participated in this "hermeneutic turn",[25] but the participant-orientation of the study of law goes further than that.

To say that law is a participant-oriented discipline is to suggest that academic legal culture is imbricated with insider attitudes, partly because of its close association with a practising profession, partly because a major function of legal education and scholarship is taken up with servicing that profession in practical ways, but also because putting oneself in the shoes of different actors within a given legal system is widely accepted as a necessary part of understanding law. The culture of academic law seems to be markedly different from that of history or philosophy or anthropology not only because it includes many practical or applied concerns, but also because even where the purpose is understanding or "external critique" there is a widespread tendency for jurists to identify with one or more kinds of participant within a particular legal system.[26] Even the term "legal science" is most commonly applied to the study of one body or system of law rather than to law in general.

Academic lawyers are overtly participating in their legal system when they make recommendations for law reform or are involved in "policy-oriented" research or professional training. Much of legal theory involves offering general advice to participants in the form of prescriptive working theories of adjudication or legislation or "fact management" or even advocacy.[27] It is perhaps less obvious that exposition of legal doctrine is also a form of participation in a legal system and that the expositor has a variety of functions that typically, and usually overtly, extend beyond "mere description". Since exposition is still the predominant mode of legal scholarship it is worth looking at its nature and the roles of the jurist as expositor in some detail.

EXPOSITION REVISITED

Exposition may have declined in relative importance and prestige in the period of diversification, but it is still a very important part of legal scholarship. Some would maintain that it is still the core of the discipline. If this is so, it is odd to find it dismissed as a largely descriptive pursuit, interlarded with a few intellectual puzzles or that it involves no more than the ordering of an established corpus of knowledge.[28] It is easy to refute some of the cruder elements in these charges, but difficult questions arise about the purposes, nature and methods of exposition of doctrine, or as it is called in civilian systems, legal dogmatics. And what, if anything, can the enterprise claim to have added to the sum of human knowledge?

If one considers the greatest achievements in the expository tradition, none fits the picture of mere description and arrangement. Let us consider briefly Blackstone's *Commentaries*, the great Harvard treatises of the Langdell period, the *Restatements* of the American Law Institute, and the most celebrated modern English treatises.

Blackstone's Commentaries

The *Commentaries* was designed as an institutional work which could form the basis of the study of English law in the universities.[29] But, as we have seen, Blackstone failed in his educational aim of securing the establishment of a School of English Law at Oxford. He is often held up as the first great expositor who attempted to give a systematic account of English Law as a whole.[30]

It is difficult to see how one can read The *Commentaries* as purporting to provide a neutral or objective or even relatively detached account of English law. On the contrary, the essence of the work is a sustained argument in support of the traditional common law and a particular interpretation of the English constitution as embodying an explicit political ideology. Blackstone's main purpose was educational, but he made no pretence of providing a value-free description: quoting Aristotle, he presented jurisprudence as "the principal and most perfect branch of ethics."[31] Throughout, Blackstone liberally distributes reproach and approbation within his vision of an idealised tradition.

It is because Blackstone failed to distinguish between the roles of expositor and censor and presented the common law in a largely favourable light that Bentham attacked him so sharply. Similarly, in addition to giving an accessible account of the common law "to gentlemen of independent estate and fortune", the success of the *Commentaries* is attributable in part to its political appeal in England and, for different reasons, in the colonies. The *Commentaries* was not, and did not claim to be a merely descriptive work by one who "has no concern with any other faculties of the mind than the apprehension, the memory, and the judgment", as Bentham mocked it.[32] Rather it was an ideological treatise arguing for the resurrection and conservation of traditional common law, the values it embodied, evolutionary development and legislative restraint. It was not so much a legitimation of the status quo, as many have suggested, as a plea to restore, preserve and strengthen an ancient tradition which was under threat and which had already been damaged, first by the Normans, and more recently by ad hoc legislation. The enduring significance of Blackstone's "exposition" is illustrated by the fact that it was chosen as the first target of attack for "trashing" by one of the pioneers of American critical legal studies.[33]

American treatises

One can interpret the greatest works of American expository scholarship in similar fashion. The first generation of treatise writers saw as one of their primary tasks the production of a body of literature which could be a vehicle both for the education of intending lawyers from all over the country and for the unification, simplification, and rationalisation of the received common law and its adaptation to the circumstances of the New World.[34] Harvard was a national, not just a local law school. Under Langdell's system students mastered the fundamental principles and methods of the common law. The great generation of treatise writers of the late nineteenth and early twentieth century—Beale, Gray, Wigmore, Williston, and Corbin—wrote about American Law, largely in private law fields that fell within the jurisdiction of the several states.[35] The case method freed the expositors from the constraints of the student market. In the eyes of many, one of the great achievements of the Harvard Law School in its educational and scholarly work was to detach the study of law from the particularities of any single jurisdiction—thereby preserving the unity of the common law at the national level and avoiding getting bogged down too much in local detail. This was done by maintaining the fiction that there is such an entity as American Law.

The Restatements of the American Law Institute

The dilemmas and ambiguities surrounding the nature and role of exposition are very clearly illustrated by the most ambitious expository project in the history of the common law, the *Restatements* of the American Law Institute (A.L.I.). From its establishment in 1923 the A.L.I. was an elite, national lawyers' organisation, a prestigious alliance of leading judges, practitioners and academics. Like the major treatises it supplemented, the project was a rather belated response to a series of perceived problems that had surfaced in the nineteenth century: the need to adapt the common law to American conditions; the need to preserve the unity of the common law across a multiplicity of jurisdictions; the modernisation of the law in the wake of social, economic and technical change; and the simplification of the sources of law in the face of the proliferation of authoritative materials by Federal and state legislatures, courts and other agencies.[36] The A.L.I. was also seen as an attempt by leaders of the legal profession to strengthen its control over the management and development of the administration of law by virtue of their technical expertise. The Restatement project offered academics an enhanced role and status within the legal establishment, since they would do most of the work.

From the start the objectives were reformist, but they had to be presented as apolitical. The involvement of the judiciary, the desire to produce an authoritative text that would not be a code, and the desire to by-pass the state legislatures,[37] required not only circumspection in describing the objectives but also procedures and a form that would not invite political criticism. For the enterprise to succeed it was essential that it should operate largely by consensus in a non-partisan mode, so that its products would be accepted as representing the agreed wisdom of experts on matters that were essentially technical.

Over time the A.L.I. has been involved in preparing model codes, the Uniform Commercial Code, and proposals for legislative reform. But the main instrument for its objectives was the Restatement project. A series of code-like texts was to be prepared, designed in the words of the first Director; "to present an orderly statement of the general common law of the United States. . . . The object of the Institute is accomplished insofar as the legal profession accepts the restatement as prima facie a correct statement of the general law of the United States."[38]

Even those who accepted the main objectives, methods and underlying theory of the *Restatement* acknowledged that there were practical problems in providing a correct, simple statement of the common law of over 50 jurisdictions. What is the draftsman to do if there is no case in point, or the authorities are in conflict, or if there is no succinct judicial formulation of a rule? What if some states have changed the law by statute or if a recent case from a court of high authority in one jurisdiction purports to overrule or depart from previous authority? or if local conditions are not uniform throughout the various states?[39] When in doubt is the conscientious draftsman to choose the predominant opinion or to predict what the courts are likely to do or to choose what s/he considers to be the "best" opinion? And what if the law is clear, but the Reporter or professional opinion generally consider it to be bad for some reason?[40]

Some of these problems were solved by devices such as comments. Others were glossed over. In the course of time the Institute gradually weakened its insistence on being strictly confined to restating the law as it is. By 1990 *Black's Law Dictionary* contained the following definition of the *Restatement*:

> "[a] series of volumes authored by the American Law Institute that tell what the law in a general area is, how it is changing, and what directions the authors (who are leading scholars in each field covered) think that the change should take."[41]

This open approach drew fire from traditionalists who complained that it was a deviation from the original purpose of merely stating what the law is.[42] Others, while welcoming greater openness, objected that the distinctions between describing, choosing a better opinion, noting a "trend" and making recommendations are blurred in practice.[43] The principal theoretical criticisms that were made of the first *Restatements* were directed at a number of assumptions: (a) that it is possible to describe the law as it is in neutral terms; (b) that it is possible to declare the principles of common law independently of authority; (c) that it is possible to make meaningful statements of legal rules without reference to their rationales; (d) that it is possible to make accurate and meaningful statements of legal rules without reference to the practical context of their operation.[44]

These debates are enduring, and they illustrate an important point. Serious scholarly exposition typically involves the careful analysis of apparently conflicting authorities; an abstraction from the data, usually reported decisions, of a rule which explains them; and a marshalling of the data and arguments to persuade the interested audience that the preferred rule is indeed the established rule. Both critics and defenders recognised that the *Restatements* involved more than exposition and that exposition involves more than description. Whatever the merits of the American political debate, the process produced expository works which have been cited (usually with approval) by courts in over 110,000 cases.[45] It is naive to criticise the *Restatements* for not being "purely descriptive"; the A.L.I. was careful to avoid areas of "hot" political controversy and it produced influential texts which were scholarly, systematic, usable and representative of a high degree of expert opinion on technical matters. The processes were arduous, the investment of talent was enormous and eventually consensus or compromise was reached by "civilised discourse and reasoned dialogue".[46] The *Restatements* represent exposition by negotiated consensus among experts.

English Textbooks and Treatises

It is not necessary here to try to trace in detail the complex history of expository and related works in England. A common version might be summarised as follows: Blackstone's *Commentaries* was an outstanding example of a particular genre of literature, the institutional text or treatise, which attempted "to give a comprehensive but elementary treatment of a whole system of law treated as a national law."[47] Such institutional works flourished at various periods in Continental Europe, Scotland and the United States. The *Commentaries* was kept alive by a series of generally competent editors, but bred no major successors, largely because of the late development of the study of English Law in the universities. Instead for two centuries the legal system continued to be dominated by pragmatic, particularistic, case-oriented practitioners; such secondary literature as there was rarely rose above the status of practitioners' compilations which were used for ready reference rather than as authorities. The pioneers of English academic law in the late nineteenth century had to establish their professional legitimacy "in the eyes of sceptical universities and a largely hostile profession" by claiming a special body of expertise of which they had a monopoly.[48] The jurist could systematise the chaotic common law through scientific exposition and analysis.[49]

The genre of literature that emerged was not institutional works dealing with the whole system or large areas of law, but rather more detailed and modest student texts dealing with quite narrowly defined fields of substantive law: Anson on Contract, Pollock on Torts, Kenny on Criminal Law.[50] These books were held out to be systematic, largely uncritical introductions to the general principles and concepts of particular branches of law. More particular than institutional texts, they were not sufficiently detailed or comprehensive to be very useful as practitioners' reference works, which continued as a distinct genre. They rarely achieved the professional standing of the great American treatises, which were freed from the constraints of the English tradition because they were not designed to be relied on by students nor were they confined to the law of a single jurisdiction.[51]

Within a relatively short time the role of jurist as expositor hardened into an orthodoxy which dominated English academic law into the 1970s and beyond. In Sugarman's words: "[E]xposition, conceptualization, systematization and the analysis of existing legal doctrine became equated with the dominant tasks of legal education and scholarship."[52]

As polemical myth-making this story has been useful, but as history it is over-simple and somewhat Whiggish. A more balanced account of the period 1870 to 1970 would need to pay due regard to several countervailing themes: first, neither English nor American academic law has been completely dominated by a single monolithic orthodoxy as the story suggests. At every stage in its history law as a discipline has been the subject of tensions and controversy. None of the small band of pioneers who are credited with at least establishing a foothold for law in the universities were narrow-minded hacks: it would be a travesty of history to suggest that Pollock, Stephen, Anson, Dicey, Bryce, Salmond and Holland were merely or even mainly writers of textbooks. Maitland, who could hardly be accused of being a narrow expositor, clearly saw that the production of sound introductory texts was a necessary first step towards getting the study of English Law established. This account of the "expository orthodoxy" does not readily accommodate Jurisprudence, Legal History, Roman Law, Comparative Law and Public International Law all of which featured in curricula and legal literature. Nor does it fit scholars such as Maine, Maitland, Holdsworth, Vinogradoff, and later Friedmann, Montrose, Kahn-Freund and Lawson, to say nothing of the strong English tradition of Public International Lawyers and Romanists. Exposition is local and particular, as Bentham pointed out; our tradition of academic law has been consistently quite cosmopolitan and not as uniformly positivistic as the legend suggests.

Leading English expositors have rarely been content with merely providing structured information for students. Some of the pioneers of the textbook tradition, such as Fitzjames Stephen, Chalmers and Pollock saw their works as a prelude to codification.[53] Others intended their books to be useful as works of reference and sources of arguments for practitioners. Scholars involved in the higher exposition have regularly tried to rationalise and systematise particular branches of the common law on the basis of principle. Since 1945

136

the expansion of law schools has increased the number of producers. This opened the way for legal scholars to upgrade and, in
some instances to take over, leading practitioners' treatises such as
Chitty on Contract and Benjamin on Sale.[54] Many of these are now
edited by teams of academics and practitioners or, in some cases,
entirely by academics. In a few areas legal scholars have been
credited with making major contributions to the development of
whole new fields, such as Administrative Law, Restitution and Intellectual Property.

The undergraduate or other primary text imposes severe constraints on authors in respect of length, detail and depth. Involvement of scholars in the production of practitioners' treatises has
freed them from some of these constraints, but has correspondingly
imposed inhibitions on speculation, criticism and genuine innovation. By their nature practitioners' treatises need to be cautious
works of reference reliably grounded on authority.[55] The best works
of the genre sometimes transcend some of these limitations to make
incremental advances in legal doctrine, but on the whole legal
scholars have to find other outlets for sustained criticism or radical
rethinking. Furthermore, English legal culture is as resistant as ever
to codification, grand theories or even institutional works on the
Scottish model that purport to treat legal doctrine as a whole or
large areas, such as Public Law or Private Law, in a comprehensive
manner.[56] It is hardly an exaggeration to say that Blackstone was
the last as well as the first great English institutional writer.

In the modern period three factors differentiate the situation of
English and American expositors. First, English textbooks and treatises deal with the home-grown law of a single jurisdiction, whereas
the American treatise writers had to grapple with problems of
adaptation and maintaining unity across the various states and with
the problems posed by federal law. Secondly, as we have seen, in
England law schools developed later and had less prestige and a
different role from those in the United States. And, thirdly, the
Langdellian system freed American legal education from overreli-
ance on expository textbooks; the pedagogical emphasis was on
development of analytical skills applied to primary sources rather
than acquisition of knowledge of the law of one jurisdiction. As a
broad generalisation, at least until recently, the expository textbook
has been the dominant form of educational work in England at
both degree and professional levels, whereas in the United States
the main vehicle within law schools has been anthologies of cases

or cases and materials, often edited and presented with a remarkable degree of sophistication. Thus the role of expositors in the two systems was, in some respects, significantly different.

Against this background let us reconsider the charge that expository legal scholarship is "mainly descriptive". This is a pejorative way of implying that an intellectual activity is unoriginal, or claims to be mechanical, "value free", or "objective". To attribute this to what I have called "the higher exposition" is no less crude than suggesting that history merely describes the past. As with the writing of history, even the most mundane kind of exposition involves selection, interpretation, arrangement and narration in the author's own words—operations that involve choices at every stage. Legal exposition no more involves "mere" collection and ordering of an established body of knowledge than historiography involves collecting and classifying given facts (themselves activities that involve choices). Like scholars in many other disciplines, expositors tend to be impatient with theorising about their enterprise and prefer to get on with the job. What is at stake in recurrent debates about exposition is in part a matter of priorities, but at a deeper level it relates to the validity of the methods, the nature of "the knowledge" produced, the uses to which it is put, and standards for evaluation and criticism. In much the same sense as historians make history, expositors construct legal doctrine, but for different purposes.

As in history, so in law, words like "creative" are double-edged. Some of the underlying concerns of historiography are quite similar, but there are, of course, significant differences, not only in respect of subject-matter and methods. In particular, there is a difference of role: expositors serve a variety of functions at different levels: some produce convenient works of reference for practitioners and elementary texts for students; some simplify, rationalise and systematise legal doctrine; and a few are a vehicle for legal development, by putting forward semi-authoritative answers to unsolved questions, or starting-points for legislative reform or codification, or as a means of maintaining the unity of the common law across jurisdictions and developing it *sub silentio* independently of legislatures. What is common to all these roles is that, far from being detached external observers or scientists, expositors are active participants in the legal system.

The most common complaint by our expositors has been that English jurists are not accorded the status of their Continental European counterparts. Recently, however, the contributions of expository scholarship to common law systems have received explicit, if rather belated, judicial recognition, both in England and the United States. The context and the tone of these pronouncements suggest some revealing contrasts.

In England in the 1980s the lead was taken by Lord Goff, first in his Maccabean Lecture entitled "The Search for Principle"[57] and subsequently in another public lecture on "Judge, Jurist and Legislature", in which he said:

"It is difficult to overestimate the influence of the jurist in England today—both on the formation of the views of young lawyers and in the development of the law. Indeed, we now live in the age of the legal textbook. It is the textbook which provides the framework of principle within which we work. The prime task of the jurist is to take cases and statutes which provide the raw material of the law on any particular topic; and, by a critical re-appraisal of that raw material, to build up a systematic statement of the law on the relevant topic in a coherent form, often combined with proposals of how the law can be beneficially developed in the future. . . . For all practical purposes, textbooks are as informative as any code could be, indeed more so; and they lack all the defects of codes, since they can be changed without difficulty as the law develops, and they encourage, rather than inhibit, the gradual development of the law. To put it shortly: propositions of law in a textbook need not aspire to completeness; they may be expressed to be subject to doubt; they may be changed without legislation; and judges are at liberty to depart from them, if they are persuaded that it is right to do so."[58]

This is the authentic voice of the common law, a professed gradualist and pragmatist, sceptical of codes, and seeing the search for principle as a collective, evolutionary process. It is worth pausing briefly to compare this statement with some recent public pronouncements by two prominent judges in the United States, both of whom are also former academics. In 1987, Judge Richard Posner published an article on "The Decline of Law as an Autonomous Discipline".[59] Posner's central theme was that traditional expository scholarship had declined in prestige and self-confidence within the academy in the previous 25 years. He attributed this to the breakdown of consensual politics, the rise in prestige and authority of "scientific and other exact modes of enquiry"[60] and the felt need of the most imaginative legal scholars to be innovators rather than imitators. Posner, who had himself contributed to the decline through his energetic promotion of economic analysis of law, welcomed the development of inter-disciplinary approaches, but nevertheless concluded: "Disinterested legal-doctrinal analysis of the traditional kind remains the indispensable core of legal thought, and there is no surfeit of such analysis today."[61]

It is particularly striking that a leading exponent of one kind of interdisciplinary approach should re-affirm from the bench the centrality of traditional expository work. Posner's statements need to be seen in a wider context. Since the late 1970s American law journals have been flooded with introspective articles about the nature of legal scholarship, trends in legal thought and the health of law schools. There have been several strands in these debates[62]; especially germane in the present context is the complaint, not unprecedented in history, that academic law and legal practice have grown further and further apart.

A particularly interesting example is an article by Judge Harry Edwards published in 1992 in the *Michigan Law Review* entitled "The growing disjunction between legal education and the legal profession"[63] in which he made a strong plea for a return to "practical doctrinal scholarship" as the core of the discipline. The article stimulated eighteen responses in a symposium in the same journal.[64]

Edwards' thesis is that American law schools are moving in the direction of pure theory, while law firms are moving in the direction of pure commerce, leaving a vacuum in respect of both technical competence and ethical responsibility. No doubt mindful of the furore provoked by Dean Paul Carrington when he suggested that critical legal scholars, like unwanted aliens, should emigrate to other parts of the academy,[65] Edwards is careful to acknowledge a role for "theory" and to accept that law schools should accommodate and tolerate innovative approaches. But, he implies, these should be treated as belonging at the periphery rather than the core. He explicitly singled out multi-disciplinary work as one of these peripheral activities and lambasted the dilettanteism of academic lawyers who dabble in areas in which they have no formal training. This is not a new complaint: when Law and Economics becomes economics by lawyers it may just pass muster; when lawyers indulge in literary theory one raises an eyebrow; when Law and Psychiatry becomes psychiatry by lawyers one dives for cover.[66] In expressing these concerns, Edwards resurrects the idea of "practical doctrinal studies" as the core of the discipline of law in both research and teaching.

At first sight these pronouncements by three prominent judges suggest that legal scholarship is moving in different directions in England and the United States. Lord Goff praises English legal scholars for their recent contributions to legal development and practice and promises them an enhanced status. Posner and Edwards, on the other hand, accuse American law schools of abandoning their role. There are significant differences, but the underlying similarities may be more significant: first, in both countries legal scholarship has diversified. Goff focuses almost exclusively on the contributions of traditional expositors and, in this context, barely mentions other kinds of work. Posner and Edwards on the other hand were reacting to the diversification of legal scholarship. They may be right about a decline in prestige of traditional doctrinal scholarship, but it is quite misleading to suggest that it has been abandoned.[67] Secondly, all three judges either assume or assert that exposition is the core of legal scholarship and that the main role of jurists is to serve the legal system—especially the higher courts—by assisting in the rationalisation, simplification and interstitial development of legal doctrine. Thirdly, all agree that this role is important, but it is essentially subordinate. In the common law system power and authority is divided beteen the legislature, the executive and the judiciary in complex ways. Jurists are useful, but they have no official constitutional position.[68] In the common law system the role of the expositor is honourable, but strictly subordinate—more like poodles under the bench than lions supporting the throne.

REACTIONS AGAINST EXPOSITION AND THE SEARCH FOR ALTERNATIVES

Academic polemics require recognisable opponents. From the mid-1960s law teachers who were dissatisfied with the state of academic law began to construct a target to attack—they called it by various names: "black letter law",[69] "the expository orthodoxy",[70] "the textbook tradition",[71] and, later, "classical legal thought"[72]. The central charge was that English academic law had been dominated by a monolithic orthodoxy which was narrow, conservative, illiberal, unrealistic and boring.

As I was one of those who helped to create this story, I should take some responsibility for it, without re-fighting old battles. In

1974 I suggested that the unifying feature of the socio-legal movement in this country has been dissatisfaction with the orthodoxy, but the sources of dissatisfaction were diverse. At least five different complaints against the Expository Tradition needed to be distinguished. First, there was the complaint of the practitioner against the academic—that what was taught and written by academic lawyers was seriously out of touch with the realities of legal practice. Secondly, there was the complaint of the liberal intellectual—especially the liberal educator—that the expository orthodoxy with its emphasis on uncritical exposition, rote learning and technical detail, was philistine. Thirdly, the treatment of positive law as an essentially stable body of rules, fostered or reinforced the inherent conservatism of most people professionally connected with the law. Reformists, radicals, revolutionaries and sceptics of various kinds could unite in reacting against an intellectual approach which appeared to encourage uncritical acceptance of the status quo. Fourthly, there was the complaint that the expository approach was *narrow*, not only in respect of the range of subjects treated as important (for example, family law, labour law, criminology, and penology were neglected) but also in the range of questions asked about any legal field and the kind of techniques and source materials thought to be relevant to answering them. Finally, there was the complaint that many of the concerns of academic lawyers were trivial, judged by whatever criteria of significance the complainer chose to adopt. Academic lawyers, it was said, delighted in playing verbal chess games with the rule against perpetuities as it affected Blackacre, a country mansion with six maids' bedrooms, while glossing over entirely the problems of the urban tenant.[73]

On that occasion I went on to suggest that "[t]here has yet to be a clear recognition that a shared sense of dissatisfaction did not necessarily have roots in shared concerns and shared values."[74] Accordingly, one could expect considerable differences of opinion about what would be considered satisfactory alternatives to the dominant tradition and that it was unlikely and undesirable that a single new orthodoxy would replace the old one.[75]

These interpretations were advanced 20 years ago. Much has happened in the intervening period. In retrospect this account of a confusing pluralism succeeding a dominant and narrow orthodoxy still seems broadly correct. However, it needs to be glossed in a number of ways.

First, the British protagonists of broader approaches to the study of law challenged the dominance of the Expository Tradition but, except for a few Marxian critics, did not fundamentally deny its validity or legitimacy. The central precept of those who favoured realism or contextual approaches or socio-legal studies was that for most purposes the study of rules alone is not enough.[76]

However, Marxian scholars and the critical legal studies movement, which came into prominence after 1977, offered a much more radical critique, at least to start with.[77] According to one recent interpretation of a complex story, critical legal studies went through three phases[78]: a global critique of law from the outside, as exemplified by Marxist attacks on all bourgeois legality and strongly sceptical attacks on the claims to rationality or coherence of the whole Western legal tradition. Then American critical legal scholars, using deconstructive techniques borrowed from postmodernist literary theory, attacked the form of particular fields of law from within the academy, for instance, by showing the internal contradictions and incoherence of received doctrine in traditional fields such as contracts. Later, especially after the collapse of socialism, there appeared to be a drawing back, partly in response to accusations of nihilism, partly out of an awareness that critical scholars who were themselves law teachers might "be caught in the potentially inauthentic position of both propounding and denouncing the law."[79] By the early 1990s critical legal studies in the United States and other common law countries had diversified and, in the eyes of some, had outlived its time.

Secondly, on the positive side, the past 20 years have seen a period of expansion, intellectual ferment and diversification far beyond what one might have expected in 1974. On the whole the main trends in the common law world have been set in the United States, but United Kingdom-based scholars have played a significant part in fields such as legal philosophy, criminology and regulation. In America the foreground has been dominated by two major movements—economic analysis of law and critical legal studies— which are normally represented as the right and left wings of a politicised jurisprudence, with an outstandingly able group of political and legal philosophers, such as Rawls, Dworkin, Raz, MacCormick and Sen, defending the liberal democratic centre from these challenges from the right and the left. But the diversification of academic law went much further than that. What is important in the present context is that critical legal studies and economic analysis were only two parts of a much more complex picture.

Developments in legal theory can at least be treated as reflecting

143

the extent of the changes in the past 20 years.[80] By 1974 Ronald Dworkin had recently succeeded Herbert Hart in Oxford and the first phase of the revolution in legal philosophy could be said to be over. Bentham Studies were just becoming established. Law and Economics had hardly ventured beyond the University of Chicago[81]—the first edition of Richard Posner's *Economic Analysis of Law* was published in 1972.[82] Few, if any, academic lawyers or legal theorists in 1974 had conceived or heard of, let alone participated in, critical legal studies, feminist jurisprudence, critical race theory, law and semiotics, the Law and Literature Movement, socio-biology, or autopoiesis.[83] One might say, by way of counter-examples, that the sociology and anthropology of law and historical jurisprudence have been further marginalised within law schools, despite the contributions of a few individuals.[84] Secondary treatments of legal theory have yet to catch up with developments in the history of ideas.[85] Nevertheless, one might also say that the intellectual ferment in legal theory which began in the fifties never lost momentum, although it has diversified and fragmented in confusing ways.[86]

In England during this period American trends and fashions were closely observed, Marxist legal studies waxed and waned, and, not surprisingly, much closer contact was established with Continental Europe. Whether one looks at publishers' lists, postgraduate programmes, new law journals, or specialist associations and groups, one finds a diversification of interests and approaches and a general intellectual liveliness which is all the more remarkable for having coincided with a period of almost continuous economic crisis in higher education.

To trace the intellectual history of the discipline of law in England (or more broadly) since 1945, and especially since 1970, would require at least a substantial book. Diversification has occurred in respect of theory, methods and subject matter. The range of subjects studied has increased dramatically and many traditional areas have been transformed.[87] Legal History, Contract, Family Law, Human Rights, Public Law, and Evidence are all examples of specialisms with their own stories, which are interconnected in various ways.

The extent of change can be illustrated by socio-legal studies. In December 1993 the Centre for Socio-legal Studies at Oxford celebrated its twenty-first anniversary. The list of publications emerging from the Centre alone included over one hundred books and several hundred articles. Shortly afterwards the Economic and

Social Research Council published a report on socio-legal studies in the United Kingdom which showed a healthy spread of socio-legal work across both institutions and subject areas.[88] The report identified 265 academics involved in funded socio-legal research, of whom two-thirds were based in 46 law departments, 13 of which had six or more active researchers. The Socio-legal Studies Association, founded in 1990, already had over 300 members and, equally encouraging, the field was proving particularly attractive to younger scholars. The report identified a need for significantly improved research training in the field, a point that reflects a known historical weakness in academic law.[89] It is a bit disappointing that socio-legal studies is not established in many other departments than law and that genuinely multi-disciplinary, as opposed to interdisciplinary, work has not extended very far beyond the Oxford Centre.[90] But there is a sense of euphoria in the air and a growing sense that socio-legal studies is now firmly established. This upbeat mood is tempered with caution in the first conclusion of the ESRC report:

"Over the last 20 years, the UK socio-legal research community has produced a substantial body of knowledge about the operation and effects of law in society. The community stands poised to make major developments in the advancement of the subject and in the understanding of legal processes as they affect economic and social behaviour. This potential must be defended and enhanced in the context of a reduction of funding for social science research in general, exacerbated by the termination of the major funding commitment of ESRC to the Oxford Centre. There is, therefore, a need for universities and the research community to ensure that adequate core funding is provided to maintain the development of the field."[91]

This conclusion suggests that socio-legal studies reflect the situation of academic law in this country: it is coming of age and achieving critical mass and has enormous potential, but it is approaching a critical point when it could either continue to develop or it could decline.

The third gloss that I would put on my earlier interpretation concerns coherence. Socio-legal studies and critical legal studies are merely two of a number of striking new developments in the study of law. Pluralism and diversity are the themes of the time. There have been attempts to rethink traditional fields in a broader way, but they have yet to become established.[92] One striking feature of the scene is the survival of exposition, perhaps with diminished status, but still widely considered as central both in teaching and scholarship. As we have seen, it may even be due for a revival. To some extent it has assimilated some of the ideas of the broader approaches and has become more self-conscious and sophisticated; Judge Edwards' conception of "practical doctrinal scholarship" is not as narrow or unreflective as earlier versions of the orthodoxy.

Whatever its limitations, no serious rival has emerged to challenge the claim of this tough and coherent tradition to be the core of academic law. This is hardly surprising in a period of diversification and pluralism, but the question arises whether it is any longer sensible or useful to make claims that there is a core or centre of the discipline. That is the subject of the next chapter.

Notes

[1] Tony Becher, *Academic Tribes and Territories* (1989) at p. 30.

[2] W. Twining, "Goodbye to Lewis Eliot", (1980) 15 J.S.P.T.L. (N.S,) 2.

[3] P. S. Atiyah, *Pragmatism and Theory in English Law* (1987, Hamlyn Lectures) at p. 7.

[4] "[I]t is not easy to see that the law itself is a discipline in the usual sense. What truths do lawyers as such come up with? What are the great legal discoveries of the past ten years, or fifty years, or even a hundred? There do not seem to be any." *Invitation to Law* (1988) at p. 178. This passage, as do many similar ones, seems to conflate legal practice and legal scholarship. Becher himself suggests that the notion of discovery "seems out of place in academic law", *op. cit.* at p. 5. My own view is that collectively lawyers can claim a creditable record in respect of *inventions*, and that to equate scholarship with *discovery* of truths implies a dubious analogy with the natural sciences which would disqualify most disciplines in the humanities and much work in the social sciences that claims to be scholarly. JJM at pp. 136–140.

[5] Becher at p. 8.

[6] esp. p. 156.

[7] "Participants at our Quebec Regional Consultation spoke of the predominance of *recherches ponctuelles* (isolated, narrowly focused and rather random research), and of the absence of *recherche sublime* (research that involves finding higher levels of explanation and integration through conceptual and empirical analysis). Perhaps this pattern of attention to the technical and neglect of the fundamental gives the reason for the ambivalence so many seem to feel toward the question of legal research: what we have in abundance does not satisfy, it preoccupies." (*Law and Learning,* Report to the Social Sciences and Humanities Research Council of Canada by the Consultative Group on Research and Education in Law (Chair: Harry Arthurs) (Ottawa, 1983), at p. 75. The same report usefully distinguishes between academic research and research done by practitioners in connection with providing professional services to clients as follows: "However, our concern is not with the limited and ephemeral works produced by these activities. We are interested in articles, books, reports and studies that

together constitute a body of literature available in the public domain with a pertinence beyond the particular moment at which it was prepared." (*ibid.* p. 65). Of course, some such works, e.g. written briefs for important cases before the American appellate courts, often have strong claims to be scholarly.

[8] Becher, *op cit.*, p. 48, citing J. Law (1976).

[9] *Law and Learning, op. cit.* In contrast to nearly all such official reports the Arthurs Report focused on legal scholarship and its relationship to the needs of the profession and the public rather than mainly or exclusively on legal education. The Report does, however, contain an excellent discussion of the relationship between teaching and research. Four linked empirical studies were undertaken: John S. McKennirey, *Canadian Law Professors* (1982); *Canadian Law Faculties* (1982); *Sources of Support for Legal Research* (1982); Alice Janisch, *Profile of Published Legal Research* (1982). The account in the text, which is a summary of a summary, does not do justice to the relative sophistication of the original research, which analyses activities and publications in terms of subject-matter, perspectives and methods. While the report and some of its recommendations were controversial, the underlying research was widely praised as an advance: see for example, J. Schlegel (review) in (1984) 36 *Stanford L.Rev* 1517 (comparing the Canadian study favourably to American studies).

[10] Arthurs, at pp. 65–66.

[11] *ibid.* at p. 65

[12] At p. 66. Some might cavil at this rather broad definition, which includes more intellectually ambitious expository works; the report recognised the difficulty and, indeed, combined the doctrinal and theoretical categories in its figures for monographs.

[13] *ibid.*

[14] *ibid.*

[15] See the chart at p. 126. This picture was constructed by relating these four categories to two main kinds of influences on legal research: first, methodology or intellectual perspective, ranging from "traditional doctrinal, research "in" law which treats law as its subject"; and interdisciplinary research "*on*" law which treats law as its object.". Secondly, the constituency or desired area of impact, ranging "from the academic or scientific constituency, the world of ideas, and the professional or practical constituency, the world of action". *ibid.*

[16] The term has been used by Judge Harry Edwards in his recent criticism of American law schools for failing to perform adequately their traditional function of systematic exposition, analysis and development of legal doctrine for the benefit of practitioners and courts, discussed below at pp. 140–141.

[17] At p. 157. One of the main conclusions of the Report was that the short-term demands of the practising profession and involvement in "law reform research" dominated Canadian legal scholarship at the time. Clearly the academic community was meeting real needs, but the emphasis on these two kinds of activity had negative consequences for Canadian legal scholarship as a whole: first, "fundamental research into the values, operation and effects of law, has been largely neglected" (at p. 154); secondly, some of this activity was of a kind that could as well be done by academically less well-qualified people. Canadian law schools are essentially professional schools on the American model; the Arthurs Report repeatedly emphasised that fundamental research was an essential foundation for ensuring that law schools enhanced "the reflective, critical and analytical abilities of their students".

[18] Professor Aubrey Diamond undertook a less ambitious general survey in 1978, "Research in Law: A Report to the Council of the S.P.T.L." (1979) SPTL *Newsletter,* No. 13 (March 1979) pp. 1–18; there has since been a more detailed report on socio-legal studies by the Economic and Research Council: *Review of Socio-legal Studies: Final Report* (1994). Several Heads of Law Schools kindly gave me access to their submissions to the Universities Funding Council for the 1992 Research Assessment exercise and these generally support the theme of diversity.

[19] *Law from Oxford University Press, January-June, 1994.* (Catalogue, dealing almost entirely with new publications): During the period Jan.-March, 1994 I received catalogues from over 20 U.K. publishers who maintain significant lists in law.

[20] See above, Chap. 2.

[21] Above, Chap. 1.

[22] On the importance of clarifying standpoint, role and context as a preliminary to such exercises see HDTWR Chap. 2 and ANALYSIS, pp. 120–121.

[23] The current emphasis on "skills" includes direct, usually elementary teaching of such operations as interviewing, negotiating, drafting, cross-examination, and "counselling" in different simulated contexts. This is specifically related to pre-paration for practice and is a relatively recent development. See below, Chap. 7, section (d).

[24] R. G. Collingwood, *An Autobiography* (1939) Chap. 7; *The Idea of History* (1946).

[25] *e.g.* D. N. MacCormick, *H.L.A. Hart* (1981), Chap. 3.

[26] In the Anglo-American system during this century there has been a strong tend-ency to move away from general towards (more-or-less) particular jurisprudence: for example, to be more concerned with American legal thought or common law reasoning than with legal thought and legal reasoning in general. This is a theme for another occasion.

[27] Even legal theory is affected by this tendency. For example, Jeremy Bentham's Science of Legislation offers guidance to law-makers; Karl Llewellyn explicitly developed prescriptive working-theories for appellate judges and advocates. When Holmes suggested that law students should adopt the standpoint of the Bad Man, he can be interpreted as criticising the tendency of academic lawyers to identify too closely with appellate court judges and other participants in the higher reaches of the legal system and to neglect the more down-to-earth per-spectives and situations of ordinary citizens and office lawyers. Ronald Dworkin builds not only his theory of adjudication, but his whole interpretative legal theory around a model judge, Hercules, who works within a given system. Her-cules not only provides a role model for actual judges, but also represents all those who are concerned with correct interpretation of law. One does not need to accept Dworkin's particular theory of interpretation and argumentation to agree with him that these are activities undertaken by participants within particu-lar legal systems. See below, Chap. 7.

[28] Becher, *op. cit.,* at pp. 5, 8, 30–31.

[29] John W. Cairns, "Blackstone, an English Institutist: Legal literature and the rise of the nation-state", (1984) 4 *Oxford Jo. of Legal Studies* 318.

[30] Of course, Blackstone had some notable forerunners, for example, Hale, Wood, Finch and Gilbert.

[31] 1 *Comm.* 27.

[32] J. Bentham, *A Fragment on Government* (ed. Burns and Hart, CW, 1977), Preface, at p. 397.

[33] Duncan Kennedy (1979), *op. cit.* Chap. 1 n. 4.

[34] M. Rheinstein (1962), discussed KLRM pp. 3–5.

[35] Some, such as Thayer and Wigmore, claimed to be writing about Anglo-American law.

[36] KLRM pp. 3–7.

[37] *ibid.* pp. 275–276.

[38] William Draper Lewis, Introduction to *Restatement of Restitution* (1937) at p. 9 (the same formulation was used in several places). The original intention was to have a series of treatises to accompany the restatements, but this was never carried out. The standard procedure was to appoint a Reporter, usually a leading academic, and an advisory committee of experts. Successive drafts were to be widely cirulated among the legal profession for comment and a final agreed draft was to be presented for consideration and approval by the Council of the Institute.

[39] These issues were raised by Professor John Wade, "The Restatement (Second): A Tribute." (1985) 13 *Pepperdine L. Rev.* 59, at pp. 74 ff.

[40] Early on in the Project, one distinguished Reporter complained that the ALI rules required that "(we) can never adversely criticize a rule which we find we have to state. Such by-law presents a very unpleasant dilemma to a Reporter. He must either state a good rule which he knows perfectly well is not the law; or he must state a bad rule and by his very statement entrench it further." Barton Leach, "The restatements as they were in the beginning, are now and perhaps thenceforth shall be", (1937) 23 A.B.A.J. 517, at p. 519.

[41] Black's *Law Dictionary* (6th ed. 1990) p. 1313.

[42] *e.g.* W. Noel Keyes, "The Restatement (Second): Its misleading Quality and a Proposal for Its Amelioration," (1985) 13 *Pepperdine L. Rev. 23* (1985).

[43] The political context virtually required that the A.L.I. should adopt a set of theoretical assumptions that smacked of the previous century. By the 1920s the idea that judges merely declare the law and do not make it and the idea of a single American common law had both been sharply attacked and the assumption that legal doctrine could be meaningfully described in terms of abstract rules was increasingly being questioned by "legal realists". In the circumstances it was particularly difficult to maintain a sharp positivist distinction between the law as it is and the law as it ought to be, but the pretence had to be maintained. A more robust critique of the *Restatements* as a waste of talent on "toys of the trade" is advanced by Lawrence Friedman, *A History of American Law* (2nd ed., 1985) at pp. 674–676. Recently, greater openness has also attracted more overt political criticism: a former federal judge has attacked the A.L.I. for being an unaccountable, unelected elite involved in quasi-legislation "without obtaining any input from Congress and/ or the State legislatures, without obtaining input from the broad-based representative interests of the masses of ordinary citizens, and without giving any meaningful consideration of any kind to the social, economic and political interests of the various minority groups in this country." Paul A Simmons, "Government by Unaccountable Private Non Profit Corporation", (1992) X *Jo. of Human Rights* 67. A few areas such as products liability and corporate governance have become overtly politicised. On torts see Stephen D. Sugarman, "A Restatement of Torts", 44 *Stanford L. Rev.* 1163 (1992); on corporate governance, see J. Seligman, "A sheep in Wolf's clothing: the American Law Institute Principles of Corporate Governance Project", 55 *Geo. Washington L.R.* 325 (1987).

[44] Similar criticisms were made of the Restatement of African Law Project in the

1960s, William Twining, *The Place of Customary Law in the National Legal Systems of East Africa* (1964), Chap. 2.

[45] The American Law Institute *Annual Report* (1990); Simmons, *op. cit.*, quotes significantly higher figures.

[46] Lewis, *op. cit.*, n. 38.

[47] Cairns, *op. cit.* at p. 24.

[48] David Sugarman, "Legal Theory, the Common Law Mind and the Making of the Textbook Tradition" LTCL Chap. 3, at p. 29.

[49] *ibid.* at pp. 28–29, citing Dicey and Pollock.

[50] Pollock tended to be more overtly critical than most expositors of that generation. On Dicey, see below, n. 53.

[51] See above n. 34.

[52] *ibid.* at p. 31.

[53] A.W.B. Simpson, "The Rise and Fall of the Legal Treatise" (1981) 48 *University of Chicago L. Rev.* 632, reprinted in *Legal Theory and History: Essays on the Common Law* (1987) Chap. 12 at p. 307. Simpson adds: "Dicey's *Conflict of Laws* (1896), continuously revised by later editors, is perhaps the best known of the works that have perpetuated this format to the present day." *ibid.* Dicey's *Law and the Constitution* (1st ed., 1885) really belongs to a different genre and, perhaps for that reason, is better known outside legal circles than most orthodox textbooks.

[54] P. Birks, "The Historical Context" in Birks (ed) *Reviewing Legal Education* (forthcoming).

[55] On the sad fate of Charles F. Chamberlayne's five volume treatise on evidence that did not conform to these conventions see RE at pp. 61–65.

[56] T.B. Smith, "Authors and Authority," (1972) 12 J.S.P.T.L. (N.S.) 1 (Presidential Address). English law continues to be largely impervious to systematisation and theorising on the grand scale. This applies as much to legislation as to judge-made law, see Lord Goff, discussed below.

[57] Robert Goff, "The Search for Principle", Maccabean Lecture (1983) LXIX *Procs. British Academy* 169; "Judge, Jurist and Legislator", Child and Co., Oxford Lecture (1986), reprinted in (1987) *Denning Law Jo.* 79.

[58] *ibid* at p. 92. Robert Goff is a former law teacher, co-author of one of the most highly regarded modern treatises—Goff and Jones on Restitution—and a respected Lord of Appeal in Ordinary. His gracious recognition of the influence of doctrinal scholarship in the English legal system and of the complementary roles of judges and jurists has since been echoed by some of his brethren on the bench, e.g. Lord Woolf, *Protection of the Public: A New Challenge* (1990) (Hamlyn Lectures 41), Chap. 1. Not surprisingly it has been welcomed by the objects of his praise. His statements have been interpreted as almost the first sincere and open acknowledgment that legal scholars have a significant practical contribution to make to our legal system.

[59] R. Posner, "The Decline of Law as an Autonomous Discipline: 1962–1987", 100 *Harvard L. Rev.* 761. "Autonomy" is used here in a weak sense to refer to law as "a subject properly entrusted to persons trained in law and in nothing else." (at p. 762). Posner elaborated on the theme in "Conventionalism: The Key to Law as an Autonomous Discipline", (1988) 38 *University of Toronto Law Jo.* 333.

[60] At p. 792.

[61] *ibid* at p. 777.

[62] There has been a general, protracted controversy about "critical legal studies";

there have been polemics between rival groups or schools; there have been reflections, more or less programmatic or introspective, within movements such as feminism, critical race theory or law and literature; and there has been a strong sense of student dissatisfaction about their law school experiences.

[63] Harry T. Edwards, "The growing disjunction between legal education and the legal profession", (1992) 91 *Michigan L. Rev.* 34. The author's main concern was with professional ethics and competence; he attacked the legal profession for being too venal and the law schools for being too theoretical.

[64] Symposium on Legal Education, (1993) 91 *Michigan Law Review* no. 8.

[65] P. Carrington, "Of law and the river", (1984) 34 *Jo. Leg. Educ.* 222, and symposium in (1985) 35 *ibid.* pp. 1–26.

[66] *cf.* William Twining, "The Great Juristic Bazaar" (1978) J.S.P.T.L. (N.S.) 185, at pp. 194–196.

[67] For example, the following statement by Professor George Priest of Yale is best treated as rhetorical exaggeration: "Today authorship of the legal treatise has been cast off to practitioners. The treatise is no longer a credit to those competing on the leading edge of legal thought." (1983) 33 *J. Legal Educ.* 437.

[68] A. W. B. Simpson, *Invitation to Law* pp. 127–130.

[69] "Black letter" refers to black or Gothic type which was often used in formal statements of principles or rules at the start of a section, typically followed by a commentary.

[70] W. Twining, "Some Jobs for Jurisprudence", (1974) 1 *Brit. Jo. Law and Society*, 149, at pp. 161–164.

[71] Sugarman, *op. cit.*, n. 48 above.

[72] *e.g.* Betty Mensch, "The History of Mainstream Legal Thought", in David Kairys (ed) *The Politics of Law* (1982). Later, under American influence, the target was expansively renamed "liberal legalism", although "liberal" has rather different associations on each side of the Atlantic.

[73] This is a condensation of the analysis in "Law and social science: the method of detail" (1974) *New Society*, 27 June 758, at p. 760.

[74] *ibid.*

[75] This interpretation was analogous to my account of the American Realist Movement as a reaction to a similar dominant orthodoxy, which took a different form in the United States: Langdellism. There the reaction was rooted in a variety of concerns that were so diverse that I concluded that most attempted generalisations about the ideas and achievements of the American Realists were false or trivial or both. See generally, KLRM and TAR.

[76] TAR pp. 362–363; see further below, at pp. 174–177.

[77] M. Kelman, *A Guide to Critical Legal Studies* (1987) is the best survey of a complex movement, up to the mid-1980s. While the leaders of the critical legal studies movement claimed to be the heirs of American Realism, I am inclined to treat this as a rhetorical ploy to claim a respectable ancestry for a line of attack that was more politically committed, more genuinely radical, and more intellectually ambitious than the brands of realism espoused by the leaders of the Realist Movement such as Llewellyn, Frank and Cook. Recently, American critical legal scholars after a series of fierce political battles within a few law schools and in the law journals, have tended to adopt a more moderate tone and to retreat from strong versions of scepticism, but I personally think that to claim that the movement is an extension of Realism underplays both the radicalism of their challenge to the common law tradition, including broader approaches, and their originality, at least within law.

151

Legal Scholarship and the Roles of the Jurist

78 Costas Douzinas, Peter Goodrich, and Yifat Hachamovitch, *Politics, Post modernity and critical legal studies* (1994), Introduction.
79 *ibid.* p. 13.
80 This passage is adapted from my "Remembering 1972" (forthcoming) in D. Galligan, *op. cit.* Chap. 2, n. 57, which contains a more detailed overview of developments since 1972 and extensive references, which are not reproduced here.
81 On the complex history of the Law and Economics Movement, see Neil Duxbury, "Law and Economics in America" (forthcoming).
82 Recently Posner has ebulliently sought to be re-labelled: see, for example, R. Posner, *Law and Literature: A Misunderstood Relation* (1988); *The Problems of Jurisprudence* (1990); *Sex and Reason* (1992).
83 On autopoiesis see G. Teubner, *Autopoietic Law: A New Approach* (1988); Symposium in (1992) *Cardozo Law Rev.* and above Chap. 5, n. 36. For references to the other developments, see "Remembering 1972", *op. cit.*
84 For a survey of legal anthropology up to 1987/8, see F. Snyder, "Anthropology, Dispute Processes and Law", (1988) 8 *Brit. J. Law and Society* 141; on historical jurisprudence see generally Alan Diamond (ed.), *The Victorian Achievement of Sir Henry Maine* (1991).
85 RB *passim.*
86 A similar list could be made for developments in legal education. In the past decade or so a series of buzz-words and phrases illustrate the pace of change: judicial studies; in-house trainers; access; the skills movement; training the trainers; distance learning; computer-based instruction; expert systems; the reflective practitioner; and legal literacy are all terms that have entered the standard vocabulary of legal educators.
87 On the expansion of the London LLM, to cover about 150 subjects, see University of London, *LLM Review: Second Interim Report* (1992).
88 Economic and Social Research Council, *Review of Socio-Legal Studies Final Report* (1994).
89 This finding has been corroborated by a small survey by P. A. Thomas (1994) 12 *Socio-Legal Newsletter* p. 1. On research training of law teachers see Appendix below.
90 One important exception is the Human Rights Centre at the University of Essex, which has moved increasingly into multidisciplinary work in an area traditionally dominated by lawyers.
91 *op. cit.* at p. 47.
92 See further RE. Chap. 11.

7. The Quest For a Core

"but there ain't-a-going to *be* no core" (Mark Twain)[1]

Sociologists of knowledge tell us that some disciplines are convergent tightly-knit communities "in terms of their fundamental ideologies, their common values, their shared judgements of quality, their awareness of belonging to a unique tradition . . . {and} are likely to occupy territories with well-defined external boundaries."[2] Others are centrifugal.

At some points in the history of the Anglo-American tradition, law as an academic discipline could have been described as cohesive and centripetal: the object of study was legal rules and the role of the jurist was to systematise, to rationalise, and to expound legal doctrine. However, at no stage was this view unchallenged. As we have seen, from the late nineteenth century in the United States, much later in England, the predominant view came under regular and increasingly open attack from critics who seemed to have little in common except a shared sense of dissatisfaction with the prevailing orthodoxy.

It should not be surprising to find in an expanding discipline: (i) few who accept the idea of an autonomous discipline in a strong sense; (ii) increasing pluralism, including differentiation of specialisms and multiplicity of perspectives; and, *per contra*, (iii) scholars agonising and debating about the nature of their enterprise: is it in any way unique or distinctive? What are its parameters? Does it have a centre or core or essence?

In the current intellectual climate, it is tempting to dismiss questions about the core or essence of a discipline as misguided or plain silly, to be treated no more seriously than the quest for a non-existent Holy Grail or where the rainbow ends. Why assume that Law—or History or Sociology—has or should have a settled core? I am inclined to share such scepticism, but the theme is sufficiently persistent and there is enough at stake to make it worth looking at some salient examples of attempts to define the core in

153

somewhat different contexts and to try to tease out some of the concerns that underlie their persistence. I have chosen to inspect six contenders: conceptions of legal science; law as a branch of rational ethics; the core subjects debate; ideas about law as craft and technology; do-as-you-like pluralism; and the idea of rules as a necessary focus of legal study. This chapter ends with a brief consideration of a different, but related, question: what, if anything, can the discipline of law offer that is unique or special to general understandings?

REDUCTIONISM—A SCEPTICAL TOUR

(a) Purification—Legal Science

The word "science" is often used to claim academic status for a subject: domestic science, police science, policy science, scientology, for example. History in the nineteenth century and most social sciences in the twentieth have been concerned, sometimes obsessively, with establishing their "scientific" credentials. Law has not been immune from such hang-ups. A central issue of legal theory in civil law systems centres on the epistemic basis of "legal science"; the term is less common in the more relaxed Anglo-Saxon tradition.[3] However, especially between 1870 and the mid-1930s, American academic lawyers under German influence were susceptible to analogies with the physical sciences: "If law be not a science, a university will best consult its own dignity in declining to teach it", intoned Christopher Columbus Langdell in 1887, and proceeded to suggest that the lawyer, like the botanist, must select, classify and arrange his specimens—in this instance reported cases.[4] Analogies were invoked promiscuously with botany, chemistry, physics, geometry, and biological evolution. Experimental Jurisprudence, the states as legislative laboratories and, above all, the idea of law as social engineering litter the literature.[5] Enthusiastic decision-theorists, Bayesians and socio-biologists continue the tradition.

We can readily dismiss many of the analogies as spurious and the underlying assumptions about science as naive, but we should not underestimate the persistence of the aspiration to try to emulate the physical sciences in respect of such values as order, system, cumulation, rigour, replicability and objectivity. There are concerns about both validity and professional respectability. Even the softest discipline needs to claim to be disciplined.[6]

154

The most common model for "legal science" is the idea of systematic, objective, neutral exposition of the law as it is. Establishing a theoretical foundation for "legal dogmatics", as it is called in the civilian tradition, is one of the moving forces behind legal positivism. But here we need to tread carefully. Our greatest positivist, Jeremy Bentham, insisted on a sharp distinction between Expository Jurisprudence, concerned with the systematic description of the law as it is, and Censorial Jurisprudence, concerned with the criticism and construction of law as it ought to be on the basis of utility. Bentham saw exposition as particular to a given system and a rather lowly pursuit; legislation was the noble and universal science: "The *Expositor*, therefore, is always the citizen of this or that particular country: the *Censor* is, or ought to be the citizen of the world."[7] Bentham, the radical positivist, distinguished the is and the ought mainly for the sake of the ought; his only contribution to legal education was to advocate a School of Legislation.

It is incorrect, therefore, to see English legal positivism as essentially conservative and uncritical. However, the positivist distinction between law as it is and law as it ought to be was later used both to ground a neutral expository, descriptive science of law as the dominant form of legal study and, sometimes, to confine legal studies to exposition. It is a short step from insisting on a sharp distinction between description and prescription to maintaining that one should describe before one ventures to criticise.[8] It is only a slightly longer step to move on to say that legal scholars, and especially law students, should only be concerned with description. It is not for fledgling practitioners to reason why or to criticise their elders.[9]

The tradition of teaching and scholarship that purports to confine itself to the exposition and analysis of posited law has been the subject of diverse attacks, on such grounds as that it is narrow, reactionary and dull.[10] There is, however, a more fundamental reason for rejecting it: it is just wrong. Two of the greatest positivists—Holmes and Kelsen—can be used to make the point.

In his classic address to law students "The Path of the Law",[11] Holmes advised them to wash the law in cynical acid and to adopt the standpoint of a bad man, an amoral actor whose only concern is to predict the likely legal consequences of any action he takes: "If I do this, what will happen to me?"

Holmes had two specific targets in mind: the tendency of students to substitute their own prejudices or values or wishes for mastery of technical detail; and an over-logical and abstracted view of the law, associated with Langdell's Harvard, fostered by concentrating too much on the reasoning of judges in the upper reaches of the legal system. The first prong of Holmes' attack involved a clear separation of the description of the law as it is from prescription of what the law ought to be. His was a particularly strong version of legal positivism. But in arguing for a more realistic approach, Holmes was attacking the idea of legal discourse as a closed system: judges make law (a heresy at the time)[12]; policy is relevant to interpretation; "the man of the future is the man of statistics and the master of economics"[13]; indeed, Holmes emphasised the relevance of history and the social sciences generally to both understanding and arguing about law. Holmes is rightly seen as one of the great precursors of the movement to link law and the social sciences and of scepticism about legal reasoning as a closed system. Far from seeking to impose closure by washing the law in cynical acid, he was one of the leading advocates of opening up law to the social sciences.[14]

If one reads "The Path of the Law" as recommending the adoption of a realistic, bottom-up perspective and a picture of law as the product of other people's power, the advice has much to commend it. The Bad Man needs to cast a cold eye on law in order to cope with the (predominantly urban) legal jungle. The Bad Man is, inter alia, a version of *homo juridicus*—a calculating rational actor operating within a man-made system over which he has no control, but which is a fact of life, a given.

However, if Holmes is interpreted more broadly as advancing a general theory of law which includes the claim that law can be described and explicated solely in terms of brute fact and predictions of what courts will do in particular cases, then it is vulnerable to quite devastating attack. Two of several lines of criticism will suffice here. First, as Herbert Hart and others have shown, equating legal rules with predictions may fit the standpoint of the artificially constructed Bad Man, but it just does not fit the standpoints of the legislator, judge, advocate, law enforcer or good citizen, none of whom is solely or even mainly concerned with predicting judicial decisions. Rules can be used to guide, persuade, control, construct, or justify actions. And the outside observer cannot describe or interpret a legal system solely in terms of brute fact, any more than one can describe chess or cricket solely in terms of physical behaviour. To understand such practices one has to consider their rules from an internal point of view.[15] Secondly, Holmes' Bad Man is not as "realistic" as he appears at first sight: if he relies solely on rules as aids to prediction and focuses only on judicial decisions, he will not fare very well. The jungle survivor or street-wise actor is concerned to predict many other decisions and events, for example the reporting of a crime, investigation by the police, the likelihood of suspicion falling on him (whether he did it or not), the decision to prosecute, the likelihood of a plea bargain and so on. The bad man has to predict many events and he uses other aids to prediction in addition to rules. Washing law in cynical acid may dissolve not only moral biases but also rules, decisions and "reality" itself. Holmes helped to broaden our perspectives on law, but he did not provide a coherent theory of law or a workable basis for its study.[16]

Holmes tried to purge the study of law of ethical elements in order to promote clarity of vision. But he was also concerned to show the relevance of history, economics, statistics and the social sciences generally to the understanding of law. Hans Kelsen (1881–1973), on the other hand, sought to separate legal knowledge rigidly from both ethics and all the social sciences—indeed from all other disciplines. Like Holmes, Kelsen insisted on a sharp distinction between law and morality; but he was also concerned about the creeping contamination of legal science by psychology and sociology. For an objective legal science to be possible it had to be doubly pure.[17]

For many jurists Kelsen is the greatest legal positivist. More attention has been paid to him than to any other jurist this century: the "Kelsen industry" includes biographies, rival interpretations, and a host of critics. Let me rush in with a heretical interpretation that suggests that Kelsen's Pure Theory of Law provides the most cogent support for the idea that a pure expository science of law is impossible.[18]

Kelsen's central question was: "Is an objective legal science possible?" If one treats this as an epistemological question about the possibility and nature of legal knowledge, it can be interpreted to mean: "If pure knowledge of law is possible, what would it be knowledge of?" Kelsen's answer is a unitary system of norms, hierarchically arranged, and deriving their validity from a single basic norm.[19] What this implies is that pure legal knowledge is knowledge of a formal structure of norms. It is neither empirical nor grounded in ethics. However, Kelsen himself emphasised that this structure is independent of content; as soon as one attributes substantive content to a single norm, impurities inevitably enter in.[20] If by exposition of doctrine we mean the activity of describing its

157

content, it follows that all such exposition is "impure". To put the matter simply: Kelsen tells us what is presupposed by any purportedly "objective" statement of what the law is, but he also implies that the only pure legal knowledge is knowledge of formal structure, not content. If "science" encompasses an *activity* as well as a form of knowledge, then Kelsen's science can have no scientists—one cannot *do* pure exposition. On this interpretation, Kelsen's expository science self-destructs. Any actual expositor who claims to be applying Kelsen's method and to be doing pure science is misusing him. The architect of the Pure Theory is, on this interpretation, the leading authority for the view that objective, pure exposition is impossible.

I share the opinion that Holmes and Kelsen are among the most important figures in our heritage of Jurisprudence. But neither provides much practical help on the problems of legal scholarship as an activity nor a satisfactory basis for the core of law as a discipline. Realism opens Pandora's box and allows all disciplines to escape.[21] Cynical acid destroys the subject-matter; genuinely pure science induces paralysis; other claims to scientific purity are spurious.

(b) Subordination

A second response to the problem of developing a coherent theory of legal scholarship is a different kind of reductionism. Subordination is substituted for autonomy. Before the Enlightenment, Theology was Queen of the Sciences in the Western tradition. Law was just one subordinate enterprise within Theology. This is exemplified by the Thomist tradition of Natural Law and by other religious conceptions of law, such as one or other school of Islamic Law. What is rendered unto Caesar, how it is interpreted and what is valid or obligatory are determined by a higher law.

Since the Enlightenment the pecking order has been the subject of endless competition. Sociology, Social Darwinism, political economy, various schools of psychology, ethics, general philosophy, linguistics and more recently biology have all staked claims to leadership or even hegemony: "Law is a form of applied ethics"; "Law, as a social institution, is part of sociology"; "All law is politics"; "Law is superstructure, determined by its material base, and as such is to be explained by political economy"; "Psychology, as the science of human behaviour, is the key to law". The incantations are almost endless, subject to some circular law of fashions. Of the many attempts to treat law as a sub-branch of some other discipline, the most persistent, and still the most important, is the claim that it is a branch of applied ethics.

Normative conceptions: law as a branch of rational ethics

Apart from Natural Law, the two most powerful modern attempts in the common law tradition to ground the systematic study of law in a theory of political morality are Jeremy Bentham's Science of Legislation and Ronald Dworkin's liberal democratic theory of law as interpretation.[22]

Bentham's Science of Legislation, like all of his thought, is grounded in a particular version of utilitarianism. His "theory of fictions", which was also rooted in utility, encompassed a theory of language, a theory of knowledge and a method of analysis.[23] As we have seen, Bentham distinguished between Censorial Jurisprudence (concerned with law as it ought to be) and Expository Jurisprudence (concerned with law as it is). Censorial Jurisprudence, Bentham's main interest, involves the systematic application of utility in criticising existing laws and institutions and in designing new ones.[24]

Bentham is in the process of restoration to his rightful place as one of England's greatest jurists, but during the formative period of English academic law he exerted little direct influence on its development.[25] It was John Austin, Bentham's disciple, who was treated as "the father of English Jurisprudence" and his version of Expository or Analytical Jurisprudence was adopted and interpreted in such a way that it became largely divorced from any theory of value. Bentham's radical Censorial Jurisprudence was displaced for almost a century by a more scientistic Analytical Jurisprudence and legal positivism became associated with detached exegesis of law as it is.

Hart displaced Austin in the 1950s and helped to revive scholarly interest in Bentham, but his successor at Oxford, Ronald Dworkin, re-introduced a normative theory of law into English legal thought. Dworkin's general theory is complex, sophisticated and somewhat elusive and I shall not attempt to summarise it here.[26] Rather I shall try to consider some implications of his general views for legal scholarship.

In developing his ideas Dworkin has ranged far beyond law and has drawn on general philosophy, economics, literary theory and, above all, political philosophy. But he nevertheless finds a core for the discipline in the idea of law as a special form of social practice:

"Of course, law is a social phenomenon. But its complexity, function, and consequence all depend on one special feature of its structure. Legal practice, unlike many other social phenomena, is *argumentative*. Every actor in the practice understands that what it permits or requires depends on the truth of certain propositions that are given sense only by and within the practice; the practice consists in large part of deploying and arguing about these propositions. . . .This crucial argumentative aspect of legal practice can be studied in two ways or from two points of view. One is the external point of view of the sociologist or the historian, who asks why certain patterns of legal argument develop in some periods or circumstances rather than others, for example. The other is the internal point of view of those who make the claims."[27]

While both points of view are essential to understanding law, the external point of view is dependent upon an understanding of the internal perspectives of participants:

"The historian's perspective includes the participant's more pervasively, because the historian cannot understand law as an argumentative social practice, even enough to reject it as deceptive, until he has a participant's understanding, until he has his own sense of what counts as a good or bad argument within that practice. We need a social theory of law, but it must be jurisprudential just for that reason."[28]

In short, external study of law is dependent upon its internal study, which in turn is dependent on morality. Thus, for Dworkin, an external historical or social scientific account of law which ignores the internal point of view is "impoverished and defective, like innumerate histories of mathematics."[29] But why the emphasis on argumentation? To put the matter simply: one cannot understand, expound or apply legal rules without interpreting them and the best interpretation is that which is justified by the strongest argument. Argument about a contested question of law depends upon a two-stage process: it must fit the authoritative sources of law, what has gone before, but very often arguments about fit are not dispositive. In such "hard cases" any problem of interpretation must be resolved by reference to the underlying principles which justify the practices of law in a given system. These justificatory principles are principles of political morality which give a legal system its coherence and "integrity":

"Law is not exhausted by any catalogue of rules or principles, each with its own dominion over some discrete theater of behavior. Nor by any roster of officials and their powers each over part of our lives. Law's empire is defined by attitude, not by territory or power or process. . . . It is an interpretive, self-reflective attitude addressed to politics in the broadest sense. It is a protestant attitude that makes each citizen responsible for imagining what his society's public commitments to principles are, and what these commitments require in new circumstances."[30]

One need not accept in detail Dworkin's theories of adjudication, interpretation or justification to agree that exposition—in the sense of articulating propositions of law—involves interpretation and that choice of one interpretation in preference to another depends on justification. Similarly one need not agree with Dworkin's own account of law as a form of social practice to accept that "external" descriptions and explanations of a social practice have to take account of the internal points of view of participants.

Dworkin's general theory gives the jurist a distinctive role: to provide the most persuasive interpretation of a given legal system in terms of its internal coherence and its underlying justificatory principles of political morality. On this view any external account of law in terms of other disciplines is dependent on an internal, rational, argumentative jurisprudence in which systemic integrity, interpretation, and reasoning as well as rules and principles are central concepts.

Not surprisingly, Dworkin's theory is controversial. Apart from some of its details, each of the main elements has been challenged: a few behaviourists and economic analysts maintain that it is possible to give descriptions and explanations of legal behaviour of high predictive value without reference to the internal points of view of the participants involved[31]; others have challenged the systemic nature of our own or other so-called "systems"—the common law, says Brian Simpson, is more like a muddle than a system[32]; critical scholars and others have challenged the claims to coherence of Western "liberal" systems; and there are various kinds of sceptics about the alleged rationality of legal argumentation[33]; what many of the critics have in common is a view that Dworkin's perspective tends to give an idealised, aspirational account of law that has the tendency to gloss over the harsh realities of actual legal systems: it is a noble dream about law that does not provide an adequate vocabulary for dealing with its seamier side or with bottom-up perspectives. The Bad Man reasons, but does he argue? Others have doubted whether Dworkin's perspect-

161

ive either reflects the practice of expositors or provides them with a usable guide. I am not here concerned with the validity of these criticisms. What is significant in this context is that Dworkin places interpretation and argumentation about questions of law at the centre of his theory of law and offers one possible non-positivist basis for treating legal doctrine as the core of law as a discipline.

(c) A Body of Knowledge—the Negotiated Core

To most English lawyers, practising and academic, the word "core" refers to the subjects prescribed by the legal profession as granting exemption from the first or academic stage of qualification for practice. Balancing academic freedom and autonomy with professional control over entry is a delicate business, which almost inevitably in our system involves a compromise. Over the past 25 years conflict over this issue has sometimes soured relationships between academics and practitioners. In my view the conflict has been largely unnecessary, neither side comes well out of the story, and the issue has diverted attention from serious consideration of the nature of law as a discipline.

The modern starting-point for defining a "core" of undergraduate legal education is the Ormrod Report.[34] The context was a well-intentioned attempt to prescribe minimum conditions for recognition of law degrees for purposes of professional exemption in a way which would not unduly inhibit experimentation and pluralism at undergraduate level. The Committee recommended that any person holding a full-time law degree that included five subjects— Constitutional Law, Contract, Tort, Land Law and Criminal Law— should be deemed to have satisfied the "academic stage" of professional formation.[35] These "basic core subjects" were chosen on two grounds: first, that they were in fact already offered in all existing law degrees for purposes of exemption under the old system; and, secondly, "because it is difficult to devise an adequate course in English Law which does not include them."[36]

The first ground was unduly conservative; the second was intellectually dubious. Nevertheless the Ormrod formula might have been accepted as a reasonable compromise, if it had been implemented in both letter and spirit. Unfortunately, it was not. The first principle of curriculum planning, as with the selection of the World's Greatest Ever Cricket Team, is "Add one, Drop one". It is strange that a profession traditionally dominated by ex-public schoolboys never grasped this principle. The standard cricket team, outside Papua New Guinea, has only eleven players (and possibly a twelfth man) and has a balanced mixture of batsmen, bowlers, and a wicket keeper. One or two all-rounders are a bonus. The standard English law degree has twelve subjects, spread over three years of study.[37] The original Ormrod formula listed five subjects, with English Legal System there *sub silentio* because it was an almost automatic selection. This was equivalent to allocating half the places to rather stodgy batsmen, leaving the academics free to choose the other half. Some law schools wished to make one or more other subjects compulsory: most commonly Jurisprudence (the wicket-keeper?), sometimes Roman Law or Legal History or Comparative or Foreign Law or even a non-legal subject, such as Economics. Other subjects were listed as options, many of which looked suspiciously like additional batsmen.

The Ormrod settlement was subverted in a number of ways: first and most insidious was the "creeping core". The Bar and then the Law Society added Trusts in the seventies; recently they have pressed for the addition of EC Law, again without suggesting what should be dropped.[38] From time to time possible further additions were aired in England, sometimes because some senior practitioner had just come across a young lawyer who knew nothing of Mareva Injunctions or VAT or F.O.B. contracts. Equally important, most students would naturally choose options with an eye to their perceived vocational relevance, or to make life easier in their fourth, vocational year.

Student culture made its own interpretations of the conflicting messages that would come down from the profession on the practical importance of this or that substantive law subject or a European language or a knowledge of accounts.[39] By 1994 the *de facto* "core" effectively filled nearly two thirds of many curriculums and most students also chose vocationally "important" options. As staff-student ratios declined, more and more under subscribed options were felt to be in danger of being squeezed out; Welfare Law, Sociology of Law, Roman Law, Public International Law and Legal History were among those thought to be at risk. Meanwhile, in the "real world" new fields of law were opening up: Administrative law expanded in scope and importance; Restitution, Human Rights, Environmental Law and a host of other subjects attracted attention. In 1965 the inter-collegiate London LLM listed 30 options; by 1992 the list had grown to nearly 150.[40]

During the late 1980s a new theme developed: skills came into fashion and lists of desirable skills grew exponentially. One symptom of this further pressure on the undergraduate curriculum is worth remarking: some leading city law firms liked, or even pre-ferred, non-law graduates because they allegedly had uncluttered minds and better developed intellectual skills.[41] The legal profession had discovered belatedly that law graduates could not bowl. The academics countered by arguing that they were in the intellectual skills business too, so that soon the poor law student was faced with a steadily lengthening list of core *and* important subjects *and* a growing lists of desirable skills *and* messages that law degrees were not highly valued anyway. For the majority the period of study remained the same. In thirty years of diplomatic relations with the practising profession, I can only recall one public suggestion by a non-academic that a core subject might be dropped (it wasn't).[42] I never heard it suggested that one requirement might be that every law graduate should have studied at least one subject in depth.

The academics do not come out of the story much better. They fought attempts to prescribe the detailed content of core subjects and their methods of assessment, with mixed success; some law schools adopted rather free or cavalier interpretations of the official requirements; some negotiated private deals with the professional bodies; some resorted to other devices. By and large we stone-walled—not without success: for example, EC/EU law has yet to be officially added to the list of core subjects more than 20 years after the United Kingdom became a party to the Treaty of Rome. But for the most part the academic community submitted, out of what combination of conservatism, apathy or lack of self-confidence is a matter of opinion.[43] Perhaps the biggest failure was educational: academics are meant to be professional educators; the official leadership of both branches of the practising profession changes annually, and often has little sustained interest or expertise in education.[44] Only rarely did the academic lawyers assert their status as professional educators and advance a coherent and cogent rationale for undergraduate legal education and a principled solution to the problem of curriculum overload. Perhaps the biggest error was not to challenge the assumption that the "core" of under-graduate legal education could be defined in terms of coverage of subject-matter. I am afraid that I am one of those who think that the city law firms were often justified in preferring non-law graduates to law graduates, for some undergraduate legal education as currently practised can seriously damage one's intellectual health.[45]

The long-running conflict over the "core" was exacerbated by a semantic confusion: for some, the term referred to the irreducible minimum of knowledge that might be expected of a fledgling practitioner or a trainee—like basic anatomy in medicine; for some it referred to those foundation subjects which were necessary or useful building-blocks for the study of further subjects at the academic or vocational stage—it is difficult to study Labour Law or Commercial Law with no prior knowledge of Contract; for some, it was a way of trying to ensure some common ground among entrants to the vocational stage (a vain aspiration, since most law graduates have forgotten most of the details of what they were supposed to have learned in their first two years); for some, it really did represent some golden thread—the core as the centre or essence of English Law.

We are here concerned mainly with this last sense. On one view, echoed by the Ormrod Committee, it is difficult to conceive of a degree in English Law that does not include all of the original five or six subjects. A significant variant of this is the idea that these particular subjects represent a tradition or consensus or canon, albeit imposed, or a compromise which at least had the merit of providing a stable convention about the basics of the discipline. Furthermore, it could be argued, these subjects were as good vehicles as any for developing common law ways of reasoning and analysis. Torts, for example, may not be an indispensable prerequisite for "the legally- educated person", nor even for every intending practitioner, but it is widely regarded as an excellent vehicle for developing the analytical skills of "thinking like a lawyer" which many regard as the true core.[46] It is also a subject that almost every past law graduate has in fact studied and as such is part of the traditional canon of basic legal subjects.

There is more than a grain of truth in the last two views, but this idea of a subject-based core is vulnerable to some powerful lines of criticism: first, the list of subjects is quite arbitrary, with a distinct bias towards the problems of the propertied classes: why is knowledge of Torts or Trusts to be considered more important than Human Rights or Civil Liberties or Local Government or Welfare or Labour Law or Family Law? Why are theory, context and history excluded from the core? Why should a law degree focus solely on English Law (with a smidgen of EC law) in today's world? And, most important of all, can the "core" of a discipline be defined solely or mainly in terms of coverage of subject-matter?

In the late 1980s attempts were made to move towards defining the core curriculum for purposes of professional recognition in terms of fundamental principles and/or basic concepts rather than fields of law.[47] The professed intention was to make more space for variety and experimentation in undergraduate degrees. The first efforts produced a hostile reaction from academic lawyers. The debate continues and, at the time of writing, the issue is actively under consideration by the Lord Chancellor's Advisory Committee. So far the debate has revealed a quite broad consensus at a general level, but lack of agreement about what concepts and principles should be treated as fundamental or common, and some scepticism about the feasibility of basing criteria for recognition of degrees on such an abstract foundation. There are, however, signs of a greater willingness than in the past to move away from a knowledge-based core in this context. Recently the quality of discussion of the issues has also markedly improved and better data are available. However, what has been at stake has so far been much more a matter of delimiting spheres of influence as a political matter than any serious intellectual enquiry into the nature of a discipline. Perhaps the best that can be hoped for in this context is a reasonable compromise based on informed negotiation about the complex issues concerning the allocation of responsibility for professional formation of intending practitioners.

(d) Skills, Crafts and Technology[48]

In the early 1990s the Inns of Court School of Law in Gray's Inn Place offered the only postgraduate vocational course for those intending to practice at the English Bar. If you had visited it on a normal working day, you would probably have found groups of students doing practical training exercises on such matters as case-work skills, conference skills, negotiation and advocacy. Others might have been working on their own on exercises on legal research, opinion writing and drafting. Almost none would have been attending lectures or tutorials on substantive law. Although there is still formal instruction on Evidence and Procedure, the Bar Vocational Course, which began in 1989, represented a radical switch from emphasis on knowledge to emphasis on skills. The selected skills are developed largely through practical exercises, which as far as is feasible simulate the kind of work that young barristers can expect to do in the early years of practice. This represented a genuinely sharp break from the past in objectives, methods, and spirit. In 1993 the Law Society introduced a new

Legal Practice Course, taught in a number of centres, which moved in a similar direction, although it claimed to maintain more of a balance between knowledge and skills than the Bar Vocational Course.

These reforms could be interpreted as the belated introduction of the Ormrod Report after a delay of 20 years. They are in fact part of an international skills movement that has a long history, but which gained momentum throughout much of the common law world in the 1980s. Concern with "skills" has been a persistent theme in the Western educational tradition, as is illustrated by the long and involved history of the study of rhetoric. Langdell's revolution at Harvard in 1870 is generally interpreted as representing a radical switch of emphasis from knowledge to the direct learning of a limited number of intellectual skills. For more than a century the idea of skills has been at the centre of internal debates within American legal education about objectives, priorities, methods, competence, and competing ideologies. Perhaps the second important development in the United States was the move to broaden the range of skills developed in the academy by linking educational objectives to analysis of what lawyers in fact do.[49] On the negative side, the failure to develop "clinical lawyer schools", as Jerome Frank and others had urged, was probably as significant.[50] A sharp distinction between know-what and know-how is sometimes challenged by educationalists; nevertheless, such switches in practice do involve substantial changes.

Outside North America, the idea of direct teaching of lawyering skills through simulation and clinics was slow to catch on. The predominant view of legal practitioners was that legal practice was a mixture of innate talent and ineffable art that could only be spotted and developed through practical experience with live clients. Hard luck on the clients, but that is life. This view is still sufficiently widespread that formal skills teaching has been largely confined to the most elementary levels and, outside North America, advanced and specialist training and continuing legal education remain largely underdeveloped. Formal training is almost entirely restricted to minimum competence in respect of some basics.

One impetus behind the recent skills movement was a search for alternatives to apprenticeship: in some newly independent African countries it was realised that the conditions for apprenticeship just did not exist; elsewhere traditional apprenticeship came under sustained attack. In England the profession's response was gradually to improve and tighten up the apprentice system and, after Ormrod, the vocational year was designed to bridge the gap between the academic stage and apprenticeship rather than to replace it. Given the increasing difficulty of legal practice, the survival of apprenticeship in an improved form was almost certainly a healthy outcome, but it delayed the development of formal skills training in this country. When the new courses were eventually introduced, they were able to build on an extensive body of experience in the Commonwealth and the United States, as well as in industry and other occupations.[51]

The modern skills movement, though diverse and controversial, is guided by a recognisable orthodoxy. This might be summarised as follows[52]: One of the main objectives of legal training is to enable intending practitioners to achieve minimum standards of competency in basic skills before being let loose on the public; what constitutes such skills depends on a job analysis of what lawyers of different kinds in fact do; lawyer-jobs can be analysed into transactions or operations, which can be further broken down into tasks or sub-operations; a skill or skill-cluster denotes the ability to carry out a task to a specified standard. Minimum, acceptable competence is to be distinguished from excellence. It is the main function of primary legal education and training to ensure that all entrants to the profession exhibit minimum competence in a range of skills, measured by actual performances which satisfy articulated criteria under specified conditions. Problem-solving is, in this view, seen either as one of the most important basic skills or, as some would have it, the master skill under which all lawyering tasks can be subsumed. Finally, there is an ethical dimension: the standard lists of skills include ability to recognise and to resolve ethical dilemmas.[53] Issues of ethics, values and professional responsiblity are linked to the learning of each skill—hence the idea of "a pervasive approach" to professional responsibility.[54]

Linking professional training to job-analysis makes obvious sense. Some of the early efforts were open to the criticism that they were too wedded to a crude form of bureaucratic rationalism that emphasised observable behaviour and discrete, measurable outcomes, while down-playing intuitive, holistic and more subtle aspects of competence.[55] There has been a tendency to produce longer and longer lists of skills without much analysis of the relations between them nor any serious attempt to establish priorities. A more discriminating use of occupational psychology and the sociology of the professions is gradually beginning to underpin these new developments.

Sociology has taught us that legal professions tend to be highly stratified and much more fragmented and diverse than has sometimes been assumed.[56] It no longer makes sense, if it ever did, to talk of *the* skills of *the* lawyer—legal practice is just too varied. In England in recent years legal practice has been changing and diversifying at a pace that it has made even the best sociological studies out of date. Diversification has created considerable dilemmas within the Ormrod structure, especially at the vocational stage. One central issue is: how to provide basic training at that stage for people from varied backgrounds who will disperse into a variety of types of practice which themselves will be in process of continual, often rapid, change?

A switch from knowledge to skills does not necessarily solve the problem of determining a core for training purposes. Instead of asking: what should every lawyer know? the question becomes: what should every lawyer be able to do? But if legal practice is both varied and changing, is this a meaningful question? One common response to the question is to move to a more general level: vocational training should emphasise transferable skills rather than specific techniques—for example, ability to express oneself clearly both orally and in writing rather than how to write a particular kind of letter or draft a specific legal instrument. If one asks: "is there a common element to all such generic skills?", it is tempting to suggest that they can all be subsumed under one master-skill: problem-solving.[57]

At a consultative conference on "the initial stage" of legal education organised by the Lord Chancellor's Advisory Committee on Legal Education and Conduct in 1993, as part of the search for a new core, participants were asked: what should every lawyer know? What should every lawyer be able to do? Semi-seriously I suggested that it might be interesting to substitute historian for lawyer in this context. It would be strange to look for a common core of knowledge that was shared by historians—unless one adopted some Tory politicians' conception of history as a collection of established facts. On that view the dates of the Kings and Queens of England might be said to be the basic, quintessential core of English History. If one switched to skill, one might say that every historian should be able to solve historical problems and present his or her findings in an appropriate form.

The analogy was rejected in discussion as not very helpful, because "[t]he skills that were common to all historians were of a very general nature, for example, only general research skills. It was essential to their task that they also had a great deal of specialist knowledge of particular areas."[58] On the other hand, lawyers, like other professionals, were responsible for dealing with the immediate practical problems of members of the public, who expected them "to have instantly available a core of knowledge which would enable them to deal with common problems."[59] This response is revealing. The point of the analogy was to question two assumptions underlying the questions that had been put to us: (a) that there is a shared body of knowledge that every lawyer needs to know; and (b) that the basic skills shared by all lawyers can be stated at a more specific level than "problem solving". In short, under modern conditions, can any practising lawyer any more than any historian claim to be a generalist? Of course, historians and practising lawyers differ in many ways: for example, lawyers have to deal responsibly with immediate practical problems; clients have expectations about their knowledge and competence; if these expectations include an encyclopaedic knowledge of the law and general all-round competence to deal with any legal problem they are usually unrealistic. As with knowledge, so with skills, the idea of a core of legal competence looks fragile.

The idea of problem-solving is undoubtedly very useful in analysing the nature of lawyers' work; it may well be the case that there are some common elements in respect of attitude and generic intellectual skills; there is a close historical association between liberal education and transferable intellectual skills, dating back to the days of Greats at Oxford and the gentleman amateur. One might even venture a bold generalisation: the role of any individual lawyer or law firm is to help clients to further their own objectives and to solve their problems within the limits of the competence of the lawyer or firm and the legal and ethical constraints upon their role. But it is impossible without more to translate such generalities into practical training programmes or even prescriptions for liberal education. The competent practising lawyer and the legal scholar, like the good historian, often needs to be able to master a great deal of detailed knowledge relevant to their specific situation. Both need to know and respect the extent of their own ignorance. The historically and the legally educated person both need experience of solving highly specific historical and legal problems respectively—but doing history and doing law are in fact extraordinarily varied activities. Ability to master large amounts of detail and to handle mixed masses of data[60] is common to many kinds of prob-

The Quest For a Core

lem-solving—how much detail is appropriate is context specific. By itself the idea of problem-solving is too general to be very helpful.[61]

(e) Pluralism—Let Many Flowers Bloom

This selective tour of a few prominent attempts to construct a coherent core for the discipline of law reflects a variety of concerns and purposes: Kelsen's Pure Theory, for example, is primarily an epistemological quest for a distinct form of legal knowledge within a quite strong conception of the autonomy of disciplines. Ronald Dworkin's philosophical assumptions and his legal theory are significantly different from Kelsen's, but both emphasise the idea of law as an integrated normative system. Dworkin locates the distinctive feature of law in an argumentative attitude that is part of an activity; Kelsen identifies what might be unique about legal knowledge and legal science as a product rather than a practice. Attempts to define a core curriculum for general or professional legal studies in terms of a settled body of knowledge, basic concepts or basic legal skills operate at a different level and are more pragmatic and contingent: they are mainly efforts to develop a coherent and appropriate system of initial preparation for legal practice in the context of one particular legal culture and higher education system. Judge Harry Edwards in arguing for a return to "practical doctrinal scholarship" as the primary activity of American law schools is concerned with both professional training and the provision of important services to practitioners and judges by institutions that are assumed to be there mainly to serve the profession. Given time, we could explore other attempts to establish cores or coherences for the legal academic enterprise or particular sectors of it for specific purposes. The examples I have chosen illustrate the diversity, the fragility and the persistence of such efforts.

In the post-modern era there is a general tendency to emphasise contingency and to resist closure. There is a more general scepticism about the autonomy of disciplines. So why not agree that the possibilities are infinite and accept unfettered pluralism? There are other factors that may contribute to the growth of pluralism: the academic legal enterprise is now sufficiently large and its subject-matter so diverse as to require some division of labour and more opportunities for specialisation; the principle of free enquiry encourages multiple perspectives and a free market in ideas; some attempts have been made to counteract the tendencies of the rigid departmental system in our universities to reinforce "artificial bar-

171

riers" between disciplines and inhibit the growth of inter-disciplinary co-operation and new intellectual configurations; in law, post-modernists, it has been noted, are naturally attracted by legal pluralism[62]; it might even be suggested that the common law, with its emphasis on the pragmatic and particularities, is at its best when "muddling through", which may be pluralism under another name.[63]

In earlier chapters I have tried to describe the new pluralism in academic law and I have not concealed my general liking for it. Pluralism is even becoming respectable. For example, the Lord Chancellor's Advisory Committee in its 1994 consultative paper on the initial or academic stage of legal education explicitly made diversity a key-stone of its approach and has suggested the abandonment of a knowledge-based core for law degrees.[64] However, significantly, it has tried to set some limits to unfettered pluralism and talks in terms of substituting a "prescribed common element" for the core rather than totally abandoning it.[65]

The temper of the times may be strongly anti-reductionist, but this in turn breeds a reaction. There is, for example, a common vocabulary for attacking do-as-you-like pluralism: terms like eclecticism, dilettantism, even nihilism are frequently invoked by commentators on the intellectual scene. Gunther Teubner, himself a leading exponent of a form of systems theory, neatly sums up one important aspect of the situation:

> "Since modern society is characterized on the one side by a fragmentation into different *epistèmes*, on the other side by their mutual interference, legal discourse is caught in an 'epistemic trap.' The simultaneous dependence on and independence from other social discourses is the reason why modern law is permanently oscillating between positions of cognitive autonomy and heteronomy."[66]

For most of my career I have been committed to developing broader and more varied approaches to the study of law both as a theorist and activist. The labels and slogans attached to this endeavour—such as "realism", "law-in-context", "socio-legal studies", "broadening the study of law from within"—are not particularly significant; indeed, they have sometimes been a handicap because they have invited attempts to define them in theoretical ways which are generally misconceived. I do not believe that the ideas associated with realism and related terms are on their own sufficiently precise or specific to ground a distinctive theoretical or methodological perspective for law as a discipline.[67] Rather the aim has been to free legal studies from the grip of a rather narrow orthodoxy rather than to replace it with a new one. Nevertheless, there are both theoretical puzzlements and practical problems that need to be confronted by those who are sympathetic to the general enterprise. At this stage in the development of academic law I believe that many of these problems are unresolved. Substantial progress has been made, but there is still an unfinished agenda.[68]

One problem for those concerned with broadening the study of law is how to keep a general sense of direction and particular enterprises manageable. The central idea of mainstream American Realism was encapsulated in the proposition that for most purposes, especially for understanding legal phenomena, the study of rules alone is not enough.[69] This raises questions about what is enough? If the purpose is quite limited and clearly defined, it may be quite easy to provide a workable answer. If the purpose is more general or open-ended, then almost endless vistas and lines of enquiry may open up. This is, of course, not peculiar to law. I have sometimes called this the Pandora's Box Problem.[70] The metaphor needs to be used sparingly, for Pandora, the first woman, fashioned by Hephaestus on the command of Zeus, is notable not only for her curiosity. The story of her box (or jar) is nicely ambiguous. According to Hesiod, Zeus gave Pandora a jar that contained all manner of miseries and evils; when, contrary to instructions, she opened it they flew out all over the world and contaminated it; when the lid was replaced, only Delusive Hope remained. Those who are more sympathetic to the social sciences will prefer the later version which, instead of miseries, substitutes blessings which would have been preserved for the human race had the jar not been opened by one of its members. Both versions share one moral: unless you rein in your curiosity, things get out of control.[71]

I suspect that one reason for the seeming fragmentation and pluralism of modern legal studies is a reluctance to confront some of the problems of broadening academic law in a coherent way that combines appropriate theory (generally middle order) with explicit concern for method. In the professional sector the skills movement has made some progress in this direction for relatively clear and limited purposes. It is early days and there are some distinct limitations: the job analysis of lawyers' operations is still rather crude; concern with minimum competence has overshadowed the exploration of excellence; and the predominating educational theory is too bureaucratic-rational for my taste. Nevertheless, the new skills orthodoxy is beginning to build up a coherent picture of many tasks undertaken by lawyers and what is involved in doing them reasonably well. That is at least a start. In this area professional training is ahead of undergraduate legal education in respect of theory as well as practice.[72]

(f) Something To Do With Rules?

The preceding sections illustrate both the persistence and the contingency of attempts to find a single core or essence for law as a discipline. To try to purify legal knowledge of all non-legal elements or to treat the discipline of law as merely a sub-branch of another field of study or to define a core in terms of a settled body of knowledge, even if only settled by convention, or to locate the core of professional practice in a common set of generic skills are all too simple. One cannot reduce a whole discipline to a single formula.

The sociology of knowledge teaches us that academic division of labour is historically contingent. The academic ethic suggests that it is contrary to the spirit of free enquiry to prescribe artificial boundaries between disciplines. In jurisprudence it is now generally accepted that attempts to delimit the field by seeking a general definition of law are doomed to fail; the subject matter is too varied and elusive.[73] So our picture of a discipline needs to be sufficiently flexible and open-ended to encompass a diversity of subject-matters, perspectives and methods and to impose no artificial constraints on potential lines on enquiry. On the other hand, the idea of a discipline does suggests some limits to do-as-you-like pluralism. One may acknowledge grey areas and paradigm shifts, but there are some activities which clearly count as studying law and some which do not.

In the context of an attempt to explore the current state and future potential of the academic legal enterprise in England, it may be enough to resort to robust common sense, without pursuing too many theoretical hares. Just as it is difficult, though not impossible, to imagine mathematics without numbers or psychology without some concept of psyche or mind (however contested), so one may ask: is it possible to conceive of the study of law without some notion of rules or norms? In other words, is not a focus on rules a necessary, if not a sufficient, condition for an activity to count as studying law?

This is a jurisprudential minefield, but let me try to deal with it in a relatively simple way. To start with a semantic point. Terms like "rule" have many usages. For example, when Dworkin attacked Hart's concept of law as a system of rules, he restricted the term to categorical precepts that have an all-or-nothing quality in contrast with principles, which are more open-ended but are, in his view, an integral part of law.[74] However, "rule" is often used in a broader sense, as a generic term which encompasses all kinds of general prescription, including principles, precepts, maxims, guidelines, standards, conventions, and customs. In this usage it is synonymous with the more technical "norm". The broader usage best fits the claims that rules are a central and necessary focus of legal studies or that law is a normative discipline.[75]

Such claims have broad support from jurists who are usually seen as having quite different theories of law; but they have not gone unchallenged. For example, with one possible exception, none of the jurists discussed in this chapter denied the centrality of rules in law or its normative character. Bentham, Hart, Kelsen, Natural Lawyers, and Dworkin, for example, have different conceptions of law, but all affirm its normative character. Holmes and other American Realists have sometimes been accused of giving an account of law in terms of brute fact, using terms such as habit and prediction in a non-normative sense. The standard defence is to concede that such an account would be mistaken, but to maintain that this is a misinterpretation of their ideas: Holmes's Bad Man who is only concerned with prediction is just one legal actor among many[76]. Similarly the recent shift of emphasis in legal education from knowledge of legal doctrine to "skills" does not involve denial of the importance of doctrine nor the abandonment of the idea of "rule". Negotiation, advocacy, drafting, and other lawyers' operations not only take place "in the shadow of the law" but are also constituted and regulated by statutes, conventions, guidelines and other norms. They are largely rule-governed activities.

It is worth pausing here to make some points about "rule-scepticism", which has often been the source of unnecessary misunderstandings and distortions. I have suggested that the central precept of "realism", "law in context" or other movements to broaden the study of law can be rendered: "For the purpose of understanding law, and for most practical legal purposes, the study of rules alone is not enough." One way of justifying this proposition can be stated succinctly: rules are not self-creating, self-identifying, self-articulating, self-interpreting, self-applying, self-implementing or self-justifying. It is almost invariably misleading to treat rules as things in themselves without reference to the contexts of their creation, articulation, operation and so on; any account of such rule-handling activities has to include extraneous factors (which may include other rules, but is not confined to them). What other factors are relevant or significant, what is "enough", or what appropriately counts as context typically depends on the specific purpose and context of a particular study or other activity. The maxim "the study of rules alone is not enough", itself a rule-of-thumb, far from denying the importance of rules, assumes that they are in some sense central.[77]

Secondly, there are many varieties of "rule-scepticism". The term is sometimes applied to those who emphasise the elusiveness or ambiguity of rules or the many other conditions of doubt that give rise to difficulties in their interpretation and application. Legal pluralism, which emphasises the co-existence of different "rule-systems", is sceptical of "monist" theories which try to integrate all legal (or other) rules within a single, internally consistent, system. These are examples of scepticism about certain claims about law, but they involve no necessary commitment to strong scepticism, such as the idea that all talk of rules is illusory or meaningless.[78] Most alleged "rule-sceptics" in jurisprudence, including most realists and critical legal scholars, have tended to distance themselves from strong versions of scepticism or nihilism.[79] However, even the possibility of strong rule-scepticism can be accommodated within the idea of law as a normative discipline, just as moral scepticism or strong relativism can be treated as part of ethics—a challenge to basic assumptions about the enterprise as a whole.[80]

To say that rules, in a broad sense, are a central focus of any meaningful study of law may be correct, but on its own it is not much more informative than the claim that problem-solving is central to legal practice. Law is by no means unique in having rules as a central focus; ethics, logic and linguistics could make similar, though not identical, claims.

Furthermore, one fruitful way of looking at rules or norms is as responses to problems.[81] From this perspective, rules are prescriptions and in law, as in medicine, it is generally sensible for diagnosis to precede prescription.[82] Rules may be necessary and central to the study of law, but in many contexts they are not a good *starting-point* for analysis. Moreover, what constitutes a "problem" is relative to standpoint, depending on the vantage-point, role, values and purposes of the person(s) for whom something is problematic, whether they be participant or observer or in-between. On this analysis, conceiving of law in terms of rules or norms leads directly back to the idea of problem-solving, which we have seen is itself both problematic and open-ended.

In the first chapter, I adopted Karl Llewellyn's law-jobs theory as a useful framework for considering the subject-matter of the study of law from a broad point of view. The legal records project illustrated how this theory can be illuminating and useful for a specific purpose. The law-jobs theory conceives of law (or law-government) as an institution specialised to meeting certain problems or needs. It treats rules as only one aspect of institutions.[83] In my view, the law jobs theory deserves to be refined and used more than it has been to date, not least because it offers one way of providing a broad and flexible framework for legal studies. But it is only one from our rich stock of theories and it comes from a particular sociological tradition, functionalism, which has its own limitations and which is highly controversial.[84] The pluralism of our stock of theories confirms that we may have to accept, and I would suggest, welcome a corresponding pluralism in our intellectual enterprises.

The question remains: what, if anything, is there that is unique or special that the institutionalised discipline of law as we know it can add to our understanding of social life or to human knowledge in general? That is the subject of the next section.

LENSES OF THE LAW

The crew was complete: it included a Boots —
A maker of Bonnets and Hoods —
A Barrister, brought to arrange their disputes —
And a Broker, to value their goods.

A Billiard-marker, whose skill was immense,
Might perhaps have won more than his share —
But a Banker, engaged at enormous expense,
Had the whole of their cash in his care.[85]

When Lewis Carroll was asked why all the members of his crew for hunting the Snark had occupations beginning with B, he replied: "Why not?"[86] When pressed about the meaning of the Hunting or what a Snark is, he regularly said that he did not know.[87]

If I am asked what can the discipline of law contribute to general understanding or our intellectual life, I am inclined to adopt a similar posture to Carroll's. If asked why I would include a law-trained person in some multi-disciplinary team that was setting out to study a particular society or to sit on a committee on social science research, I might well reply: "Why not?" And, at a more abstract level, it may be wise not to stay for an answer for questions about the meaning or purpose of the pursuit of truth.

Some quite mundane reasons could be given to justify such seeming evasions: what combination of knowledge, skills and experience is likely to be useful for an enquiry or project depends in large part on the nature and purpose of the enterprise; there is no single prototype of "the academic lawyer"; and, as Carroll's Baker reminds us, individual character may be as important as occupational skills in determining suitability for a task.

Earlier, I suggested that initial scepticism about the search for a core or essence of the enterprise of studying law is justified at a general level, but that there may sometimes be good reasons, intellectual or pragmatic, for settling on a canon of basic subjects or concepts or a list of fundamental skills or some other "core" for specific, contingent purposes. If at a general level one finds a common focus in rules or problem-solving or institutions, for example, far from identifying what is unique about legal studies, this illustrates the extent of the overlap and the continuities between legal and other enquiries.

Such mild scepticism is not evasion, if one believes that academic enquiry is both open-ended in respect of purposes and open to many interpretations. The subject-matter of law is so wide and so fluid, and the purposes of its study so varied that refusal to give definitive or reductive general answers is fully justified. But it would be unsatisfactory, having offered a guided tour of my home ground, if I refused to venture any opinions at all about the value of what is on offer.

One of the main themes has been that neither legal education nor legal scholarship can afford to be self-contained. Throughout I have emphasised the continuities between law as a subject of study and other disciplines and between law as practice and other practical activities. I have suggested that law as a subject is not as impenetrable nor as mystifying as it has sometimes appeared, but rather it is an important part of everyday social life. It might be objected that I have said a good deal about the history, needs and internal problems of law schools, but I have not directly addressed the question: is there anything unique or special that the institutionalised discipline of law has to offer to outsiders? Indeed, one might even ask: what, if anything, do academic lawyers have to offer to the social understanding of law itself?

As with the search for a core, I do not think that such questions are susceptible to useful answers at a very general level. This is not to denigrate the achievements and potential of what in this country is a relatively young discipline. The newspaper exercise suggested that reading texts with legal lenses may suggest questions or insights that might be overlooked by others. Law viewed as technology has a long history of inventions, devices, concepts and solutions to problems: not only are there great monuments such as Justinian's *Institutes*, The Code Napoleon, or the Constitution of the United States, but also more mundane inventions, such as the trust, the letter of credit, and many procedures for decision are legal artefacts that are taken almost as much for granted as the telephone or the paper-clip. But most of these are collective, largely anonymous, products of a craft-tradition rather than the work of great individual scholars, practitioners or law-givers[88]; and nearly all of them could exist in a country without law schools.

There is, of course, a substantial heritage of scholarly and theoretical literature about law, some of which deserves to be more widely known. There may not be a Nobel Prize for law, but from time to time academic lawyers have made important contributions to other fields: Maitland to medieval history; Hart and Honore' on causation; Llewellyn and Hoebel's case-method in anthropology; Dicey and others on constitutional theory are examples. But these are mainly particular achievements. If pressed for an answer at a general level the best that I can do is suggest that the main thing that academic lawyers have to offer is local knowledge of an extraordinarily interesting and important subject-matter and of a rich, largely under-exploited accumulation of primary sources.

Some of my colleagues might object that this underplays the special qualities of the legal mind, or in James Boyd White's bold phrase, the legal imagination. Let us pause to consider this suggestion.

It is sometimes said that the main function of a university legal education is to develop the skills of "thinking like a lawyer". This phrase has attracted a good deal of criticism, not least because it suggests a number of negative associations: narrow-minded; unreflective; tricky; manipulative; venal; or any of the other qualities that provide a basis for anti-lawyer jokes.[89]

179

Within the legal community a distinction is sometimes drawn between "lawyerlike" (positive) and "legalistic" (negative) qualities.[90] This can be interpreted as an attempt to isolate the more admired aspects of "the legal mind". One can identify the qualities which are commonly valued in this context from the ever-growing lists of intellectual skills that are produced in connection with modern skills training. The intellectual qualities that are expected of "the good lawyer" in this context include ability to express oneself clearly both orally and in writing; ability to distinguish the relevant from the irrelevant; ability to construct and present a valid, cogent and appropriate argument[91]; ability to identify issues and to ask questions in a sequence appropriate to the particular context; general problem-solving skills; library research skills; and, increasingly within legal education, ability to spot ethical dilemmas and issues.[92]

A striking feature of standard lists of such intellectual skills is that almost none of them is unique to law: skills of analysis, synthesis, reasoning, communication and problem-solving are aspects of clear thinking which are valued in most disciplines and which are sometimes claimed as transferable. They are, of course, combined in different ways with different priorities in different contexts. The 'case for law' as a good basis for general education rests in large part on the claim that the subject-matter of the discipline is potentially an excellent vehicle for developing such general intellectual skills[93]; conversely, in the English context, the justification for allowing non-law graduates to follow an accelerated route to qualifying as practitioners is grounded on the premise that the basic intellectual skills required of lawyers can be developed as well by other disciplines and all that they need extra is a bit of legal knowledge, some specific techniques, and socialisation into the milieu of one or other kind of legal practice. On this view, the phenomenon of some law firms preferring nonlaw graduates can be interpreted as an implicit criticism of the practice of much undergraduate legal education.

Within legal education these intellectual skills are supposed to be acquired through the study of a body of primary materials which, as we have seen, cover most areas of social life, are well-documented and accessible.[94] We have also seen that in practice only a small part of these materials are regularly exploited for educational and scholarly purposes within law schools.[95] Trial records, legal instruments and many other legal records are neglected by academic lawyers as well as scholars in other disciplines. On this interpretation there is little that is unique or special about "the legal mind" except the ability to apply some general intellectual skills in some specific kinds of context.

I have suggested that if there is anything that is unique or special that academic lawyers have to offer at a general level to colleagues from other disciplines it is local knowledge of an important area. Let me conclude by illustrating this by one last case-study taken from one of my fields of special interest, evidence.

In an important recent book on *The Evidential Foundations of Probabilistic Reasoning* David Schum, a psychologist, has attempted to synthesise basic ideas and insights about evidence and inference from, among others, law, philosophy, logic, history, probability theory, semiotics, artificial intelligence and psychology.[96] Evidence and inference are of concern to any discipline and practical activity in which conclusions and decisions are reached on the basis of incomplete information.[97] In practical affairs accountants, actuaries, air traffic controllers, detectives, doctors, engineers, insurers, intelligence analysts, meteorologists, and sailors are among those who have to make decisions on the basis of inferences from evidence. Problems of evidence, proof and probability have accordingly been much debated in a variety of disciplines. In popular culture problems of inference are at the core of detective stories and other mysteries. Sherlock Holmes regularly features in the literature of several disciplines.[98]

Schum states that legal scholarship on evidence "forms the major source of inspiration for anyone interested in a general study of the general properties and uses of evidence".[99] Schum commends the study of evidence in law to other disciplines especially in respect of dealing with complex bodies of evidence and reconstructing unique particular events, and in relation to some particular aspects of inference, such as cascaded inferences (inference upon inference), ways of testing the authenticity and credibility of evidentiary sources, ancillary evidence and second-hand or indirect evidence, such as hearsay. The general theme of his analysis is that the complexity of inferential tasks has often been underestimated in some disciplines or treated with resignation in others, whereas in law we have been forced as a practical matter routinely to grapple with at least some of these difficulties. A rich body of scholarship, claims Schum, has grown up around these practical activities; much of it is of direct relevance to scholars and practitioners in other disciplines and activities concerned with evidence and inference, but it has to date only been exploited spasmodically.

For example, when we have masses of information we do not know how to deal with it:

> "Our current methods for gathering, storing, retrieving, and transmitting information far exceed, in number and effectiveness, our methods for putting this information to inferential use in the drawing of conclusions from it."[1]

Schum gives credit to John Henry Wigmore, the American legal scholar, for making major strides in filling this "methodological gap" by devising a method for marshalling and structuring a mixed mass of evidence within a single argument. In so doing, Wigmore anticipated modern developments in respect of influence diagrams and fuzzy logic.[2]

It is pleasing to hear a distinguished outsider making such claims for the relevance of one's subject to other disciplines. On the whole I agree with Schum's thesis, but I would enter a few caveats. First, he is perhaps too generous in giving credit to the contributions of evidence scholarship rather than to the practical context of law. As Schum himself observes, the courts have been a clearing-house for almost every variety of evidence and for expert witnesses from many fields.[3] In dealing with "mixed masses" of different kinds of evidence from varied sources, courts and lawyers have regularly had to ask questions about the credibility, reliability and authenticity of the sources and how the evidence relates to the issues in dispute, especially in respect of relevance and weight. Nearly all disputed cases involve problems of proof which typically have to be tackled dialectically by interested, often skilled, adversaries. Because some cases involve a great quantity of evidence, practising lawyers have had to develop methods of analysing and marshalling complex masses of data and presenting them in a clear and orderly fashion.[4] Until recently most disciplines have tended to over-simplify by underestimating the complexity of most inferential tasks. If law has been less prone to fall into this trap, it is largely because its raw materials, real life cases, force at least some of these complexities to the surface in the crucible of adversarial argument.

However, the record of evidence scholarship is rather uneven. During the past century Anglo-American legal scholarship has focused almost entirely on the Law of Evidence, especially the artificial rules of admissibility. With a few notable exceptions, it has until recently neglected the wider aspects of evidence and proof.

The Law of Evidence is a rather disorderly, technical and unappealing subject that is especially puzzling to non-lawyers. By focusing on it, legal scholars may have inadvertently obscured the potential interest of the broader field of legal proof to outsiders. This is an example of academic law not living up to its potential.[5]

However, in the work of Bentham, Wigmore and other pioneers and in "the new evidence scholarship" there is nonetheless a great wealth of literature of general interest, even if it has been underexploited within legal education. Furthermore, the logic of judicial proof and the Law of Evidence by and large share a common body of key concepts, and there is a good deal of illumination to be had from the experience and learning that have been built up around such concepts as hearsay, corroboration, presumptions, circumstantial evidence, prejudicial effect, and standards of proof, despite the narrow focus and the tendency to exaggerate the importance of the Law of Evidence as a body of rules.

Another caveat is that "the new evidence scholarship" is a genuinely multi-disciplinary enterprise. Law may have a lot to offer, but equally it has already learned a great deal from other disciplines and could learn even more. Psychologists have told us about the reliability of confessions and different kinds of testimony, especially identification evidence and testimony of child witnesses in sex abuse cases.[6] Forensic science has made great advances in such areas as DNA, the analysis of traces, and the use of modern technology in police investigation. Students of linguistics and semiotics, such as Umberto Eco, have illuminated aspects of evidence discourse. Jonathan Cohen, a philosopher, has provoked a major series of debates in law, statistics, psychology and diagnostic medicine about Baconian or inductive probability. Probability theorists are trying to fill a gap in our understanding of how the probative force of evidence might be systematically assessed and combined. Developments in computer applications promise to make very significant contributions to problems of processing and marshalling masses of evidentiary data; and though some of us are sceptical about the likely contribution of the computer to decision-making, every sceptical move is seen as a challenge to be surmounted by more refined analysis.[7] Last, but not least, David Schum himself, a psychologist, who has taught engineers, intelligence analysts, and law students among others, has contributed as much illumination to law as he has gleaned from it.

Finally, Schum rightly points to the analytical complexities of arguments about evidence in legal and in other contexts. But there is a further aspect that needs to be stressed: contextual complexity. At a multi-disciplinary conference in Boston in 1986, the subject was Probability and Inference in the Law of Evidence.[8] At one stage there was a series of rather sharp exchanges between proponents of different theories of probability—all non-lawyers. Professor Richard Lempert, a distinguished sociologist of law and evidence scholar, commented that as a lawyer he felt like a Belgian peasant observing a war between the Great Powers being fought out on his territory. Later several commentators have developed the analogy to make the point that in carrying controversy and enquiry from one discipline into the territory of another it is important to have some local knowledge of the terrain.[9] To lawyers some of the legal examples used by non-lawyers in debating issues of probabilities and proof do not make sense because they ignore procedural and other "local" factors that lawyers would take into account in actual cases. This raises a general issue fundamental to inter-disciplinary work. I have argued elsewhere that psychological research into eyewitness identification has focused too narrowly on the reliability of such evidence in court to the exclusion of a wide range of other issues of both theoretical and practical importance, because psychologists have uncritically assumed a formalistic, jury-centred and essentially naive picture of the problem of eyewitness identification.[10] Similarly, some of the standard examples used in debates about mathematical and non-mathematical probabilities do not make legal sense and probably do not illustrate the points for which they are used, because they overlook procedural and policy considerations which bear on lawyers' perceptions of the problems.[11] Schum is correct in saying that problems of inference and evidence arise in a wide variety of contexts and that much can be learned from looking at these problems across disciplines. But in all of these contexts local knowledge is essential in order to grasp the complex interactions between logical and contextual factors. That is why one needs local guides.

Notes

[1] Mark Twain, *Tom Sawyer Abroad* (1894) Chap. 1.

[2] Becher, *op. cit.*, at p. 37. A useful survey of the literature on "the quest for order" in most disciplines is Colin Evans, *Language People* (1988) Chap. 8.

[3] The greater interest of civilians in "legal science" is variously explained: the longer history of the university study of civil law, a greater concern about scientific status or about practical influence or more contingent factors. In the Anglo-American tradition few lawyers subscribe wholeheartedly to a view of law as an

autonomous discipline in a strong sense. Nevertheless, a persistent undercurrent of unease about the nature of the academic enterprise is visible in the literature, occasionally surfacing to the level of explicit debate. For example, Jim Harris, *Law and Legal Science* (1979) and Nigel Simmonds, *Decline of Juridical Reason* (1984) can be read as attempts to articulate coherent theoretical bases for legal exposition, the former in positivist terms, the latter as a critique of positivism.

[4] *op. cit.* Chap. 5, n. 1.

[5] Hohfeld, who had a background in chemistry, suggested that his fundamental legal conceptions were "the lowest common denominators of the law". Cook drew on analogies from physics, Underhill Moore tried to apply a particularly rigid form of positivist psychology to the behaviour of humans confronted with rules, and the illustrious Roscoe Pound, whose first book was on the phytogeography of Nebraskan plants, moved on from improbable attempts to produce taxonomies of social interests and of jurists to popularise the idea of law as social engineering, a form of naive instrumentalism that still survives in some quarters. See further, KLRM Chaps. 1–4. On the use of "scientific analogies" by English academic lawyers see D, Sugarman, LTCL Chap. 3.

[6] See generally Becher and Evans, *op. cit.* n. 2 above.

[7] J. Bentham, *A Fragment on Government* (Hart and Burns, ed. CW 1977) at p. 398.

[8] On the fallacy of the Way of the Baffled Medic see above, Chap. 4, n. 10.

[9] For one example of this kind of attitude, see W. T. S. Stallybrass, "Law in Universities", (1948) 1 J.S.P.T.L. (N.S.) 157.

[10] See above, Chap. 6 at p. 141–142.

[11] O.W. Holmes Jr., "The Path of the Law" (1897) 10 *Harvard L. Rev.* 457.

[12] On the hostile reaction to such a suggestion made by Arthur Corbin of Yale as late as 1914, see KLRM at p. 33.

[13] Holmes, *op. cit.*, at p. 469.

[14] See below, n. 16.

[15] H.L.A. Hart, *The Concept of Law* (1961) Chap. 7. A sophisticated and amusing development of such ideas (with a post-modern gloss) is David Fraser, *Cricket and the Law* (1993).

[16] On the ambiguities of Holmes as a man and a thinker see R. Gordon (ed.) *The Legacy of Oliver Wendell Holmes Jr.* (1992); on the Bad Man, see further HDTWR pp. 69–73, (1973) 58 *Cornell L. Rev.* 275.

[17] Joseph Raz, "The Purity of the Pure Theory" in Tur and Twining (eds), *Essays on Kelsen* (1986) at p. 80, citing Kelsen's *The Pure Theory of Law* (1967) (trs. Knight), p. 1. Kelsen acknowledged that the sociology of law, as well as psychology and politics, could contribute to the understanding of law. His concern was to isolate a form of knowledge, not to restrict what law students study.

[18] The argument is developed in *Essays on Kelsen, op. cit.*, introduction by the editors at pp. 19–34.

[19] Hans Kelsen, *Introduction to the Problems of Legal Theory* (trs. B. and S. Paulsen, 1992).

[20] Tur and Twining, *op. cit.*, pp. 15–29, esp. 27–28.

[21] See below at p. 173.

[22] See especially, *Law's Empire* (1986).

[23] Ross Harrison, *Bentham* (1983).

[24] There is some disagreement among Bentham scholars as to whether Bentham was a consistent act-utilitarian and, if so, whether that grounded a coherent theory of adjudication or of interpretation and application of positive laws. Insofar as he was an act-utilitarian, that left little space for detached or neutral interpretation and

exposition of the law as it is, independent of utility. My own view is that Bentham's conception of Expository Jurisprudence, though relatively undeveloped, was almost as directly dependent on the principle of utility as Censorial Jurisprudence. That is contested. What is clear is that Bentham advanced a utilitarian theory of positive law that was based on and given coherence by a particular version of political morality. See further, RB at pp. 107–108.

25 There is an extensive controversy about Bentham's "influence" on reform in the nineteenth century, but this does not bear on his clearly marginal role in the development of academic law in England.

26 An excellent introduction is S. Guest, *Ronald Dworkin* (1992).

27 *Law's Empire* p. 13. "Legal practice" is not here confined to legal practitioners, but embraces all actors within a legal system; Dworkin is using history and sociology as examples of external points of view.

28 *ibid* p. 14.

29 *ibid.*

30 At p. 413.

31 For a balanced account, see C. Veljanowski "Legal Theory, Economic Analysis and the Law of Torts," (1986) LTCL Chap. 12.

32 A.W.B. Simpson, "The Common Law and Legal Theory" (1973), reprinted in LTCL, Chap. 2, C. Sampford, *The Disorder of Law* (1989). Autopoiesis is one sophisticated attempt to revive the idea that legal thinking is systematic in an important sense, see above Chap. 5, n. 36.

33 RE Chap. 4.

34 See above Chap. 2.

35 See para. 108.

36 See para. 49.

37 The main variant is that some law degrees provide for "half subjects", but patterns are changing with the advent of "modularisation" and "semesterisation" and may change further if professional pressures on the academic stage are relaxed.

38 The proposal requires the approval of ACLEC which began a major review of legal education in 1993. This could lead to a different system of recognition of degrees.

39 William Twining, "Preparing Lawyers for the Twenty-first Century" (1992) 3 *Legal Education Rev.* 1.

40 Above, Chap. 6, n. 87.

41 The system which allows non-law graduates to "convert" in one year has been sharply attacked, *e.g.* P. Birks, "Short Cuts" in *Reviewing Legal Education* (forthcoming, 1994). The ACLEC Consultation Paper on *The Initial Stage* (June, 1994) reasserts the view that the law degree should not be the only route of entry (4.27), but leaves open the question whether one academic year is sufficient for a conversion course for non-law graduates.

42 The Marre Committee, *op. cit.*, Chap. 2 n. 17 (1988) recommended "that consideration be given to teaching trusts and land law as a composite subject", *op. cit.* at p. 119 (para. 13.19–13.24), thereby returning to the Ormrod conception of five core subjects.

43 At one level the core subject issue was of more symbolic than practical importance in that the Ormrod Committee recommended the recognition of all existing law degrees and there is no record of a single honours law degree being refused recognition. Practical problems arise with some mixed and modular degrees.

44 In recent years the Law Society's strengthened secretariat has provided greater continuity, but the governance of the Bar still suffers from its complexity and rapid turnover of key personnel.

The Quest For a Core

45 The seriousness of "the CPE problem" can easily be exaggerated, despite the increasing popularity of that route. Comparing CPE holders with all law graduates is not comparing like with like, as the former tend to be highly selected from graduates with good degrees, to be older and highly motivated and to have the short-term advantage of having studied the core subjects immediately before the vocational stage.

46 See below at pp. 179–81.

47 See the ACLEC Consultation Paper, *op. cit.* n. 41.

48 Some of the themes in this section are developed at greater length in JJM at pp. 141–155.

49 The main pioneering efforts were J. H. Wigmore, "The job-analysis method of teaching the use of law sources" (1922) 16 *Illinois L. Rev.* 499; H. Lasswell and M. McDougal, "Legal Education and Public Policy: Professional Training in the Public Interest" (1943) 52 *Yale Law Jo.* 203; K. N. Llewellyn, "The Place of Skills in Legal Education" (1945) 45 *Columbia L. Rev.* 345.

50 On Antioch, see T. Anderson and R. Catz, "Towards a Comprehensive Approach to Clinical Education" 59 *Washington U. Law Qtrly* 727 (1981).

51 See generally, N. Gold, K. Mackie and W. Twining (eds.) *Learning Lawyers' Skills* (1989).

52 For a fuller discussion see JJM at pp. 136–55.

53 The most important recent example is the ABA Task Force Report, *Legal Education and Professional Development—An Educational Continuum* (The MacCrate Report, 1992) Chaps. 4 and 5, esp. pp. 203–207.

54 The teaching of professional ethics illustrates rather clearly one difference between a professional school which can be expected to inculcate professional values and an academic institution which might find the ethical dilemmas of practising lawyers intellectually interesting, but might consider it inappropriate to "indoctrinate" students with a particular set of professional values. The ACLEC Consultation Paper on the Initial Stage cautiously suggests that one outcome should "be to enable students to show awareness of the ethical issues raised in the study of law" (*op. cit.* at 4.8).

55 JJM at pp. 146–147.

56 Abel and Lewis, *op. cit.*, Chap. 2, n. 21.

57 The idea can be traced back at least to 1943 when Lasswell and McDougal boldly declared: "We submit this basic proposition: if legal education in the contemporary world is adequately to serve the needs of a free and productive commonwealth, it must be conscious, efficient and systematic *training for policy-making*", *op. cit.*, n. 49 at p. 206. Policy-making in this context was used almost synonymously with problem-solving to produce the classic image of the American lawyer as all-purpose fixer.

58 Lord Chancellor's Advisory Committee, Review of Legal Education: First Consultative Conference, 9 July 1993, *Report*, Discussion Group 4.

59 *ibid.* One can only generalise about "common problems" at fairly high levels of abstraction; if by "common" is meant routine or frequently arising, these vary according to types of practice; if by common is meant shared or similar, the similarities can only be identified at a high level of abstraction.

60 TEBW Chap. 2, *Analysis, passim.*

61 Since the mid-1980s "skills" have been the most prominent fashion in legal education and training. As the initial excitement dies down a more judicious balance between skills, knowledge and perspectives may be achieved and a greater sophistication may develop about the relationship between know-how, know-

The Quest For a Core

what and know-why. There is still a need for sustained research and development and for more attention to be directed to advanced and specialised training.

62 "It is the ambivalent, double-faced character of legal pluralism that is so attractive to post-modern jurists", Gunther Teubner, "The Two Faces of Janus: Rethinking Legal Pluralism" (1992) 13 *Cardozo L. Rev.* 1443.

63 A.W.B. Simpson, *Invitation to Law* (1988) at pp. 70–76.

64 *op. cit.*, n. 41.

65 *ibid.*

66 Gunther Teubner, "How Law Thinks: Toward a Constructivist Epistemology of Law" (1989) 23 *Law and Society Rev.* 727, at p. 730.

67 TAR and JJM.

68 RE, Chaps. 1 and 11.

69 Above p. 143.

70 *e.g.* RE pp. 24–27.

71 This version is drawn mainly from 20 *Enc. Brit.* 675 (13th edn. 1911), citing Hesiod, *Works and Days 54–105* and Babrius *Fab.* 58. It is not interpreted here as the anti-feminist myth that Hesiod may have intended. (Robert Graves, *The Greek Myths* (1955), Vol. 1, at pp. 145, 148–149.); *cf.* G.N. Gilbert and M. Mulkay, *Opening Pandora's Box: A sociological analysis of scientists' discourse* (1984).

72 JJM at pp. 142–147.

73 above, Chap. 1 at p. 16–19.

74 R. Dworkin, "The Model of Rules" (1967) 35 *University of Chicago L. Rev.* 14 (variously reprinted as "Is law a system of rules?").

75 HDTWR Chap. 2.

76 Twining (1973) above, *op. cit.* n. 16.

77 This is a very condensed summary of ideas that are elaborated in HDTWR and other writings, especially RE, *passim*, Chaps. 4, 6 and 11.

78 Even talk of rules as fictions can be interpreted as a form of constructivism—*e.g.* that rule-statements, like concepts, language, history and knowledge are human constructs—which is not necessarily a form of scepticism (RE Chap. 4); *cf.* Bentham's theory of fictions.

79 For example, Arthur Corbin was attacking contemporary expository accounts of legal doctrine for being too abstract, rather than rejecting the possibility of exposition (KLRM at p. 32); Jerome Frank argued for the improvement of legal rules; and Karl Llewellyn, often labelled the leading "rule sceptic", was the architect of a major code, and drafted an almost complete book on "The Theory of Rules" which he did not publish. He would readily have agreed that concepts like institution, process, practice and craft cannot be adequately elucidated without reference to some basic generic concept of rule or norm.

80 On internal and external scepticism, see R. Dworkin, *Law's Empire*, *op. cit.*, pp. 78–86.

81 HDTWR Chap. 2. This is not to be interpreted as strongly rationalistic or individualistic: responses to problems may be individual or collective, immediate or evolutionary, conscious or unconscious and so on.

82 Above, the Way of the Baffled Medic, Chap. 4., n. 10.

83 "[A] sound sociology [of law] plays not alone, as Timasheff suggests, between the two poles of power and ethics, but between six poles which I prefer to call Might, Right, Skills, Rules, Results and Law's People." In Kocoureck (ed.), *My Philosophy of Law* (1941) at p. 197. At a different level, the concept of institution can itself be elucidated in terms of rules, see above n. 79.

84 For a defence of Llewellyn's theory against some standard attacks on functionalism, see JJM. at pp. 131–136.

[85] Lewis Carroll, *The Hunting of the Snark*, Fit the First (1876).

[86] Martin Gardner, *The Annotated Snark* (1974 ed.) at p. 53n.

[87] *ibid.* pp. 21–22.

[88] Above Chap. 6 n. 4.

[89] There is an extensive literature on this topic. One of the best discussions is in Chap. 4 of *Law and Learning* (the Arthurs Report), *op. cit.*, above, Chap. 6.

[90] HDTWR, *passim* (index under legalism).

[91] Although some lists include such items as "ability to analyse facts and to be able to construct and criticise an argument on a disputed question of fact" (Marre report, *op. cit.* at p. 114), little more than lip-service is paid to this in the practice of legal education and terms like "legal reasoning" and "thinking like a lawyer" usually refer only to analysis of and arguments about questions of law—one of the great failings of the narrow, expository tradition. RE Chap. 2.

[92] Above, n. 53.

[93] Above Chap. 3.

[94] Above Chap. 5.

[95] *ibid.*

[96] David Schum, *The Evidential Foundations of Probabilistic Reasoning* (1994).

[97] Schum: "In any inference task our evidence is always incomplete, rarely conclusive, and often imprecise or vague; it comes from sources having any gradation of credibility." *ibid.* Preface.

[98] *ibid.* pp. 477–481 and *passim*.

[99] At p. 6.

[1] At pp. 4–5.

[2] *ibid.* at pp. 7–8. In the mid 1980s Schum regularly presented one of Wigmore's charts to classes of scientists and engineers and asked them when they thought that it was first developed. The earliest guess was usually about five or six years ago. In fact Wigmore first published a paper on the subject in 1913. This was a semi-formalisation of what litigators have to do all the time. Ironically, it did not catch on with practitioners because it appeared too elaborate and cumbersome; but by today's standards it seems somewhat simplistic (personal communication from D. Schum).

[3] pp. 58–59.

[4] It may be objected, that evidentiary issues in courts relate mainly to unique past events rather than to problems of establishing scientific laws and other generalisations on the basis of incomplete evidence. There is an intimate relationship between arguing from particular evidence to particular conclusions and trying to induce generalisations from particular instances. But the problems are not identical. Insofar as this is so, it too sets some important limits on Schum's claims for law.

[5] RE Chap. 7.

[6] Sally Lloyd-Bostock, *Law in Practice* (1988) contains a useful survey from an English perspective of a field that has been dominated by American scholars.

[7] One of the most enthusiastic decision-theorists who has taken an interest in law is Ward Edwards, *e.g.* "Summing Up: The Society of Bayesian Trial Lawyers" (1986) 66 *Boston U. L. Rev.* 937. His work is discussed extensively by Schum who attributes to him the dictum: "People should think, machines must decide".

[8] Symposium on "Probability and Inference in the Law of Evidence" (1986) *Boston Univ. L. Rev.* pp. 377–952.

[9] *e.g.* Terence Anderson, "Refocusing the New Evidence Scholarship", (1991) 13 *Cardozo L. Rev.* 783–791.

[10] RE Chap. 5.

[11] ANALYSIS at pp. 440–41; RE pp. 362–363; on the rodeo problem, see above Chap. 5, n. 32.

EPILOGUE

Roland Barthes' marvellous essay on the Eiffel Tower begins: "Maupassant often lunched at the restaurant in the Eiffel Tower though he didn't much like the food: *It's the only place in Paris, he used to say, where I don't have to see it.*"[1] The Tower, says Barthes, is a universal symbol of Paris, but "[t]his pure—virtually empty—sign—is ineluctable, *because it means everything*".[2] For example, the Tower transgresses the habitual divorce between seeing and being seen; it escapes reason just because it is an utterly useless monument; yet Gustave Eiffel felt compelled to justify his creation on the basis of its scientific uses in terms that seem quite ridiculous.[3] Paris looks at the Tower and visitors to the Tower have a bird's eye view of Paris. Seeing Paris from the Tower is an exercise of the intellect which constructs a panorama, a map and a past. To regard Paris from above is an act of intellection that imposes a structure on the swarming humanity and unplanned terrain below; and "to perceive Paris from above is infallibly to imagine a history."[4] The Tower is a vantage-point, but, even though there is nothing to see there, it also has an inside which is at once technically intriguing, banally commercial and rather comfortable.[5]

In choosing the title *Blackstone's Tower* to symbolise the world of the English Law School, I took a risk. Symbols are tricky, open to many interpretations, some of which can subvert their own text. Legal culture is somewhat resistant to fanciful images. Law schools might invite comparison to an ivory tower or a Victorian folly or the Tower of Babel, but I hope that I have said enough to undermine such interpretations. Comparing the modern English law school with the Eiffel Tower may seem far-fetched, except that it might suggest some contrasts: the former is almost invisible and somewhat opaque; far from being unique, it is only one structure among many in the academic landscape; it has grown and is still growing by fits and starts, conspicuously lacking a single architect; and it attracts few tourists. However, I find Barthes' essay quite suggestive: a tower has both an inward and an outward aspect;

attempts to account for it solely in terms of rational utility tend to be absurd; and adopting a bird's eye, top-down, view is an exercise of the mind: the intellect constructs and imposes a structure; the imagination reminds one of history and the complexities of human experience. Beyond this it is probably sensible to leave my audience to create their own meanings. I have stuck with the title because it links four main themes in this attempt to interpret the world of the English law school from the inside.

First, Blackstone's Tower is a vantage point from which to look at law, in all its variety and elusiveness, from a number of levels and angles. If one looks outwards one can construct a panorama and a map—which is both necessary and of limited use.[6] If one looks inwards, one finds in the library an extraordinarily rich storehouse of texts, stories and ideas; the law library has two striking characteristics: first, the primary sources—legislation, law reports, other original documents—greatly outnumber the secondary writings and are constantly renewed by fresh problems, decisions, and rationalisations from the world outside. More than in most disciplines academic lawyers feed off these primary texts rather than each other. However, secondly, what regularly reaches the library represents only a small, and in many respects untypical, part of what is going on outside. As we saw in the legal records project, the variety and extent of legal documents are not reflected in library holdings. The neglect of routine legal documents in legal education is a symptom of a more general tendency.[7] At least until recently, academic law had been quite restricted in both scope and depth—most academic attention has been focused on parts of lawyers' law and lawyers' action, which are themselves only part of the law and law in action. It is widely accepted that in order to get to grips with the particularities of law one has to go into the field or streets or courts to observe or to participate or both. To adapt Holmes, to understand the life of the law requires both logic and experience. But the law school is quite comfortable, the library is an absorbing treasure-house and many who venture out never return. In short, at this stage in its evolution Blackstone's Tower has marked limitations as a vantage-point.

The second salient characteristic of the modern English law school is that, despite a long tradition, it is in most respects a recent creation. Indeed, it is only just beginning to come of age. Historically the main reason for this has been that the study of English law was a relative late-comer to universities, and the pioneers had to devote most of their energies to establishing their credentials with two reference groups who had different sets of expectations: the legal profession and the university community. It is only since the 1970s that law schools have achieved both critical mass and sufficient acceptance within the academy to start to build the capacity and the self-confidence to set a more ambitious agenda both functionally and intellectually. This enormous and belated expansion has happened at a time when universities, the legal profession and the legal system have all been changing rapidly in a relatively unfavourable economic climate. It is uncertain whether in the next phase law schools will consolidate, or expand further or retreat back into being very modest institutions with a quite limited role.

The third characteristic of the modern law school is that by and large it has been assimilated into the university. As such its commitment is and should be to the academic ethic, that is to the advancement, stimulation and dissemination of learning, broadly conceived—what I have called know-why, know-what and know-how.[8] Academic lawyers conform quite closely to the profile of academics in general; their duties are defined in terms of teaching, research and educational administration, and their career development is determined by standard academic norms. Like many other disciplines, law has been endemically introspective, with recurring debates about objectives, priorities, and methods and about the nature of the enterprise. Expansion has created the conditions for diversification of several kinds: subject-matters, clienteles, methods and perspectives.

In respect of ideas there is a relatively new, and to my mind healthy, pluralism; to say that this is a house of many mansions, like most clichés is at best a half-truth, which glosses over the persistent concern to try to find a core to the discipline, or at least to make it more homogeneous. It is naturally tempting to try to subsume the discipline under some single conception of law as a system of posited rules or universal moral principles or problem-solving techniques or to make it a sub-branch of sociology or politics or ethics or theology. Such forms of reductionism appeal to some, but are unlikely to win a consensus in our post-modern world.

Those who, like myself, welcome a degree of diversity are resistant to attempts to re-impose an old orthodoxy or create a new one. Yet there are genuine and persistent concerns about identity both on the part of individual law teachers and about the discipline as a whole—if we cannot claim a core, is there a sufficient sense of community based on at least a family of concerns about disputes, order, problems, rules, values, concepts, facts, power, decisions, processes and social context? The activity variously called exposition or practical doctrinal scholarship or legal dogmatics remains prominent, despite a series of attacks that have challenged its validity as well as its pretensions. The role of the jurist as expositor is assured, even within the common law tradition, but the claims of the censor, the empirical researcher, the craftsman, the technologist, the internal sceptic and the outside observer are also persistent. The relationship between all of these roles and claims is uneasy and rarely has a satisfactory integration been achieved, as is illustrated by the relative failure to date to construct stable coherences in attempts to broaden the study of law from within.[9]

There are also grounds for fearing that if academic law should be cut back, a power struggle would ensue in which some of the most interesting activities and lines of enquiry that have secured a niche would be marginalised or squeezed out almost entirely by some narrowly vocational orthodoxy. Not only socio-legal studies, critical theory, sociology of law, legal history, the study of foreign legal systems, and criminology, but also emergent fields, large areas of legal practice, and the whole range of legal subjects that affect ordinary people without regularly involving lawyers are all areas which could suffer by a contraction of the academic enterprise or a narrowing of its vision.

A fourth characteristic of Blackstone's Tower is that it seems to exclude outsiders. Although accommodated within the university, the law school is still often regarded as an outpost, or a forbidding fortress or an exclusive club. Law students are reported to be standoffish and cliquey; law teachers, according to Becher, are "variously represented as vociferous, untrustworthy, immoral, narrow, arrogant and conservative, though kinder eyes see them as impressive and intelligent."[10] Even if unfair, these are troubling images. As we saw in the first chapter, law features on the front pages of newspapers, yet it is almost invariably hidden at the back of book shops and booksellers seem reluctant to place anything that looks like a "law book" in other sections, under for example feminism or history or politics, however relevant and readable it may be.[11] Yet books relating to law are to be found throughout the book shop as long as they do not carry the dreaded label.

Nowhere is this exclusiveness more apparent than in university law libraries: even where the law library is not physically separate, it must seem esoteric and unwelcoming to most outsiders. And, as we have seen, most readable books related to law—novels, plays, accounts of famous trials, "journalistic" works however excellent—tend to be excluded, as do many important kinds of legal documents. Perhaps the first important ritual of socialisation of law students is their initiation into the mysteries of this inward, exclusive, selective sanctum.

One of the great myths is that law is a discipline that is difficult to penetrate. Volumes have been written about the self-interested mystification of law by lawyers and about jargon, persiflage, verbosity and unnecessary use of latin and law french. Historians testify to the difficulty of interpreting legal records and regularly praise Maitland, who was a lawyer, for having unlocked their secrets.[12] Non-lawyers often regard the alleged mystery of the law with awe as well as resentment.

Yet there are counter-examples: Blackstone wrote his *Commentaries* so that the principles of common law could be part of the equipment of any English gentleman; in the nineteenth century jurists were much more part of the intellectual mainstream than they are today.[13] English academics of my generation have had to grin and bear it when very senior judges and other members of the legal establishment used to boast that they had had no legal education, thereby implying that law teachers did not have a real job. This was sufficiently common to be known as "the look-at-me syndrome".

Today England is one of the few jurisdictions in the world in which a law degree is not a necessary qualification for practice. There is a growing industry of do-it-yourself law books and materials, for dealing with problems of conveyancing, probate, divorce, consumer claims, and domestic violence. Legal awareness programmes, law in schools and law days are designed to make law more accessible to ordinary people. And most citizens have to cope with law daily as a practical matter. Yet, ironically, one rarely finds do-it-yourself books or "law for non-lawyers" in a university law library, for such concerns have traditionally fallen outside the purview of university law schools. Developments in new technology may help to break down some of these barriers.[14]

Blackstone's Tower, then, is a vantage point from which traditionally only parts of law have been regularly observed and studied; as it has expanded in size it has broadened its focus; it has been absorbed into the university, but it is in many respects still seen to be somewhat apart; it is a relatively young institution which has yet to develop a clearly defined role. It is rapidly approaching a point where important decisions will have to be taken as to whether it should continue to diversify and expand, or consolidate or even contract. As we have seen, power over decisions about legal education is widely diffused and it will not be law schools alone that will determine their destiny.

Historically, the shape and scale of legal education in England, as in many other countries in the common law world, have been largely demand-led. In an increasingly market-oriented and privatised context the law school community will need to be both realistic and flexible in responding to actual and perceived needs and demands. However, if one accepts that almost everyone in society needs some legal education from cradle to grave, then it seems likely that the potential demand will always exceed what law schools, especially university law schools, will or can supply. That in turn suggests that individual institutions should be able to choose from a range of potential customers or clients, and where to concentrate their energies. To that extent they have the opportunity to control their own destinies, provided that they have a clear sense of direction. There is, of course, a constant tension between the noble ideals of the academic ethic and the commodification of education, but one has to be pragmatic and realistic about the economic underpinnings of the academic enterprise.

In the short-term the immediate fear is that the contraction of the legal profession and the severe reduction of opportunities to obtain a professional qualification may lead to a drastic fall in the demand for places on undergraduate degrees. The future of the legal profession and of legal services as we know them is very uncertain. But if the law degree continues to be perceived mainly as a route to legal practice, and not the only one, there could be a sharp drop in demand for applications to study law at undergraduate level.

The analysis presented here suggests two main strategies for preserving the economic base of legal education and thereby enabling law schools to continue to develop their potential. The first is to diversify and to become more wholeheartedly and regularly involved in other kinds of formal legal education—from legal literacy and teacher training to various forms of advanced and multidisciplinary studies—as the ILC model suggests. During the 1980s this kind of diversification began to occur but, I have suggested, our practice tended to outrun our self-image: many law schools still perceive and present themselves as essentially undergraduate institutions, even though many law teachers feel increasingly constrained by the standard, overloaded undergraduate curriculum. Our law schools have outgrown the three year law degree at eighteen plus.

Diversification might help to mitigate some of the economic pressures, but on its own it will not take us very far in the direction of realising the potential of our discipline. Many of the more obvious demands are for quite low level or minimalist services: an introductory course for engineers or accountants, which are too often based on a banausic and outdated view of the subject; some quick fixes to satisfy continuing education requirements; a few seminars for overworked judges. These are all useful and some are interesting. But undergraduate education is the staple of our university system and is likely to remain so for the foreseeable future. Public funding is largely based on the principle of "one bite of the cherry"[15] and, by and large, English culture has tended to regard postgraduate and advanced studies as luxuries, only relevant to a small intellectual elite.

In order to maintain a reasonable share of the undergraduate market and to break out of the straitjacket of the current curriculum, law schools will have to do a much better job of persuading the relevant constituencies that law is a good vehicle for general education at undergraduate and other levels. Law school prospectuses regularly proclaim that they offer a good general liberal education in law, but one senses that few people, including many law teachers, really believe them. There is a credibility gap between the rhetoric of mission statements and the general perception of undergraduate legal studies. Law school practices and discourses reveal either a deep ambivalence about the nature of the enterprise or an overt commitment to a narrow form of vocationalism. For example, talk of overproduction of law graduates *assumes* that numbers should be geared to training places and to the perceived needs and absorptive capacity of the private legal profession[16]; about half of single honours law degrees make all of the core subjects compulsory, although from the point of view of general education it is difficult to see why trusts or torts or EC/EU Law are better vehicles of liberal education than human rights or welfare or family or environmental law or constitutional history or fact-analysis or jurisprudence or many other potential contenders.[17]

It is quite easy to make a strong case for law as a potentially good vehicle for general or liberal education. The subject-matter is important, extremely wide-ranging, intellectually challenging and potentially interesting. It is also vocationally relevant to many spheres of activity in addition to legal practice. There is a very rich body of constantly renewed primary sources based on actual practical problems or situations; and a solid and increasingly soph-

196

isticated body of scholarship. There is an admirable tradition in law schools, much influenced by America, of taking education seriously.

However, our law schools are some way from realising their potential. It is not necessary for my argument to speculate how far English undergraduate degrees in law do provide a good general education for those who take them. My impression is that the practice is uneven, ranging from the excellent to the inadequate. The cardinal sin of making an interesting subject boring is not unknown. The overloading of the undergraduate curriculum; the preference of some law firms for non-law graduates; the ambivalence of many academic lawyers about their roles and objectives are all matters of concern.

If law schools are to flourish they need to move in the direction of the ILC model. The case for embracing this model can be restated as follows:

It is in the social interest that our law schools should be involved in the systematic advancement and dissemination of knowledge about all aspects of law from a variety of perspectives and that they should be quite large and diverse rather than contracting into a small elite that focuses mainly on the upper reaches of the legal system.

It is in the interests of law schools, law students and law teachers that they should broaden their range. Undergraduate options are increasingly being squeezed and vast tracts of law are conspicuously under-researched. Students have diverse needs and interests and should have the opportunity to choose from a reasonably broad menu of subjects, perspectives and methods. Academic lawyers need varied outlets in order to flourish.

It may be less easy to persuade the legal profession that law schools should diversify in this way, because this could be interpreted as law schools distancing themselves from the profession and weakening its influence. But the ILC multi-functional model is as much in the interests of the profession as of anyone.

At the lowest level it will relieve the so-called problem of "oversupply" of law graduates: if the profession really helped to promulgate the idea that a law degree is and should be genuinely liberal and academic in the best sense, this would maintain a broad pool of talent from which to select, take pressure off undergraduates to make premature career choices, and it would help to reduce the expectation that a law degree is an automatic passport to practice. In respect of undergraduate degrees, if only a third to a half of law graduates will in future have the opportunity to qualify, let alone to practice, it is in everyone's interest and, indeed, it is our duty to make it clear that law degrees are not an automatic passport to the legal profession; we can only hope to maintain demand if undergraduate legal education is designed, delivered and sold as being genuinely multi-functional and as vocationally relevant for many other occupations as most degrees in the arts and social sciences. It is my strong impression that this is not the message that most of our present and potential students have been receiving, especially from the practising profession.[18]

But there are more fundamental reasons than these: it is in the interests of the practising profession that law schools and law teachers should be professionally involved in teaching and researching much more than the core subjects, a few undergraduate options, and elementary skills. It is in the interests of the profession that subjects that are currently squeezed out of the overloaded undergraduate curriculum should be the object of sustained academic attention. A flourishing academic enterprise should be better placed than practitioners to be able to take a longer, broader and more critical view, to explore and develop new fields (as has happened with Restitution and Administrative Law), and to be involved in fundamental as well as applied research. Academic lawyers are much more likely to make useful contributions to legal practice and legal development, if their routine professional activities are not confined to primary education and deal with all aspects of law in our interdependent world. Law is a grown-up subject and law schools need to be given the space to develop into broad-ranging, mature institutions concentrating on what they are meant to be good at—the intellectual advancement, stimulation and dissemination of learning about law.

My argument here is about structures and attitudes and perceptions and only indirectly about practices. It is quite simply that the discipline of law should take all law for its province and view it through a variety of lenses; that the multi-functional model of the role of law schools is in the social interest and in the long run will benefit students, scholars and, not least, the legal and other professions; that law schools should be regularly involved in legal education and training at many different levels and not be confined almost entirely to primary education; that law as an academic discipline can provide an excellent basis both for enlightened vocational training and general education, also at a number of levels; that the academic stage of professional development should be

Epilogue

unequivocally academic in the best sense and that this includes an emphasis on depth and breadth of vision, as well as intellectual rigour; that legal scholarship should continue to diversify in respect of subject-matter, perspectives and methods and for this to happen it needs to stand on the shoulders of teaching; and that, finally, the study of law should be reinstated as part of our general intellectual culture and not be left to linger at the back of a few book shops.

Notes

[1] Roland Barthes, "The Eiffel Tower" in *Barthes: Selected Writings* (ed. Susan Sontag, 1983) at p. 236.

[2] *ibid.* p. 237.

[3] "Eiffel . . . scrupulously lists all the future uses of the Tower: . . . aerodynamic measurements, studies of the resistance of substances, physiology of the climber, radio-electric research, problems of telecommunication, meteorological observations etc. These uses are doubtless incontestable, but they seem quite ridiculous alongside the overwhelming myth of the Tower, of the human meaning which it has assumed throughout the world." (*ibid.* at p. 239).

[4] *ibid.* at p. 244.

[5] *ibid.* at p. 250.

[6] Blackstone, Bentham and Austin all used the metaphor of providing a map of the law.

[7] Above, p. 115.

[8] Above, Chap. 3, n. 9.

[9] RE Chap. 1 and 11.

[10] Becher at p. 30.

[11] This has been a common experience of books in the "Law in Context" series, such as Katherine O'Donovan's *Sexual Divisions in Law* (1985) and Ann Dummett and Andrew Nicol, *Subjects, Citizens, Aliens and Others* (1990), both of which deserved to reach a wider audience.

[12] *e.g.*, G.R. Elton, *F.W. Maitland* (1985).

[13] S. Collini, *op. cit.*, Preface, n. 1.

[14] Above Chap. 5.

[15] See Philip Thomas, "The Poverty of Students", (1993) 27 *The Law Teacher* 152.

[16] See above, at pp. 60–61.

[17] Esther Johnson, *op. cit.* above Chap. 4 n. 37, reported that in 1993 all of the 29 law schools surveyed offered all core subjects, 11 made the post-Ormrod six compulsory, and five more also required EC Law, which the Law Society had recommended should be added to the list of core subjects.

[18] "Preparing Lawyers for the Twenty-first Century", *op. cit.*, Chap. 6, n. 39.

APPENDIX

English Law Teachers as Academics: A Preliminary Analysis[1]

This note raises the question; are there any salient characteristics that differentiate English law teachers from the academic profession as a whole?

Let us start with a negative image. I have anecdotal evidence that some law teachers sense an underlying hostility from fellow academics and administrators, especially in the context of university politics. This may not be sufficiently marked to generate the analogue of lawyer jokes, but it is felt as an undercurrent. Becher reported that colleagues' perceptions of academic lawyers and their own self-image were generally unattractive and in some respects peculiar. He constructs a picture of members of a soft, applied, largely rural discipline that is isolated and fits uneasily in the academy. For example:

> "The predominant notion of academic lawyers is that they are not really academic—one critical respondent described them as 'arcane, distant, and alien: an appendage to the university world.' Their personal qualities are dubious: they are variously represented as vociferous, untrustworthy, immoral, narrow, arrogant and conservative, though kinder eyes see them as impressive and intelligent. Their scholarly activities are thought to be unexciting and uncreative, comprising a series of intellectual puzzles scattered among 'large areas of description'.
>
> This generally negative view seems to be shared by its victims, a number of whom diagnosed a common 'tendency towards self-denigration' and 'a sense of doubt about one's intellectual quality'."[2]

Becher's sample was admittedly very small and relates to 1980. However, there is a good deal of anecdotal evidence to support at least parts of this image. A much-quoted article entitled "The law teacher: a man divided against himself"[3] is representative of an

201

angst-ridden literature, not all of it American. The ambiguities about the role of law schools are, not surprisingly, shared by law teachers. In chapter six, I argued that the depiction of legal scholarship as largely descriptive is not only out of date, but is also fundamentally misconceived. I pass no comment on the personal qualities, except to say that I find most of my chosen profession rather congenial and I can think of very few who fit Becher's image, almost none in respect of integrity. Whether my colleagues are more obnoxious than other academics I have no means of knowing.

Without dismissing this negative picture out of hand, let me at least outline an alternative hypothesis; that English law teachers in most important respects are not very different from the rest of the academic profession in this country.

In his surveys of British senior common rooms in 1964, 1976 and 1989 Professor Halsey treated law as one part of the social sciences and humanities and law teachers remain largely invisible in his *Decline of Donnish Dominion* and its predecessors.[4] He has very kindly extrapolated the sample of 84 academic lawyers (about 3 per cent.) from his 1989 survey and made it possible to contrast them with the total of 2,674 respondents.[5] A preliminary analysis of this rich set of data produces some interesting results, including a few surprises, and a confirmation of the hypothesis that in most of Halsey's categories academic lawyers are near the middle of the academic spectrum.

Halsey's survey suggests that in almost all key respects his profile of academic lawyers in 1989 very closely resembled the profile of the academic profession as a whole, especially colleagues in the Humanities and Social Sciences. In respect of their situation lawyers were generally more bullish than the rest; they emphatically denied that the quality of teaching or of research in their discipline had declined[6]; they confirmed that there had been an increase in student numbers in their department during the past decade[7] and in the quality of applications[8] and no decline in the standards of students[9]; fewer than average would have chosen another discipline, if they had their time again,[10] but rather more might have chosen another occupation and had thought of moving,[11] which is hardly surprising, given the rewards of legal practice; lawyers were somewhat more optimistic about their own prospects of obtaining a chair, providing they were willing to move to another institution.[12] Overall, the survey figures suggest that, in 1989, morale among lawyers was less bad than the average.[13]

In respect of background, somewhat fewer lawyers had first class degrees (L.26.6/R.32.2 per cent.) and far fewer had doctorates (L.11.5/R.58.4 per cent.)[14]; on the other hand many more had either higher degrees or professional qualifications or both.[15] The poor record of law in respect of doctorates is well-documented and is a continuing cause for concern.[16] How far these disparities in the overall profile of qualifications of academic lawyers is counterbalanced by those who have a professional qualification and extensive practical experience is an open question. The figures on home, school and university backgrounds are inconclusive, but show no clear pattern of deviations for lawyers.[17] There appeared to be significantly more women law teachers than the average in Halsey's sample, but this is not clearly confirmed by other available data.[18] Lawyers are very slightly more uxorious than the average, with more marriages and fewer divorces.[19]

Academic lawyers' attitudes appeared to be close to the norm in most respects; for example, like their colleagues they appeared to be generally in favour of more part-time and mature students,[20] better staff-student ratios,[21] and less government control[22]; there was strong agreement that academic salaries were too low—the lawyers were more emphatic than the rest, but Halsey's figures do not provide evidence of support for differential salaries for law teachers on the American model.[23] Following much the same pattern as their colleagues, the survey showed strong agreement that respect for universities had declined,[24] a cautious affirmation of Oxbridge dominance[25] and reasonable sympathy for convergence of universities and polytechnics (this was before the abolition of the binary divide).[26] Lawyers seemed to be generally more enthusiastic than average about undergraduate teaching (relative to postgraduate teaching and research),[27] but this difference was not reflected in time spent on research[28] or current work[29] or numbers of publications,[30] in respect of which lawyers were somewhat above the average.

Some may be surprised to learn that lawyers were somewhat to the left of the academic political spectrum[31]; there was an unexplained bulge in the age profile of the sample, with 37 per cent. of lawyers in their thirties, compared to the average of 25 per cent.[32] Perhaps the most surprising deviation was that fewer than average academic lawyers claimed (or admitted) to doing outside paid work, especially the proportion who spent more than 25 per cent. of their time on this.[33]

Perhaps the most important point of this rather free initial interpretation of Halsey's data is that, except in respect of doctorates, few of the deviations are large or likely to be particularly significant.[34] Nor is this convergence particularly surprising. In respect of pay, promotion, terms of service and in many other ways they have been treated much the same as other academics.[35] This may be a reflection of the broader thesis that since the Second World War nearly all major public changes and decisions affecting the discipline of law in universities have been much more part of changes in higher education than of developments in legal practice and the legal system.[36] By and large this evidence suggests that academic lawyers are generally integrated into the academic profession.

There is clearly a need for further research into the academic legal profession over and above the current work by Professors Sugarman and Leighton. Becher and Halsey are almost unique in providing a basis for comparing academic lawyers with colleagues in other disciplines. Both samples are small and relate to different times (1980 and 1989) in a rapidly changing context. It is possible that by using a questionnaire technique that dealt with attitudes and context Halsey's work would tend to encourage convergence; Becher suggests that academic culture is fragmented, but this is related more to ideas.

As Becher acknowledges, sub-disciplines may be a better unit for comparison than whole disciplines[37] (commercial lawyers, legal theorists and public international lawyers belong to different clans, if not tribes) and it is probably also the case that comparing lawyers with other applied or soft disciplines would also be illuminating. A specific study would need an appropriate theoretical framework. This is clearly just a modest start.

Notes

[1] For more substantial essays on academic lawyers see "The Law Teacher as a Superstar", ALLD and "Good-bye to Lewis Eliot", (1980) JSPTL (NS) 2; see also the ILC Report, *op. cit.*, paras 217–37 and Chap. 4, n. 31–34.
[2] *op. cit.*, at p. 30.
[3] T. Bergin, (1968) 54 Virginia L. Rev. 637; a useful survey of the American literature on the theme is Douglas D. McFarland "Self-images of Law Professors" (1985) 35 J. Legal. Educ. 232.
[4] Above, Chap. 2.
[5] Halsey's main sample was larger, but this was weighted and included Scotland. The population used here covers academics in universities and polytechnics in England and Wales. This is a preliminary analysis, comparing the responses of law teachers (hereafter L) to the rest (hereafter R) in response to Halsey's questionnaire (Halsey's questions are referred to as q.1, q.2, etc.) which is printed in *Decline of Donnish Dominion* (hereafter DDD), Appendix 1. The figures are expressed in percentages, *e.g.* L 70 / R 65 means 70% of lawyers compared to

Appendix

65% of the rest. I have mainly used the total sample, without distinguishing between responses from Universities (U) and Polytechnics (P), except in one or two instances. The interpretation of the data is mine and is mainly intended to suggest some hypotheses for further research. The sample of law teachers is too small to produce results that are statistically significant, but the figures do suggest some potentially fruitful lines of enquiry.

[6] q.19g teaching has declined: disagree L 87 / R 74; q. 19h (research quality declined: disagree): L 86.6 / R 66.7.

[7] q.3. (more students) L 78.3 / R 60.8.

[8] q.4. (students applying better) L 57.1 / R 33.8.

[9] q4b. (students graduating better): the figures are complicated, but on the whole the lawyers were more positive than the rest.

[10] q.17g. L 16.3 / R. 26.2.

[11] q.17h. L. 25.5 / R 33; q.27a L 76.1 / R.69.6; cf. q.28a.

[12] qq.23a-c.

[13] See above, Chap. 2, n. 59.

[14] q.34.

[15] q.34 L 47.7 / R 25.3. These figures exclude professional qualifications, so it seems that most law teachers have at least two qualifications. These figures may not be very different for other professional subjects, such as engineering, teaching and medicine, but sit uneasily with the claims of law also to be part of the social sciences and humanities.

[16] See ESRC *Report on Socio-Legal Studies* (1994), *op. cit.*, above. Chap. 6, n.17. For a critique of Rutland's practices in respect of the Ph.D., see W. Twining "Postgraduate Studies in Law" in P. Birks, (ed.) *Reviewing Legal Education* (forthcoming, 1994).

[17] qq.32–33

[18] q.30 (men) L 78.3 / R 60.8.

[19] qq.(38a and b (U); 34a and b (P)).

[20] qq.6d. and 17.

[21] q.29a.

[22] q.29e.

[23] No direct question was asked about this issue, and the inferences from answers to questions about remuneration are inconclusive.

[24] q.19i. L. 85.4 / R.89.6.

[25] q.29c

[26] q.9 (a-i).

[27] qq.13, 14a, 14b. Complex (*e.g.* there were fewer law teachers supervising postgraduate research students: L 38.6 / R 53.1)

[28] *e.g.* q13: none L 8.6 / R 9.7; over 25% of time: L 42 / R 43.2.

[29] q.12 a L. 88.7 / R. 85.3.

[30] q.12b.

[31] qq.40 a and b. DDD Chap. 11.

[32] q.31.

[33] q.13 Nil: L 75.2 / R 63.5; over 25% of time: L. 1.1 / R 9.9. Possible explanatory factors may include the points that many academic lawyers today are not licensed to practice, that opportunities for private practice by academic lawyers are quite restricted outside London, that a number of them are involved in pro bono work (in advice centres and in legal and other pressure groups) (qq. 36–37), and that some moved to universities because they did not enjoy practice.

Appendix

[34] The sample of lawyers is too small to enable confident judgements about significance, above n. 5.

[35] This, again, in sharp contrast to the U.S. where, *inter alia*, law professors have a significant pay differential, but have to live with quite unfavourable staff-student ratios.

[36] Above, Chap. 2.

[37] Becher, *op. cit.*, at p. 6.

INDEX

207

Index

Index

Kahn-Freund, Sir Otto, 105–106
Kelsen, Hans, 157–158, 171
Kennedy, Duncan, 2
Kent, James, 98

Langdell, C.C., 25, 91–92, 154, 167
Law and Learning (Arthurs Report), 125–127, 128
"Law books" and "books about law", distinction between, 12–14, 94, 112, 193
Law and Development, 58–60
"Law in action", 9, 12–13, 16–21, 191
Law in English universities, history, before 1945, 24–26
post-war period, 26–31
1960s, 31–33
Ormrod and after, 33–43
low visibility of, 10, 25–28, 38–39, 79–80
see also LAW SCHOOLS
Law libraries (general) 67, 69, 91–118, 191
bibliographical aids, 94, 95–96
Bodleian, Oxford, 92, 94, 112
Harvard, 92
Institute of Advanced Legal Studies, 92
Jurisprudence in, 111, 112, 116–117
legal periodicals, 94, 109–111
new technology, 93, 117–118
non-lawyers daunted, 95–96, 193–194
omissions, 94, 114–115, 191, 193–194
primary sources, emphasis on, 94, 113, 115, 191, 196
Rutland, 67, 72, 93, 99, 109–110, 115–116
Law publishing, 114, 128
Law reports, 98–109
Law Quarterly Review, 110–111
Law schools, general
academic model, 53–58
admissions, 37, 81–84, 182–183
economic factors affecting, 41–42, 51, 55–56, 59, 195–196
culture, 64–85, 129–130, 203, *see also* LAW STUDENTS

Law schools, general—*cont.*
expansion, 28–29, 32, 39–40, 55, 66–67, 192
functions, 28, 51–61, 75, 83–85, 195–196
graduates
subsequent careers of, 57–58, 74–76, 83
"over-production", 56, 59–61, 195–197
ILC model, *see* INTERNATIONAL LEGAL CENTER
polytechnics, 28, 32, 33, 38, 40, 202
primary school model, 54–55, 71–72, 83–85, 198
professional model, 28, 52–58, 82–85
size, 43, 51, 78
Law Schools, particular
Bangalore, National Law School of India University at, 54
Birmingham Polytechnic, 40
Cambridge, 23–26, 29, 202
College of Law, 53
Continental Europe, 23–24, 27, 51–52, 54–55, 138–139
Gibson and Weldon, 30
Harvard, 92, 167, *see also* UNITED STATES
Inns of Court, 24, 53
Inns of Court School of Law, 53, 166–167
Kent, 40, 82
London External Division, 31, 32
Oxford, 1, 24–26, 29, 144–145, 202
Rutland, 66–85, *see also* LAW LIBRARIES
School of Oriental and African Studies, 40
United States, 10, 27–31, 51–53, 67, 73, 79, 92, 132–138, 167, 171, 200–201
University College, London, 25, 68
University of Ghana, 20
Warwick, 40, 64–65, 83
Law Society of England and Wales, 31, 35, 41, 166–167
Lawson, F.H., 1

209

Index